MOUSEJUNKIES!

MORE Tips, Tales, and Tricks
for a Disney World Fix

all you need to know for a perfect vacation

Bill Burke

TRAVELERS' TALES
AN IMPRINT OF SOLAS HOUSE, INC.
PALO ALTO

Travelers' Tales is a trademark of Travelers' Tales/Solas House, Inc., 853 Alma Street, Palo Alto, California 94301. www.travelerstales.com

Art Direction: Stefan Gutermuth
Photo Credit: © Blaine Harrington
Interior Design and Page Layout: Howie Severson

Library of Congress Cataloging-in-Publication Data

Burke, Bill.
  Mousejunkies! : more tips, tales, and tricks for a disney world fix all you need to know for a perfect vacation / Bill Burke.
      p. cm.
  ISBN 978-1-60952-022-9 (pbk.)
  1. Walt Disney World (Fla.)--Guidebooks. 2. Orlando (Fla.)--Guidebooks. I. Title.
  GV1853.3.F62B87 2011
  917.59'2404--dc23

                        2011019923

First Edition
Printed in the United States
10 9 8 7 6 5 4 3 2

To the Mousejunkies:

Amy, Randy, Carol, J, Deb, Jenna, Ryan, Walt,

John and Barry. Thank you for the invaluable help,

endless patience and support.

Table of Contents

Foreword

AT ONE TIME I THOUGHT my secret love for Walt Disney World was just that—a secret.

I still live in a nice enough house (though I probably should be mowing the lawn instead of fixating on Walt Disney World) and unfortunately I still drive a sensible car. I put my daughter on the school bus every morning and then set about my day, writing features for the *Boston Herald* or whipping up a column for a regional parenting magazine I work with. It all seems fairly normal.

Step inside that house, however, and it becomes clear pretty quickly that there might be more to this quirky, smiling fellow than meets the eye.

Would it take a sleuth to divine my Disney obsession? Not exactly. It looks like Mickey Mouse threw up in my living room. For those in the know, I'll explain it in our shared parlance: there are Big Figs and loss leader throws and framed pin sets and even a cardboard Krissa DVC tri-fold.

In fact, as I sit tapping at my computer there's a sixty-one-minute loop of the Magic Kingdom's entrance music filling the room. To my right there's a thick stack of purple credit card-sized, previously used Walt Disney resort room keys. I look to my left and there's a twisted pile of metal, leather and crystal—watches, all bearing some sort of Mouse-shaped image on their face. I call it my watch collection, but it's really more a growing monument to forgetfulness. Every time I go to Walt Disney World I forget to bring a watch. At least that's what I tell my wife, Amy. We always visit the Magic Kingdom first, and our second stop—after a coffee and chocolate croissant at the Main Street Bakery— is the watch shop, where I add one more timepiece to my collection.

In the real world, I try not to make too many unnecessary purchases. Get me anywhere on Walt Disney World property, however, and I start spending like a man possessed. Maybe it's because when I'm there I feel like there are no responsibilities in my life other than getting to our dining reservation on time. I only know that when I leave there, I like to have enough swag so that I can attempt to recreate the feeling in my own home.

For those who haven't jumped into the Disney lifestyle with both feet quite yet, let's just say that if it seems like I'm attempting to cling to a youthful existence as I hurtle into my forties, you might be right.

Spend more than five minutes talking to me and I'll figure out a way to insert Mickey Mouse into the conversation. It can be annoying, but I have no qualms about the fact that I am a hard-core Walt Disney World fanatic. I love Disney World, and I'll spend as much time vacationing there as I can without going broke.

Actually, that's a lie. I don't really care about debt. I just need my fix.

No one asks me where I'm going when I tell them we're taking a vacation. It just saves time to assume we're headed to Walt Disney World. At first people would just look at me curiously, wondering when they'd be invited to the intervention. Now it's almost expected. I think people would be disappointed if we opted to travel anywhere else.

One time, I went to a friend's house to watch a hockey game on TV. I wore a Walt Disney World hoodie that had the number "71" stitched on the sleeve, designating the year the Florida resort officially opened.

"What does that number mean?" my friend's wife asked.

"That's how many times he's been to Walt Disney World," her husband answered with a straight face.

Her response? "Oh." And she walked out of the room. She didn't doubt it for a second. My affliction is renowned.

I often wonder about why I'm so enamored of the place. So I conducted a little self-examination: Could it be the attractions? (That's part of it.) Is it the food? (Most definitely.) The customer service? (Probably.) Add about fifteen more items to that list and we'd start to zero in on why I surrendered to this addiction. I did learn a few things from the examination: I was good at some aspects of Walt Disney World travel, and not so good at others. But I knew who to turn to when I had a question. The result is Mousejunkies, a crowd-sourced compendium that talks about when to go, where to stay, and what to do.

All I knew was that the experience was so satisfying, that I thought I'd like to share what I learned from those multiple trips.

Here's What You'll Find in This Book

Mousejunkies is a travel guide with a sense of humor. My opinion might not match up precisely with yours, but the way you opt to go about your Walt Disney World vacation is just as valid as mine. As long as you have a plan. This book will provide you with information you need to formulate a strategy because you'll need one. The cautionary tales about families who arrive on Mickey's doorstep, suitcase in hand with little prior preparation are spine tingling.

The Straight Dope are tips you may be able to use on your own trip. They've come about as a result of scores of trips by the Mousejunkies in this book. (Experience breeds knowledge, and at least in my case, a load of mistakes.)

Mousejunkie U are tidbits of trivia any self-respecting student of the Mouse would want to know.

There are comments, tips, anecdotes, and advice from the group of people collectively known as the **Mousejunkies**. They're a friendly, fun group who love Walt Disney World and are excited to share their experiences with anyone from first-time travelers to fellow addicts.

Awesome/Stupid Disney Idea are the things that pop into my head while I'm staring out the window daydreaming about my favorite vacation destination. They might be awesome ideas, but there's an equal chance that they may be stupid. It's been said that there's a fine line between clever and stupid. I walk that line pretty much every day.

I hope you laugh and maybe learn something about Walt Disney World. Most of all, I hope this book transports you there. Because every Mousejunkie needs a fix now and then.

Mousejunkie Rising

WHEN THE FIRST EDITION of *Mousejunkies* was released, I hoped it would strike a chord with small pockets of Disney fanatics. I thought it might find its way into the hands of people like me who can't get enough of Walt Disney World.

I had no idea that there is such a vast Mousejunkie army—a fifth column of enthusiasts, as it were—ready to mobilize the minute Annual Passholder room rates are released. What I learned is that we are legion. Geeky, maybe, and strangely obsessed, but we've got numbers. And opinions. With the release of *Mousejunkies* came a torrent of encouragement, shared experiences and questions. I thought I'd take a moment to address a few of the more common queries:

Do You Ever Get Tired of Disney?

Silly person. I put the "junkie" in "Mousejunkie."

For the better part of a year I worked in internal communications at a global healthcare company. One afternoon, the day after returning from a Walt Disney World vacation, my supervisor asked me to join her in a nearby conference room. As I walked into the room, I saw an HR representative was already there. The company was undergoing reorganization, and with that came layoffs. Other employees were organizing job searches and unemployment registration. How did I deal with the prospect of being caught up in the ongoing economic downturn?

Two words: Disney trip.

I drove straight home, picked up the phone, and gave in to my most basic Disney yearnings. I had been back a day and here I was, making arrangements to return in less than a month's time. It even sounded crazy to me. Yet somehow, the idea of taking a spin on the Tomorrowland Transit Authority took the sting out of signing on to the dole.

To be fair, I should disclose that a large contingent of Mousejunkies were going to be there, and one of them offered the pullout couch in a room at the Boardwalk resort. I had a few months left on my Annual Pass, and a Disney gift card I had recently received would probably pay for the food during my stay. So the cash outlay would be minimal.

Of course I still had to break it to my wife that I was about to embark on a five day Disney bender. She completely understood and encouraged me to take advantage of what I had already started to call a "research trip." And by "completely understood" I mean she was stressed, not sure this was such a great idea, and a little jealous that I'd be tearing through our favorite vacation destination while she would remain behind to care for our daughter, pay the bills and otherwise remain responsible.

The woman is obviously a saint. Her patience with my idiosyncrasies and obsessive behavior is matched only by her stunning beauty. And her willingness to proofread my books.

So, in short, no.

Does Your Wife Enjoy Walt Disney World as Much as You Do?

Once we're there, sure. But when I've got our credit card in hand and I'm on the phone with a cast member booking a trip, she'll usually assume the role of "Reluctant Mousejunkie." She worries about the bills and costs associated with traveling to Disney several times a year. I worry about getting an Advanced Dining Reservation at 'Ohana or if Space Mountain will be down for refurb while we're there. Remember: I'm an addict. I'm terribly irresponsible. There is no joke tacked on to the end of that sentence. I'm not kidding.

I Booked an Off-Site Hotel. Should I Be Afraid?

Not necessarily. I prefer the amenities associated with on-site hotels, but the chances are you will have a great trip. Despite the necessity of a rental car or limited shuttle access, having to actually leave Disney property every night, and the likelihood of encountering a pack of Orlando Jumping Snakes. You'll be fine. Maybe.

Why Do You Hate Figment So Much?

He peed in my Dole Whip.

What Do Others Think of Your Disney Habit?

A former coworker once asked me: "Why go to a place that recreates a majestic lodge in the Pacific Northwest, when you can actually go to a majestic lodge in the Pacific Northwest?"

My best answer, "Well, because . . . Mickey Mouse."

I didn't win over a convert that day. But I've learned to live with the strange looks and patronizing smiles.

Is There Anything about Walt Disney World that Bugs You?

Sure. The food is insanely expensive and the Disney Dining Plan has resulted in dumbed-down selections and one-page menus. Tomorrowland is one big construction site at this point. It's difficult to get a reservation at certain restaurants. It's about two thousand miles away from my house.

At times I get particularly attached to an attraction or show and then it disappears. I still miss the Tapestry of Nations parade and the Hunchback of Notre Dame stage show. And now that the brilliant a cappella group, Four for a Dollar, has been excised from the Beauty and the Beast pre show, Sunset Boulevard is just a bit less bright.

The Mouse giveth and the Mouse taketh away.

At the same time, some things never change. It's an addiction that has no signs of abating. I have yet to discover some sort of methadone that keeps my pulse from racing every time I hear the theme from IllumiNations: Reflections of Earth. I wonder if one day there will be a convenient wearable patch that'll make Dole Whips taste like paste or make me want to vacation somewhere that's not in central Florida.

Maybe something that'll help keep my meager earnings in the bank and out of Mickey's purse.

Even if there was something that'd break the spell Walt Disney World has on me—or something that would make me act a bit more responsibly—I don't think I'd sign up for it. Besides, I like to think the profits Disney scored off my many trips to its vacation kingdom went into developing the Toy Story Midway Mania attraction or subsidized the cost of humongous turkey legs in Frontierland.

It may sound crazy to the uninitiated, but there are others out there with a habit much worse than mine. I am most definitely not alone.

In fact, I know that many other seemingly well-adjusted adults go to Walt Disney World as often, or more often, than I do. I can't get through a day without running into a fellow Mousejunkie. They're scattered everywhere throughout my life. They're my poker buddies, coworkers, family members, my UPS driver, online acquaintances and longtime friends. I even sleep with one.

I feel better knowing that I'm not alone, but it doesn't completely kill the inkling that I'm somehow seen as a social oddity, since my love of all things Disney has been outed. I don't mind. For every person who thinks I've been blinded by Disney's skilled marketing gurus, there's someone else calculating how an order of Figaro Fries from Pinnochio's Village Haus at the Magic Kingdom fits into his Dining Plan allotment. That person understands.

Our paths cross on Main Street USA. He's wearing an inexplicably stupid souvenir Goofy hat, I'm wearing a hopelessly outdated fanny pack and proudly sporting a lanyard with unnecessarily expensive collectible pins on it. We make eye contact and think nothing of our otherwise regrettable fashion choices. These things are part of the dress code at Walt Disney World, and we revel in it.

I don't have to convince a Walt Disney World guidebook reader. Chances are you're already planning a trip, have been there several times or are suffering the inevitable withdrawal that comes with the end of every Disney vacation, and you want to experience that magic again. Face it, you're either a Mousejunkie, or you're a potential Mousejunkie. There's a reason you're holding this book and not flipping through something from a more respectable section of the bookstore.

But I know not everyone shares our love for the place. All Disney addicts face the same quizzical looks and opinionated replies when coworkers or friends learn we'll be returning to Walt Disney World on vacation.

I've prepared a brief, two-page worksheet suitable for distribution.

Simply fill out the form on the following two pages, make copies, and hand it out to any naysayers, party poopers or mundane-loving coots around your workplace.

Mousejunkie

Two cubicles over
The one with the Mickey ears on top of the monitor
Your office

Dear _____,

Yes, I am going to Walt Disney World on vacation. Again. Before you
a. Roll your eyes
b. Snort
c. Offer your unsolicited opinion

Let me try to explain to you why I have decided to visit WDW for
the ____th time.

I love the magical atmosphere, incredible attractions, Broadway-
caliber shows, unmatched customer service and value for my vacation dollar.

There is nothing quite like
a. Seeing the wonder in my child's eyes when his/her dreams
come true
b. Seeing the wonder in my spouse's eyes when his/her dreams
come true
c. Seeing my dreams come true
d. Having a Dole Whip in one hand and a Fastpass in the other

Since you choose not to visit Walt Disney World, I can only assume
a. You will not be in line in front of me at Expedition Everest
b. It'll be that much easier to get an Advanced Dining Reservation
at Le Cellier

c. You won't mind covering my shift/responsibilities while I'm at
    IllumiNations: Reflections of Earth

Remember, you'll be stuck back here sitting in a conference room
while I hug
a. The lovely Princess Jasmine
b. The rugged, if slightly tipsy, Jack Sparrow

Sincerely,

_____

Your Walt Disney World-bound co-worker

P.S. Plplpblbbblbllllblllll

Mousejunkies Adapt: What's New Around the World?

Who Moved My Cheesecake?

THINGS AROUND THE FLORIDA property change faster than my friend Mousejunkie J can traverse the World Showcase at Epcot. Which is to say, rather quickly. Especially if there's a funnel cake with his name on it at the other side.

What's new? You can't book a breakfast at Spoodles or Boatwrights. You can spend your vacation in a tree house. The Share a Dream Come True parade has stepped off for the last time. You can drift off to sleep in a hotel room overlooking the Magic Kingdom. And the future plans for Fantasyland are nothing less than astounding.

This is how Walt Disney intended things to be. He was always encouraging his workers to continue "plussing" things, taking a good idea and making it better. This is why Mr. Toad went to the great swamp in the sky and why I can't get my hands on the apple streusel cheesecake at Tony's Town Square restaurant anymore. Sometimes the changes are for the better, other times they're off the mark. One thing is for sure, however, there will always be something new and different going on in central Florida.

While some of the recent changes at the Walt Disney World Resort wouldn't be considered plussing by even the most ardent Mousejunkie, some are nothing short of an utter triumph.

And this is why we must return. I've got to get into that balloon at Downtown Disney and have a look at the property from four hundred feet in the air. I want to check out the American Idol Experience at Disney's Hollywood Studios. I want to head down to the Boardwalk to see what's so great about Cat Cora's cooking. But most of all I want that weird, stale smell of Walt Disney World water—something you can only score deep in the bowels of a Disney dark ride—to lodge itself in that part of my brain that releases Technicolor, animatronic endorphins.

That's the kind of thing that never changes. If you're a certified Mousejunkie, you know exactly what I'm talking about. And even then, there are countless new experiences to tweak out on during every visit to Walt Disney World. For every classic attraction like Carousel of Progress, there's always a new astonishing example of technology and magic like Toy Story Midway Mania that sends us into new fits of wondrous rapture.

Here's a closer look at what's new across the roughly forty square miles of central Florida that began its life with the unassuming title of The Florida Project.

New at the Magic Kingdom

The largest expansion Walt Disney World's original theme park has ever seen is underway. By 2013, Fantasyland will have doubled in size, offering new attractions, themed dining and immersive experiences.

★**Awesome/Stupid Disney Idea** *A stroller parking deck located near the back of Fantasyland. Think of it. A stroller-free walk past Mickey's Philharmagic? Divine.*

Ground breaking on the massive Fantasyland expansion has already sent Mickey's Toontown Fair to Disney heaven. Or maybe theme park purgatory. It wasn't *that* good.

At press time, the expansion is in full swing. The construction wall runs from Pinocchio's Village Haus, already resulting in the removal of Ariel's Grotto, and Pooh's Playful Spot, to just about the current entrance to Toontown. Elements of Toontown will live on in the new Fantasyland. Goofy's Barnstormer, a short roller coaster perfect for breaking youngsters in, will survive the wrecking ball, and Mickey and Minnie's houses may pop-up elsewhere. A section of the Town Square Exposition Hall is being converted to house the new Mickey and Minnie meet-and-greet.

I've also been assured that there likely won't be a day when Dumbo the Flying Elephant won't be doing what it does best: carrying children through the skies of Fantasyland and causing parents to wait ungodly amounts of time in the hot sun. In fact, when all is said and done, there will be two Dumbo the Flying Elephant attractions in the park. The new attractions will be able to handle twice as many guests and will be located in

Dumbo's Flying Circus. While waiting under the new bigtop, there will be midway games and interactive activities.

What else will guests get once construction is complete? An almost unrecognizable Fantasyland.

Disney princesses will have their own themed villages in the new Fantasyland Forest. The key theme here, and throughout the new Fantasyland, is immersive experiences.

Cinderella already got her own castle, that instantly recognizable icon of Walt Disney World, but it looks like she will be getting a summer place.

At **Dreams Come True with Cinderella**, youngsters can meet the princess, dance with her, or train to become one of her knights.

At **Enchanted Tales with Belle**, guests will stand in front of an enchanted mirror, which will "transport" them from Belle's father's cottage to Beast's castle for a storytelling performance.

Beast's castle won't compete with Cinderella Castle in terms of size or scale, but it will contain the new 552-seat **Be Our Guest restaurant** ready to offer repast to hungry visitors.

A smaller, counter-service option, **Gaston's Tavern**, will also be part of Belle's village. Though calling it a 'tavern' is part of the fantasy. The Magic Kingdom is a dry park.

A Birthday Surprise for Sleeping Beauty will allow kids to take part in a sweet sixteen party for the most well-rested monarch. Guests will step inside Briar Rose Cottage where the three good fairies will preside over Aurora's surprise celebration.

The **Seven Dwarfs Mine Train** will take you on a ride into the mine "where a million diamonds shine." The coaster, reportedly bigger than Goofy's Barnstormer/The Great Goofini but smaller than Big Thunder Mountain Railroad, will feature a first-of-its kind ride system with a train of ride vehicles that swing back and forth throughout the ride. The journey will be accompanied by music from the classic Disney film and animated figures of Snow White and the Dwarves.

Princess Meet and Greet   Snow White's Scary Adventures is being evicted to make room for Princess Fairytale Hall, a Disney princess meet-and-greet.

Speaking of meet-and-greet opportunities, Mickey has taken up a new residence and guests will soon be able to schedule a time to get their photo and hug with the Big Cheese. Guests can now get a Fastpass to meet Mickey in his new home in the Town Square Theater. The Town Square Theater is inside Exposition Hall right at the entrance of the park. According to Disney, this marks the first time FastPass will be utilized for a meet-and-greet at any Disney theme park.

Tinker Bell's Pixie Hollow will shrink visitors down to pixie size and allow a meet-and-greet with Tink and her pixie friends. It'll likely be similar to the former Toontown version: populated by really, really, really enthusiastic characters who stand with their hands on their hips and probably had too much pixie coffee. Great for the kids though.

If all this sounds like gussied-up new photo ops, you might not be far off. There's no way to know until construction is complete. Even if that is the case, it'll likely look amazing, and the added interactive elements will surely outshine standing in line for a quick snapshot.

However, there is one major new attraction involved in the expansion. **Under the Sea: Journey of the Little Mermaid** will be a ride-through attraction featuring music from the popular animated film.

According to a Disney insider's report after a site-visit where the attraction was under construction, Under the Sea: Journey of the Little Mermaid will be narrated by Scuttle, from the film. Guests will ride through the attraction—down under the sea—on a Disney omni-mover similar to what is used in the Haunted Mansion attraction. Classic scenes from the film are recreated, and Jody Benson, the original voice of Ariel, has reprised her role. The attraction reportedly captures the soul of the film perfectly.

Early planning art shows a castle wall surrounding the new Fantasyland, giving it a completely new look. Expect heavy crowds as the project is unveiled.

Now that that's all been laid out, I'm going to add a caveat: Disney likes to change its mind. These plans could very well be altered, expanded, or excised.

Also among the newer offerings at the Magic Kingdom is **Dream Along With Mickey,** a show where Mickey, Minnie, and all kinds of characters must convince Donald Duck that dreams do come true. Song and dance numbers are punctuated by brief fireworks displays. The show is performed several times daily right in front of Cinderella Castle.

The current daily 3 P.M. parade (please don't ask a Cast Member what time it steps off) is **Celebrate a Dream Come True**. In this typically impressive Disney pageant, Mickey leads a colorful tribute to Disney animation, a float-laden procession of characters and live actors from Frontierland, around the Castle hub and down Main Street U.S.A.

The Straight Dope *The parade starts from one of two places: Right next to the firehouse at the City Hall Hub, or in Frontierland near Splash Mountain. Ask a cast member which end of the park the parade will be stepping off from. If you're at the far end, you won't start to see the parade until 3:20 P.M.*

It's not all Fantasyland though. The park is now host to one of the most visually surprising shows in all of Walt Disney World, "The Magic, The Memories and You."

When Disney first announced the Let the Memories Begin campaign, I was gripped by an intense indifference. Actually, it was indifference bordering on dislike. It all just seemed so underwhelming. Projecting pictures of guests on the Castle seemed to lack any spark.

When I actually saw it executed in the form of the night-time show, "The Magic, The Memories and You," I took it all back.

You'd think I would've learned by now. Disney knows what it's doing. Sure, there are missteps, like the second-half of Spaceship Earth or the What Will You Celebrate campaign, but for the most part they tend to hit it out of the park.

Let the Memories Begin is another home run. The images projected are remarkably clear, and the use of color completely remakes Cinderella Castle in a way I didn't think was possible. Then there's the soundtrack. For me, music plays a huge role in how a show, attraction or presentation works or doesn't work at Walt Disney World. And in this case, it works. Disney has again created something that can move you. And that's one of the reasons I originally fell in love with the place.

New at Epcot

That beeping, four note melody chirping out across the World Showcase is the sound of Disney's Imagineers discovering new interactive ways to involve guests in their parks.

In this case it's Disney's **Kim Possible World Showcase Adventure**. Guests pick up a "Kimmunicator" at one of several kiosks throughout the park. From there, they're invited to become secret agents and work alongside Kim's tech expert Wade Load to foil comical villains throughout the World Showcase.

I've been known to whine from time to time, especially when it comes to crisscrossing the park endlessly. Aging legs and an increasing girth will do that to a once spry young Mousejunkie. But joy! When guests are sent out into the World Showcase, Kimmunicator in hand, each mission is relegated to one of seven pavilions. This means no rushing from Mexico to Italy, back to China and off to the U.K. It's all in one country's pavilion, depending on your specific mission.

The interactive, handheld device helps guests maneuver through their quest by prompting them to complete a number of tasks. The device sets off interactive elements within the pavilions. My favorite: as you are asked to stand in an alleyway and look up the Eiffel Tower, a photo is taken and sent to your Kimmunicator. There you are, clutching the device and staring upward. The effect is impressive and leaves visitors looking around, asking, "How did they do that?"

Guests can play the World Showcase Adventure in seven World Showcase pavilions: the U.K., France, Japan, Germany, China, Norway, and Mexico, each of which promises a new adventure and a new arch villain from the animated Kim Possible series.

A lot of people loved Michael Jackson. They loved his music, his dancing, and evidently his oddball lifestyle. I am not among them. I don't have anything specific against him or his legacy. I recognize his place in pop music history, it just does nothing for me. Dance music and I are not exactly on speaking terms. For a nominal fee I will demonstrate why. I will not be held responsible for internal injuries caused by the ensuing laughter.

So it was with great ambivalence, bordering on overwhelming ennui, that I learned that **Captain EO** was returning to Epcot after a sixteen-year hiatus.

Michael Jackson stars in this seventeen-minute, 3-D film where the good Captain and his crew discover a colorless planet where they confront the forces of darkness with the power of music and dance.

The show includes two original songs, and was shot in the mid-80s involving the talents of George Lucas, Angelica Huston, and Francis Ford Coppola.

Fans of the Gloved One were ecstatic.

"I'm a huge Michael Jackson fan and I always have been," my friend Walt said upon hearing of the Captain's return. "When they took Captain EO away I remember how disappointed I was. It's great that it's back at Walt Disney World. I couldn't be happier."

Mousejunkie U *Sharp-eyed guests may be able to spot a young* Super High Me *comedian Doug Benson as an uncredited orange dancer in Captain EO.*

Captain EO is shown in the Imagination pavilion in the Honey I Shrunk the Audience Theater. Perhaps an epic battle of who is more irrelevant will break out.

Disney's smallest Audio-Animatronic, at least temporarily, entertains diners at Chefs de France at Epcot.

Six days a week, four times a day, **Remy**, the gastronomically gifted rat from the Disney/Pixar film *Ratatouille* emerges from under a silver-domed cheese platter to interact with guests. He squeaks, chirps, wiggles and dances as a maitre d' wheels Remy around to each table in the restaurant. Diners are allowed an up-close experience with the impressively designed creature, which is part of Walt Disney Imagineering's Living Character initiative.

Remy's run was originally scheduled to end in 2009, but seems to have been extended indefinitely. No word on how long he'll stick around.

New to the Mexico pavilion in the World Showcase is **La Cava del Tequila,** a cavern-like space offering my favorite kind of tequila: a lot.

Sampling the tequila and specialty margarita flights is fun, and light Mexican appetizers are offered.

New at Disney's Hollywood Studios

One of the newer attractions, depending on when your last visit to Walt Disney World was, is also among its best. **Toy Story Midway Mania,** located on Pixar Place near the back of the park, is a 3-D, interactive dark ride and game based on the successful series of films.

In this particularly eye-catching queue, as they enter the world of Andy's room, guests are "shrunk" down to the size of a toy. Winding through the line, Imagineers reveal guests' diminished size by placing them among toys and games from a time predating video games and computers: Giant playing cards, board games, a massive orange crayon here and a Lincoln Log structure there. A fistful of Barrel Full of Monkeys leads the way to an animatronic Mr. Potato Head, who acts as a midway barker. The Don Rickles-voiced spud spouts a mixture of witty puns mixed with allusions to the insult comic's classic bits. (Nothing stronger than "you hockey puck" here.) Cast members—"toys"—get everyone onboard a vehicle, where they don 3-D glasses and are whipped through several midway game scenarios where they fire projectiles to score points. The effects are convincing, the game play rapid, and the overall effect breathtaking. And true to Disney's initial philosophy, it's a game parents and children can play together.

The midway minigames are:

➤ The Pie-Throw Practice Booth
➤ Hamm and Eggs—an egg-toss game.
➤ Rex and Trixie's Dino Darts—a new scenario has been added since the release of *Toy Story* 3. This new dart tossing challenge replaced Bo Peep's Baaa-loon Pop as of May 2010.
➤ Green Army Men Shoot Camp—players break plates with baseballs while a drill sergeant sounding suspiciously like R. Lee Ermey shouts instructions and encouragement.
➤ Buzz Lightyear's Flying Tossers—a ring toss game featuring the little green denizens of Pizza Planet's claw game.
➤ Woody's Rootin' Tootin' Shootin' Gallery—a shooting gallery that could ultimately put your score over the top. (Watch for the bat that comes swinging down at the top of the screen.)

My family is fairly competitive, so the first time we piled into our ride cars, the trash talk was pointed and plentiful. The ride vehicles seat up to four people, back to back. Amy and our daughter, Katie, sat on one side, so I took the other side for myself. The ladies behind me had their game faces on, so when the car lurched forward and whipped us around the corner, I could hear them pulling on the firing strings as fast as they could.

But a technical malfunction ensured that I would emerge triumphant this day. After the first scenario in the game, our six-year-old thought she did so well that she went to high-five her mom. Her hand caught the corner of her 3-D glasses and sent them flying away in a bright yellow arc. Being a good mom, Amy removed her glasses and put them on Katie's head. Katie resumed playing, while Amy squinted and pointed her firing cannon at a blurry smudge that probably resembled something from *Toy Story*.

Meanwhile, I kept firing away behind them, unaware of my now-ensured victory.

Does defeating a six-year-old and a partially blinded woman make me feel somehow superior? Triumphant? No, of course not. (Yes it does.)

Pop star hopefuls get their shot at fame at the **American Idol Experience**. Guests with a vocal talent (or perceived talent) pre-register and audition for a producer. Three people are picked to perform in front of a live audience, and face Disney's version of Simon, Randy and Kara (or Ellen. Or Paula. Or Jennifer Lopez. Or Stephen Tyler.)

Several shows are held throughout the day, and the winners from each performance compete in a finale that night. The winner gets a Dream Ticket—a guaranteed reservation at a future *American Idol* regional audition without having to wait all day with the rest of the rabble.

Mousejunkie U *American Idol finalist Aaron Kelly was an American Idol Experience winner, and finished fifth overall in the ninth season of the television show.*

Developed with Simon Fuller's 19 Entertainment, the American Idol Experience Theater recreates the TV show's look and atmosphere perfectly. It's a fun, exciting recreation, and fans of the show will no doubt love the Studio's version.

Finally, a new 3-D version of **Star Tours** is scheduled to open in 2011. Though it remains popular, a do-over of the tired film portion of the attraction is long overdue. The new version is being created under the auspices of the head Jedi himself, George Lucas, and will reportedly include immersive elements that will usher guests to locations throughout the *Star Wars* universe.

If you find yourself near Star Tours—or even if you don't, get there—check out the **Jedi Training Academy**, located right next door. Jedi Training Academy was previously performed only during *Star Wars* Weekends, but its popularity led to its installation as a full-time, interactive attraction. A Jedi master chooses a clutch of younglings to join him onstage to learn the ways of the Force. Kids are given training light sabers and robes and are taught a few basic fighting moves. When Darth Vader and the Stormtroopers arrive, the little ones are given a chance to combat the Dark Side with their new skills. When danger is defeated, the kids return the robes and light sabers and get a small diploma for their efforts. It's an entertaining and always hilarious show.

New at Disney's Animal Kingdom

Personalized, guided treks out into the **Harambe Wildlife Reserve** in Disney's Animal Kingdom Park will now provide guests with a chance to get even closer to the action. This new immersive experience will take small groups out into the reserve, allow them more time to observe the animals in their natural surroundings, and provide a peek into an undeveloped forest area. The new tour wraps up aboard a special vehicle designed just for this experience.

"New-er" at Disney's Animal Kingdom is **Finding Nemo: The Musical**. It's a forty minute song-and-dance theatrical extravaganza that opened in 2007 and is a can't-miss for fans of the Pixar film. Inventive, colorful, and in some cases huge puppets designed by Michael Curry, who also created the puppets for Disney's Broadway production of *The Lion King*, and new musical numbers ("In the Big Blue World," "Just Keep Swimming," "Fish Are Friends Not Food" among them) make this production one of the top draws to the park. The show is performed five times daily.

New at the Resorts

As things change and new options for all budgets are introduced around the World, it becomes more and more difficult to rationalize staying off-site.

Disney's All-Star Music Resort Family Suites provide an affordable way to accommodate larger clans. More than 400 guest rooms have been converted into 215 suites at the All-Star Music Resort. Most prominently, a tour through the family suites gives the impression that you are not at a value-level resort: two bathrooms, a nice size kitchenette, a private master bedroom, two flat screen TVs, and colorful, inventive furniture make this a fantastic option for families looking to spread out without breaking the bank. (*$190 to $320 a night depending on season. Sleeps up to six.*)

Caribbean Beach Resort's Pirate Themed Rooms immerse guests in the adventure-filled world of buccaneers. Pirate ship beds and wooden "ship's deck" flooring are among the details added to 384 rooms near a zero gravity pool themed to appear like an old Spanish fort with cannons guarding the walls. (*$179 to $304 a night depending on season. Sleeps up to four.*)

But what's really new at Walt Disney World's resorts is just that: new resorts.

Disney's Art of Animation Resort, scheduled to open in 2012, will feature 1,120 family suites inspired by Disney and Pixar animated films such as *The Lion King*, *Finding Nemo* and *Cars*. There will also be 864 additional themed rooms in a "Little Mermaid" wing, according to Disney. The resort will be located next to Pop Century, which only makes sense, because it was originally constructed to be part of Pop Century.

The Villas at Animal Kingdom Lodge/Kidani Village are Disney Vacation Club resorts, but non-DVC guests can reserve rooms. All DVC resorts have a percentage of their rooms allocated for cash reservations. The Villas at Animal Kingdom Lodge are located in the original Jambo House. The villas at Jambo House are converted rooms that have taken over half of this original part of the resort. Kidani Village is a separate, new villa-only resort, located adjacent to the original Animal Kingdom Lodge. It features a smaller, more intimate feeling lobby, an adventurous table-service restaurant, Sanaa, and its own savanna. Quick-service dining is offered at the Mara in Jambo House, next door in the Animal Kingdom Lodge. Bus service is available between the two resorts. African-inspired (as if it weren't obvious) studios, one-bedroom suites, two-bedroom suites, and grand villas all feature home-away-from-home amenities. (*Studios range from $275 to $720 a night depending on season and view. One-bedroom suites range from $400 to $970 depending on season and view. Two-bedroom suites range from $720 to $1,695 a night depending on season and view. Three-bedroom Grand Villas range from $1,555 to $2,260 a night depending on season.*)

The Treehouse Villas at Disney's Saratoga Springs Resort and Spa are a unique development tucked into the wooded shores of Village Lake. From 1975 to 2002, Disney used the treehouses for guests as part of The Disney Institute and later for cast members. The older style treehouses were removed, and new, prefabricated structures have been installed. Each is a three-bedroom home elevated ten-feet off the ground. Each treehouse features cathedral ceilings and sleeps nine. They are all furnished with granite countertops and flat screen TVs. Disney calls the style "cabin casual." Mousejunkie J calls it "nice enough, but I wouldn't stay there again."

"You spend two bedroom DVC points for a three-bedroom unit. They're brand new, nicely decorated with vaulted ceilings, and they're detached units so no neighbors banging on the ceilings, walls, or floors," J said.

Your mileage may vary, but J, who likes to be in the center of the action a bit more, finds that the treehouses are a bit isolated. *(The Treehouse villas range from $555 to $935 a night depending on season.)*

The crown jewel in Disney's recent resort expansion has to be **Bay Lake Tower at Disney's Contemporary Resort**. A Disney Vacation Club resort, Bay Lake Tower overlooks, well, Bay Lake. But lucky guests can also score a room overlooking the Magic Kingdom—a more desirable, but pricier accommodation. The crescent-shaped structure offers some of the most dramatic views in all of Walt Disney World from its Top of the World Lounge.

Don't plan on wandering in to the Top of the World Lounge for a few drinks and a look-see, however. Guests have to be staying at Bay Lake Tower on DVC points in order to gain access.

The knock against Bay Lake Tower is that it feels sterile and lacks magic. I find it to be modern and clean. The rooms have a contemporary décor with modern artwork and a bright feel.

Bay Lake Tower is connected to the Contemporary Resort by a skyway bridge, and is within easy walking distance from the Magic Kingdom. *(Studio rooms range from $540 to $645 a night depending on season and view. One-bedroom suites range from $455 to $775 a night depending on season and view. Two-bedroom suites range from $645 to $1,350 a night depending on season and view. Three-bedroom grand villas range from $1,635 to $2,475 a night depending on season and view.)*

Feel guilty while kicking your feet up in a deluxe resort while Fido is sweating it out in a boarding kennel back home? (Honestly, I'm not being lazy. I have never met a dog named Fido. It's just a euphemism for "generic pet," I think.)

If you've ever wanted to bring your pet along on your Walt Disney World vacation, then lay this on your furry friend: a **Luxury Pet Resort** is being built to provide pet hospitality services such as doggy day camp, grooming and boarding. Does that sound crazy? Then try this on for size: ice cream treats and bedtime stories. For your dog. Seriously. Something tells me Pluto was in on the planning.

The facility will be run by Best Friends Pet Care.

New at Downtown Disney

The closing of the Adventurers Club and other Pleasure Island mainstays has opened the area up for some fresh shopping and dining options. Among them:

Paradiso 37: Featuring North, South, and Central American street cuisine, this restaurant sits near the grave of the late, lamented Adventurer's Club. Paradiso 37 offers thirty-seven kinds of tequila, ten signature margaritas and waterfront dining. As a new Downtown Disney option, it's perfect for those nights when I am forced, against my will, to choose something other than Raglan Road.

Cooke's of Dublin: A quick service (or, as Orlando's Irish say: food made for "take away") is part of the Raglan Road complex. It offers as a specialty, The Original One and One—hand battered fresh fish and chips served wrapped in newspaper. (Actually, paper designed to look like newspaper. This is too bad, given that I come from daily journalism and we need to sell as many newspapers as possible.) Finish off your meal with a Doh-Bar—a deep-fried candy bar. Cooke's is great for that fast meal when all the priority seating is booked at Downtown Disney.

Characters in Flight gives guests a chance to hop aboard a hot air balloon and view Walt Disney World from four hundred feet in the air. The balloon is tethered to the ground, and can carry as many as thirty guests at a time to see the Disneysphere. (Or fourteen if I'm on board.) Don't plan on flying if it gets breezy, however. Wind conditions can result in suspension of flights. The six-minute trip costs $16 for adults, and $10 for children aged three to nine.

Edgy apparel (Disney's description, which I can only take to mean "stuff kids wear" or maybe pointy shirts), Vinylmation, and accessories can be had at **D Street** at Downtown Disney's West Side.

Tren-D offers shoppers Disney-themed clothing with a designer flair. This urban-inspired shop is located in the Downtown Disney Marketplace.

New Dining Options at Walt Disney World

Contempo Café: Located on the fourth-floor concourse of the Contemporary Resort, the Contempo Café allows diners to place their orders using electronic menus and touch-screens. (Marinated beef flatbread, honey-lime chicken sandwich, chicken basil pasta.) This is the deluxe resort's version of counter service.

Kouzzina: Cat Cora's new eatery fills the old Spoodles location a Disney's Boardwalk Resort with Greek/Mediterranean-style cuisine. Cora, the first and, still, only female Iron Chef from the Food Network's *Iron Chef America*, has put together a hearty menu that stands out by its truly unique offerings. *Kouzzina*, a Greek word meaning "can we just get to the *Galaktoboureko*," (which, itself, is a Greek word for "custard baked in phyllo dough with vanilla-praline *gelato*" which is an Italian word for ice cream which typically translates to "gimme" in American English.) Kouzzina (which actually means "kitchen" serves breakfast, lunch, and dinner. (Menu items include Oak-fired pork T-bone, slow-cooked lamb shank, fisherman's stew, smashed-garlic fried potatoes, and a selection of Greek salads and sides.)

T-Rex: The full name of this new Downtown Disney restaurant is T-Rex: A Prehistoric Family Adventure, A Place to Eat, Shop, Explore and Discover. And Shop. (Because you can't get in or out without going through the gift shop.)

A prehistoric-themed eatery, T-Rex is run by the same outfit that brought the Rainforest Café to life. Picture a dino-themed Rainforest Café and you've pretty much got it. The atmosphere here is a lot of fun, with occasional meteor showers and dino activity. (Menu items include triassic tortellini, layers of Earth lasagna, bronto burger, paleozoic chicken sandwich, jurassic jerky. OK, not that last one. I just felt like playing along.)

Try to get past the really cheesy food titles. It's a lot of fun and the food is decent.

Now there are even bigger changes coming. After a few years of consistent atrophy, Pleasure Island has been put out of its misery.

Long live Hyperion Wharf.

The former nightclub district will be reborn with a nostalgic take on an early twentiety century port city/amusement pier. Hyperion Wharf, named for both the Greek god of light and the street where the first Disney animation studio was built, remained under construction at press time. Disney says the new take on this space will offer "stylish boutiques and innovative restaurants" by day, and "by night, thousands of lights will transform the area into an electric wonderland." Nearly $3.2 million is being invested into the nighttime lighting, according to reports, and the expansion will also include a waterfront entertainment area and a lighthouse structure.

Dining availability will increase by twenty-five percent at Downtown Disney. Steve Schussler, developer of Yak & Yeti, the Rainforest Cafe and T-Rex, has been tapped to create a restaurant called Mahogany Bay. The increased dining will add 1,500 seats to the Downtown Disney area, and create 1,200 new jobs. This is great news, giving more dining options to guests who don't want to, or can't, use a day on their park pass to get dinner at a restaurant inside a theme park.

Also, the Lego Imagination Center is expanding by 3,500 square feet, and we'll see new exterior models from Disney films.

The AMC Theatres at Downtown Disney are also getting a makeover, becoming Florida's first Fork & Screen Theater.

We'll also be getting new shops and "merchandise vignettes." Yes, merchandise vignettes. I remember walking around Downtown Disney thinking, "What this place needs is more merchandise vignettes." Well, dreams do come true.

Construction on the district began immediately following the announcement in early 2011, and is scheduled to be completed in 2013.

Wait. Isn't the Fantasyland expansion slated for completion in 2013? 2013 is going to be an awesome place to be. Put up those construction walls and let's get this thing going.

Bold American cooking defines **The Wave** at the Contemporary Resort, according to Disney. If by "bold" they mean "weird," then I am fully onboard.

This upscale restaurant makes the most of organic ingredients and healthy preparation. The decor is outstanding, the service is, as usual, perfect, and the drinks are certainly interesting. It's the menu that threw me a bit (for example: white bean mash in place of mashed potatoes. My answer: "Only if you take bologna paste as currency.") If you've got a bit of an adventurous palate, by all means give it a try. (Other menu items include seasonal vegetable stew, cinnamon-rubbed grilled pork, sustainable fish, and braised lamb shank.)

Rix Lounge, a nightlife spot at the Coronado Springs Resort, provides tapas-style appetizers and specialty drinks with its nightly entertainment. (Menu items include burger pinchos, cheese-and-fruit platter, smoked salmon tartar, chorizo flatbread, citrus chicken skewers.)

Located in the new Kidani Village resort, **Sanaa** is an exciting mashup of African and Indian cuisine. The expert waitstaff is fantastic at suggesting samplers and describing menu items to hesitant diners who may not be familiar with the exotic-sounding food. The restaurant has an outstanding view of the animals of the Kidani Village savanna just outside. By all means start with the Indian-style bread service: naan, onion kulcha, paratha, and paneer paratha served with several accompanying dipping sauces. (Menu items include chicken in red curry sauce, tandoori chicken, grilled lamb kefta, and for the less adventurous, Angus chuck burger.)

Epcot has a few new dining changes as well. **Via Napoli**, an authentic Neapolitan pizzeria is now serving up pie in the Italy pavilion. The three hundred-seat pizzeria is inspired by Naples 45, another Patina Restaurant group pizzeria in New York City.

Via Napoli features an open kitchen with three wood-burning pizza ovens. According to Disney, the three ovens, each decorated with an ornately carved face, represent Italy's three active volcanoes: Etna, Vesuvius, and Stromboli.

Via Napoli's pizza chefs claim the difference is in the ingredients: hand-stretched dough, water from a source that is akin to water in Naples, mozzarella imported directly from Italy, and a quick spin in the seven-hundred-degree ovens, which seal in the rich flavors.

The restaurant occupies a formerly vacant area in the back of the pavilion.

The popular **Cantina de san Angel** has also expanded dramatically, offering more seating right on the World Showcase Lagoon. The 14,000-square-foot space offers indoor and outdoor dining.

Finally, dinner at **Le Cellier** now costs two dining credits on the Disney Dining Plan.

Someone Got Green Mush on My Burger

If I'm ever sent to the electric chair, I know what my last meal will be: A burger, fries and a coke.

Although I'd rather skip the electric chair and just get the burger, if that's all right.

So when I saw Disney was unveiling a clutch of new designer burgers across the property, my heart skipped a beat, and not because I've had so many burgers that my arteries are clogged with ground beef. I just couldn't wait to see what they came up with.

I'm a little conflicted though. While I love burgers—and the more creative, the bette—I can also be picky. There are certain things I just don't want to eat, and many of these things are on these designer burgers. Your mileage, of course, may vary.

For example, one of the new burgers at Cosmic Ray's Starlight Café in Tomorrowland at the Magic Kingdom is topped with Cheddar cheese, guacamole and bacon. I can rule that one out thanks to the guac. Order it without the guac, and you've basically got a bacon cheeseburger.

The Liberty Inn, also in the Magic Kingdom, features two. First, a veggie burger with Monterey Jack cheese, avocado, tomato and lettuce. No thanks on the avocado. Oh, and a veggie burger is not a burger. If it never went "moo" then it's not a burger. It's formed veggie mash.

A second burger at the Liberty Inn is topped with smoked ham, bacon, smoked Gouda cheese, red onion, tomato, pickle, lettuce and mustard aioli sauce. We've got a winner.

At Epcot, the Electric Umbrella is serving the mushroom-blue burger with sautéed mushrooms, bacon, blue cheese, fried onion straws, lettuce and tomato The surf 'n turf burger at the ABC Commissary at Disney's Hollywood Studios is particularly unique: the Cheddar cheeseburger is topped with fried shrimp, a sweet onion ring, tomato, pickle, lettuce and their own special sauce.

Also at Disney's Hollywood Studios, Rosie's tops their Cheddar burger with fried onion rings, tomato, pickle, lettuce and special sauce. At the Backlot Express, look for a Cheddar cheeseburger topped with diced avocado, sweet onion ring, lettuce, tomato and special sauce. I can only believe Disney has invested in a guacamole/avocado plantation somewhere. Or maybe The Land had an unexpectedly good yield. Still, keep the green mush off my burger, please.

As if to taunt me: The All Star Movies resort is offering a bacon-guacamole cheeseburger.

Here's the fun part with all the new upgrades and construction: don't believe for a second that expansion or refurbs are over with these announcements. The trouble with committing something to print is that Disney will invariably announce something new as soon as this book hits the shelves.

3 Birth of a Mousejunkie

In Which a Disastrous Beginning Improves Dramatically

WE HAD BEEN ON THE GROUND in Orlando for less than an hour, and we were already rethinking our plan to vacation at Walt Disney World.

My wife and I had just battled an unruly mob while checking in to our non-Disney-owned hotel somewhere on a patch of oily, sun-softened asphalt in Kissimmee.

Then we discovered that our travel agent had dramatically misrepresented our accommodations.

And now Amy was succumbing to what was shaping up to be a disaster of a week ahead of us. There was no kitchenette. There was no shuttle ready to take us to Walt Disney World, which allegedly lay just to our west. Perhaps it lay strategically hidden behind the fried chicken shack or the crappy t-shirt shop.

There were flies. And all around us was an absolutely crushing, all-enveloping, relentless heat. It is memorable only because where there was once an air conditioner in our room, there was now a large metal box that conditioned approximately no cubic feet of air whatsoever.

In a quiet voice shaking with regret, she summed up our vacation thus far.

"I can't do this," she said.

If, at that moment, I had grabbed a taxi back to the Orlando International Airport and hopped the next flight home, this would be a very short book, perhaps called Laying-on-the-Couch-All-Weekjunkies." We certainly would have saved a lot of money. And we definitely would have avoided curious stares from people when they learned we'd be returning to central Florida. Again.

But then we would have missed so many things. Like the overwhelming nostalgia that made it feel like we were traveling back in time, watching Wonderful World of Disney as a youngster in the early 70s. Or the tangible high that accompanied being completely immersed in an admittedly manufactured world where everything exceeded my expectations. What I would've missed most, without even knowing it, would have been the relationships.

Mousejunkies are a fraternity of like-minded Disney enthusiasts who speak a shared language and have experienced similar things at a fixed location. It's almost impossible not to forge new bonds with people who have also been moved by what started out as nothing more than a simple trip to a theme park resort.

It also could have been the bread pudding at 'Ohana. Either way, our lives would be dramatically different right now if it wasn't for that decision to see our planned vacation through.

So I'm glad we decided to change hotels, brave the heat and the crowds and embark on what would become a life-changing seven days. It wasn't exactly a religious experience, but it did open up a whole new world, introduce us to new friends, and provide an all-encompassing hobby and lifestyle.

There's a reason Mousejunkies exist. People visit Walt Disney World and we return again and again, which means that Disney is doing something right. And when it all comes together, it can form a potent concoction that turns a seemingly normal individual into an unabashed, wide-eyed fanatic. It's that heady fusion that breeds Mousejunkies.

More often than not, it all starts with a lightning bolt moment. Weather, crowd levels, company, and circumstances combine into a synchronous mash that converts even the most apathetic vacationer. I know this to be fact because what else can I attribute my compulsion to sit in a giant honey pot and ride through the Hundred Acre Wood like a child?

I'll throw a few "likes" out there that might stereotype me as a meathead: I like hockey. I like mixed martial arts fighting. I like Lemmy from Motorhead, who, to my ears, is a velvet-throated crooner. And yet, thanks to my own personal lightning bolt moment, I'll hug a sweaty stranger in a bear suit and gasp at water fountains.

Here's an example of what being beaten by the magic stick will do to you: I love Peter Pan's Flight in Fantasyland at the Magic Kingdom. On the surface that might not seem like much, but such is my shameless love for all things Disney, I am powerless in the face of animatronics.

On one trip a few years back I found myself at Walt Disney with a friend named Kevin. We were in Fantasyland standing in front of Peter Pan's Flight—a dark ride that takes guests on a flying tour over London and through Neverland. I looked at Kevin, jerked my thumb toward the standby line and we took our spot among the toddlers. I'm a fairly big guy and Kevin is six foot four. The two of us squeezed into our personal pirate ship and began our pixie-dusted flight, which takes guests past the usually lengthy queue. As we glided past the screaming masses I could not look them in the eye. Here we were, two grown men stuffed into a ride vehicle designed ideally for kids a fraction of our combined size, delaying a youngster's journey into the world of Peter Pan. I avoided the accusing stares of people who had waited for the better part of an hour by staring at the wall next to us as the echoes of hot, crying children reverberated in my ears.

Then, we turned the corner and took flight over J. M. Barrie's London, whereupon I clapped my hands like a five-year-old on Pixie Stix.

A Field Guide to Spotting a Mousejunkie

What's the difference between a satisfied Walt Disney World guest and a hopelessly addicted Mousejunkie?

For Mousejunkies, Disney is a lifestyle.

A satisfied guest might feel they got a good value for their vacation dollar. A Mousejunkie has a great time and leaves no vacation dollar unspent. And if there are a few meager funds left at the end of the week, they are spent planning the next trip—which has already been booked.

In the simplest terms, a Mousejunkie is an admitted Walt Disney World fanatic. Think of it like this: fans of the Grateful Dead, Deadheads, had Garcia. Parrotheads love Jimmy Buffett. Juggalos.... Well, Juggalos are just weird. But they embrace their passion, which I can get behind. I don't get any of that, but I don't expect other people to understand the life of a Disney freak either. Unless they are one of us.

Conduct a little self examination and see if any of this sounds familiar: A Mousejunkie has Dole Whip running through his or her veins. A Mousejunkie has more than one Disney trip planned and booked at any time. A Mousejunkie can tell you what day is 180 days away from any given date. It's all part of a lifestyle that makes picking a Mousejunkie out from a crowd quite easy.

Here's a quick litmus test to gauge whether or not you might be a Mousejunkie: take a look at your browser's bookmarks. Do you see your child's school, your bank, a search engine, YouTube? Excuse my indifference, but "yawn."

On the other hand, do you see an Advanced Dining Reservation link, Mickeyxtreme.com, the Parks Blog, the WDW Today Podcast site or the DIS Boards? Well then, pull up a Mickey Premium Bar and let's talk.

Say you're on the road and you think you may be stuck in traffic behind a Mousejunkie. Take this quick visual inventory: Are there Disney antennae toppers or license plate frames? Bumper stickers are a dead giveaway: "Honk if you want my Soarin' Fastpass."

Be aware of these subtle clues, and you'll see that Mousejunkies in the wild are actually quite common.

Crowd-Sourcing the Mouse

Mousejunkies are, of course, Disney fanatics, the label people sometimes assign to themselves when explaining their love for Disney. But they're also my panel of personal experts, the people I turn to when I need to know something about Walt Disney World.

Here's the strange thing: each of these people found their way to Walt Disney World separately. None of us traveled together when we were first inducted into this fraternity of fantasy. It only emerged that we were wrestling with internal Disney needs at weddings, cookouts and gatherings. Each person traveled their own road to Disney addiction, but as time passed and our habitual vacation patterns emerged, we connected on another level.

In the following pages I'll rely on the sage advice of these people. These are the leisure ninjas who have embraced this lifestyle. Each possesses a black belt in Disney trip planning, and each has their own particular area of expertise. Ask about what time of year to go, what park to visit or which restaurant to eat at, and they'll slap a little Mickey Jujitsu on you. They're each capable of throwing a magical submission hold that'll have you flailing about in the happiest tap-out on earth.

There are a million Disney experts, but below are the dossiers on the Special Forces of this army. (Assembled mainly because I know them and can bother them endlessly for tips and information.)

I've said it before: I'm an enthusiast, but these people are true experts. All I know is I came back from that first trip to Walt Disney World, sat down in front of my computer and started typing. These people helped me make sense of it all.

Think of this roster as a Walt Disney World jury. My opinion is no more valid than the next guest's. So if there's a mob of Disney freaks and if we can reach a quorum on whether or not Citrico's is great or the ABC Commissary is awful, or whether it's smarter to use cash on a weekend rather than using Disney Vacation Club points for your room, then I'd say we've hit upon something.

These Are the Mousejunkies

Name: Mousejunkie Randy
AKA: Disney King
Profile: Randy has issues. And I mean that in a nice way.

I didn't know him prior to his Disney addiction, but from what I'm told he was always Mr. Fun. I know a lot of people that travel to Walt Disney World often, but none of them possess the rabid need to return that Randy does. Randy is an engineer by profession, and his employer could probably send his paycheck to the Boardwalk Resort and he'd never miss a deposit.

Randy once worked as a cast member in the Disney Store one night a week. By day he'd help design defense systems for the U.S. government, and by night he'd help design Disney vacation plans for store customers. He pioneered pin trading at the store, and was instrumental in launching scores of first-time ventures to the vacation kingdom.

His claim to the throne of Disney King didn't come lightly. Randy took his role at the store seriously. His enthusiasm for anything Disney was contagious.

I admire his ability to approach trip planning with the eye of a detached analyst. He can weigh financial concerns against cost-per-hour and come up with best practices in a matter of seconds.

I suspect there's something more nefarious at work with Randy, however. Legend has it that Randy's house is exactly 1,971 miles from Cinderella Castle in the Magic Kingdom, a number that reflects the same year the resort opened. It's sort of like a pixie-dust-laden version of *Poltergeist*.

Expertise: Name it. The man's brain is constantly scanning options, plans, prices, and new information to formulate the most efficient Disney vacation possible. He doesn't answer to "Disney King" for nothing. Try this experiment: The next time you're at Walt Disney World, look for a guy with broad shoulders, very short hair, a New England Patriots or Boston Red Sox jersey, and a backwards baseball hat on. That will be Randy. Just walk up behind him and say, "Disney King." Trust me, he'll answer.

"That actually happened to me once," Randy said. "I was in Disney Hollywood Studios and we had just entered the basement queue for the Twilight Zone Tower of Terror. Carol and I were just about to decide on right or left queue, when the lady behind me asked, 'Excuse me are you from New Hampshire?' I thought that my New England accent always gets worse when I am in Disney for some reason and I had been found out again. They would be asking me to 'pahk my cah in Hahvid yahd.' But that wasn't the case. I said 'Yes,' and she followed with 'Are you the Disney King, Mousejunkie Randy?' Carol let out a muffled gasp, holding in her laughter. I responded 'Well, yes I am.' She and her husband were frequent visitors to Disney World and had just read *Mousejunkies* and thought it was me. We rode in the same elevator, talked some Disney dining and got a picture."

Name: Mousejunkie Carol
AKA: Mousejunkie Mathlete
Profile: Carol is a partner at an accounting firm. She travels around the Northeast, auditing and, well, acccounting, I guess.

All I know is I don't quite understand what she does, but evidently she is very skilled at it.

But even in the suit-and-tie world of high finance, Carol's sharp eye can spot a potential Mousejunkie from across a desk.

"It's like a secret society for adults," she said. "I don't mention a word about it unless I see something from Disney in a person's office. And then it's like we have a different nature toward one another. It's like we've been friends for years. We speak the same language. My best clients are the ones that are part of this 'secret society.'"

Expertise: Carol is a connoisseur of Walt Disney World's resorts. Sure, the attractions are fun, the restaurants are nice and the shows are great, but for this discerning woman, it's all about where you lay your head. Carol and her husband Mousejunkie Randy have stayed at all but three of the twenty-four Disney-owned resorts. And with literally scores upon scores of nights spent in resorts ranging from luxury to bargain level, you'd think she's become a resort snob. Not so, this leader of lodging, this sovereign of sleep.

"I just like a resort that has a lot of activities or access to my needs," she said. "For example, the Caribbean Beach Resort has a huge food court and a nice central area with a pool and a bar. The new Kidani Village, although very nice, does not have a lot of amenities. So there is little for me to do or have at my fingertips, with one big exception: from three to four every afternoon, you can challenge Disney cast members to Wii games in the lobby."

Carol has been known to get funkier than you thought an accountant could during a highly-competitive game of "Just Dance" on cloudy afternoons.

"The best part of the Polynesian, for example, is that the quick service dining is open twenty-four hours a day. It's nice to come back from a late day at the park and be able to pick up a quick drink or snack before heading back to the hotel."

Just one note of advice: don't stand between Carol and a zebra-dome dessert at Boma in the Animal Kingdom Lodge. She may be slight in stature, but she packs a wallop.

 Name: Mousejunkie Amy
AKA: The Reluctant Mousejunkie
Profile: For someone categorized as a Mouse-junkie, Amy is pretty tough on my addiction. I suppose someone has to be.

In the interest of full disclosure, Amy also answers to the name "Mrs. Burke." We've been married for fifteen years, so of all the Mousejunkies, I know her best. She might be short, but she has the heart of a cornered badger that ate a bad-tempered wolverine. Just try adding a little debt to our family's finances, and you'll see it emerge. Her eyes take on a suspicious, and some might say violent stare whenever she sees me with a credit card in one hand and the phone in the other. That tableaux of irresponsibility can mean only one thing: I'm booking a Disney trip, and she's going to be the one to arrange payment. In our family, I'm the camp coun-selor. She's the CFO.

Don't get me wrong. She's not heartless. Far from it. The minute we're in our seats on the flight to Orlando, she becomes as Mickey-addicted as any of us. I think that's what makes her so great: she'll go along for the ride, but she's also the reason I'm writing this on a laptop in our own home, instead of using a crayon on a cardboard box in an alley. She's the responsible adult to my eternally tweaked adolescent.

"Every kid dreams of going to Disney World," she said. "I was in eighth grade when my dad showed up for our weekly visitation. He said we could go to the movies, or...go to Walt Disney World. I was totally surprised and that trip still seems like a dream.

"But I don't think I truly fell in love with the place until I was able to share it with my husband. I knew that the moment he saw all the different countries in Epcot, that he would fall madly in love. I couldn't wait to see the look on his face, because I knew deep down that it was the sort of place he'd never want to leave. He'd never been to Epcot, but I had. I knew he'd be wide eyed and loving all the sites and sounds. The Tapestry of Nations parade sealed the deal. The giant puppets combined with the music made it all incredibly magical."

Expertise: Amy's middle name is Danger. Actually, it's Rose. But Danger would fit her vacation personality better. If Mousejunkies were a military organization, Amy would be a fearless paratrooper hurtling into the unknown armed only with a dagger clutched between the wolverine chunks in her teeth. Get her on Disney property, and she'll start seeking out something fast, high, or upside down to hurtle through. When we found ourselves on a boat bobbing up and down on Bay Lake, it was Amy who jumped up when a volunteer was needed to take to the skies paragliding. She laughed heartily as a gust of wind turned her completely upside down four-hundred feet above the (in my mind) croc and snake-infested swamps below. Meanwhile, I peed a little. Nothing scares that woman. Except when I get that telltale Disney itch.

 Name: Mousejunkie Barry
AKA: The Blindside
Profile: Barry never expected to fall in love with Walt Disney World. He was sucker-punched with a white, four-fingered glove. He was unexpectedly battered with a switch ripped off the Tree of Life.

"I was fifteen years old and touring Disney World for the first time when it happened," he said. "When you're fifteen, you're perhaps both too old and too young to really appreciate the Magic Kingdom—the naiveté of youth is gone and you haven't experienced enough of the world yet to truly appreciate the escapism. I was wandering through the park looking for something interesting to do when I came upon the entrance to the Pirates of the Caribbean ride. There's no cutesy cartoons involved, right? Okay, off we go, then. As I made my way through the dungeon queue, I was being steadily wowed by the little touches: the skeletons, the dankness, the anticipation of what's to come. By the time I made it to the boat loading area, I was thoroughly enthused. The lightning bolt moment—that one moment where your spine tingles and you are at a loss for words—came when the boat shot down the falls and out into the harbor.

"As we slowly made our way past the side of the ship lobbing cannon balls across and into the water in front of us, I would have sworn that I had actually been shot out of the humid 2 P.M. sunlight of Florida and into fourteenth century at 2 A.M. I was completely blown away by the Inside-Outside—the feeling that you're actually outdoors in another world when in reality you're putting around inside a building in interesting-smelling water with convincing fake fire and robots chasing each other around. I went on Pirates no less than five more times that day and it remains my favorite ride of all time."

Expertise: A father of two Disney-loving girls, Barry has become an expert on traveling to Walt Disney World with kids. In his enthusiasm for all things Disney, Barry immediately jumped in and started using the Walt Disney World shorthand. He's also been known to make up his own: "I love my new BGSMM t-shirt." (Biscuit and Gravy Stained Mickey Mouse t-shirt.)

 Name: Mousejunkie Ryan
AKA: Teen Queen
Profile: Ryan was inducted into the cult of the Mouse at a fairly young age. It's not polite to divulge a young lady's age, but as someone in her late teens, she will serve as the teen expert throughout this book. Ryan's favorite attraction in all of Walt Disney World? "The Italian boys scooping gelato at the Italy pavilion at Epcot."

The girl knows what she likes.

Expertise: Thrill rides are about the only thing that will get this nineteen-year-old out of her resort bed at the crack of dawn. She won't say much, won't pack away the biscuits and gravy at the food court, and won't bring a whole lot of early-morning sunshine as she stares blankly while Disney's transportation system carts her ever-closer to the day's destination.

But the minute she steps down off that bus and her Chuck Taylor's hit theme park property, she comes to life. This dark-haired wisp of a teen will face down the craziest thrill ride available. The great thing about Disney thrill rides, she says, is that they tell a story—a detail most other theme parks overlook. Paired with Mousejunkie Jenna and clutching her ever-present Stitch plush, Ryan will run the Tower-of-Terror-to-Rock-n-Roller-Coaster Route of Insanity for days at a time.

She's also the loudest to mock my stubborn refusal to experience anything more thrilling than, say, Small World.

Name: Mousejunkie J
AKA: Just J
Profile: A mechanical engineer at a nuclear power plant, J is smart, successful, and just as addicted to Walt Disney World as the rest of us.

Around the office, he's the guy people turn to when there are questions regarding a Walt Disney World vacation. Above his desk is a huge digital clock which is always counting down. The Doomsday Clock perhaps? Nothing so serious. The clock is forever marking time toward J's next Disney vacation.

Also, I've known J for about thirty years. His name *really* is J. It says so on his license plate: "JustJ." He's not hiding his identity. I think.

Expertise: For J, Walt Disney World is all about the food.

An expert in touring theme parks and planning meals at Disney's table service restaurants, J has an uncanny way of recalling menus, describing flavors and maximizing dining options.

J is also known for a form of measurement known as "The Cote Pace." This is a way of gauging the speed at which one traverses Disney theme parks. The Cote Pace was initially set by J and his wife, Mousejunkie Deb. You'll know they're at Walt Disney World by the smoke trail they leave while moving from one attraction to the next. They're not rushing; it's just the natural speed they reach while touring Disney theme parks.

I was in England for ten days once, and I rented an Audi to drive to Scotland. That car seemed to naturally seek out eighty miles per hour along the M-something. (Which, I believe, equates to about 900.1 litres for our European friends). So, too, do J and Deb naturally seek out a blistering pace as they traverse Disney property.

I'm not totally convinced The Cote Pace is the best way to get around. I'm leaning towards a theory that they walk blindingly fast to see if I either collapse or if my thighs burst into flames due to chronic chafing.

We had dinner reservations at Chefs de France in Epcot on a recent trip. A friend who checked in at the restaurant called to alert us that our names had been called early. We were in the new tequila bar in the Mexico pavilion, which I believe, is approximately a jillion miles from Chefs de France. All of a sudden it became necessary to hoof it from the bowels of the Mexico pavilion to France.

This light jaunt (for everyone else in our touring party) almost killed me. I think I stopped sweating by the time the profiteroles were served.

Name: Mousejunkie Deb
AKA: Just Deb
Profile: In the real world, Deb leads a project management office for information systems within Boston's world-renowned healthcare industry. But drop her off at the Magic Kingdom and you'll find her in the back of the Main Street bakery sidling up to a chocolate chip cookie ice cream sandwich the size of her head. She seems to exude an endless capacity for vacation fun, and has put into words perhaps my favorite quote for why we are repeat visitors: "I like to think my favorite Disney memory hasn't happened yet."

Her Disney enthusiasm is catchy. However, if you are ever lucky enough to travel to Walt Disney World with Deb, don't let her tiny frame and big smile fool you. As one of the creators of the "Cote Pace," she may kill you. Must be special sneakers or something.

The Cote Pace has become such a well-known, and for some—well, for me—infamous part of our trips together, and I've come up with a plan to combat the side effects of the couple's blinding gait.

It's a studied, highly scientific response, and I'd like to share it with you now: try to be skinny. It's just a theory at this point, since I can't actually put it to the test, but I think it'll probably work.

Expertise: Deb possesses a ruthless Disney efficiency. From money-saving tips to mapping out travel routes, she's got it down. Deb can map out the best route for getting from any spot on Disney property to another, and do so in record time. It's a dramatic change from her first trip—a family vacation when she was a teenager in 1985— which had a few very un-Mousejunkie like moments.

Deb's family flew to Florida from their home in New Hampshire. It was her first time on a plane, and she looked forward to the break from the frigid New England winter. She arrived in Orlando prepared for a tropical vacation.

It snowed.

For the first time in years, there was measurable snowfall in central Florida.

On top of that, there was very little planning involved by 80s Deb.

"We were clueless," Deb said. "We rushed through the Magic Kingdom to log some vacation hours at the relatively new Epcot. After wandering through Future World for some time, we deemed the park small and lame and left.

"We had no idea we missed the entire World Showcase."

Scores of trips later, Deb is a much savvier visitor. She also counts Epcot as one of her favorite Disney destinations. But it was the first time staying on-property—at Dixie Landings (now Port Orleans Riverside)—that awakened the Mousejunkie in her.

"It was the full immersion in the magic and the theming," she said. "And never having to leave the boundaries of the World for a full week. That's what hooked me."

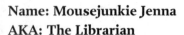

Name: Mousejunkie Jenna
AKA: The Librarian
Profile: As one who flies her Mousejunkie flag proudly, Jenna's interest in Disney World is readily apparent. Disney mementos dot her entire home. Wander into her cubicle at work, and if it weren't for the bitter Michigan cold freezing your nose hairs, or someone laughing at you because the Red Wings have won about two dozen Stanley Cups and your team hasn't won one in about forty years, you'd swear you were somehow transported to the Emporium shop on Main Street U.S.A. When Jenna goes golfing, she has a Mickey Mouse pouch on her bag. She has a Disney Vacation Club sticker on her car. She's a walking, talking Disney convention.

"I don't wear it every day, but I have a charm bracelet with one charm for every trip I have taken to Walt Disney World," she said. Which may explain her unusually developed right bicep. "Whenever I need something to occupy my brain, I default to Disney trip planning."

Expertise: Jenna is a Walt Disney World trip planning guru. As a writer, Jenna is a virtual library of Disney knowledge with an encyclopedic ability to recall even the most minor Disney detail.

And that's where Jenna's inner-librarian removes her glasses and shakes out the bun in her hair in slow motion. Trip planning is where Jenna truly comes alive.

"I have always been a planner and a list-maker, and my interests in subjects often turn into obsessions," she said. "I don't do things in half measures. When a friend and I made plans to meet for a vacation in 1999—my first trip in thirteen years—she soon let me take over the planning because I immediately began poring over books and the internet to find out everything I could. Over the years, I've continued following those resources and adding new books, sites, and experts and try not to let any new information slip by unnoticed."

"Think of me as a sort of Walt Disney World reference desk—I know a little bit about a wide range of subjects, but more importantly, if I don't know the answer to a question, I know where and how to find it."

 Name: Mousejunkie John
AKA: The Soul Man
Profile: John is a truck-driving, guitar-slinging, blues-singing father of two high-school-aged daughters, who can't get enough of Walt Disney World. Push his Harley out of the way, and you'll find the back wall of his garage is handpainted with a massive mural featuring Sorcerer Mickey. He's the only man I know brave enough to attempt creating a Dole Whip with a secret recipe based on his own handmade pineapple ice cream. None of that softserve nonsense for this multitalented Granite stater.

"During our first family trip, my youngest got to meet Cinderella in ToonTown," John said. "She was just shy of six at the time, and I must have read *Cinderella* to her at bedtime over a hundred times by then. Never had I seen a smile that big. Huge. I knew we'd be back."

Expertise: As a lifelong guitarist and singer, John is a Walt Disney World entertainment expert.

"I make sure I see British Invasion in the U.K. pavilion at the Epcot World Showcase every trip," John said. "Being a musician myself, I think they do a smashing job. So I knew when the guy who was 'Paul,' who kind of looked and sounded like Paul but didn't play lefty, was replaced with an actual lefty 'Paul,' who didn't really sound like Paul and had to wear a moptop wig. And then the guy who was 'George' left, and was replaced by the guy who had been 'John,' so they had to get a new 'John.' And, 'Ringo' seems to be someone different every time."

 Name: Mousejunkie Walt
AKA: The Mayor
Profile: Walt lives his life with flair. Traveling around the country while working on the finance side of the restaurant business, Walt has friends from every corner of the country.

If there's ever anyone in our group likely to run into an acquaintance while on vacation at Walt Disney World, it's Walt. He knows, and seems to be known, by everyone.

Expertise: Doing Disney deluxe is Walt's trademark. A Disney Vacation Club member, he and his family have nearly six-hundred points between them. There may be Mousejunkies who go more often, but there may not be any that go with more style.

"I only go once or twice a year," he said. "So I stay at the Boardwalk, I get the Boardwalk view—I do it right. When I'm there I want to treat myself to the best I can afford."

That fun comes with a price. Walt works long hours with very few days off in order to be able to visit Disney World the way he wants.

Ask Walt about his favorite trip and he's ready with an answer.

"The most rewarding trip, by far, was when I was able to get my family down there with my grandfather, and to be able to do that through Disney Vacation Club," he said. "If I could only go once in my life, and if I spent all that money on DVC, that one trip would have been worth it.

"We went with my grandfather, my father, and my nieces and nephews, and we were all able to enjoy it with him. He can't go now—he's on kidney dialysis—but it was just so rewarding. My grandfather appreciates everything in life, and he was so happy to be there. I will remember that trip for the rest of my life."

When someone books a trip to Walt Disney World, they realize fairly quickly that it takes a little more planning and expertise than a similar vacation to Six Flags might. And that's when the questions begin: When should I go? Where should I stay? Should we get the Disney Dining Plan? Where are your pants? Where can I get a massage? Where can I watch the football game on Sunday?

The Mousejunkies have, at one time or another posed these questions themselves. And they've learned the answers by trial and error. They've lived the answers and they're more than happy to share their Disney knowledge.

And then, of course, there's me. I've made huge mistakes, and I'm happy to tell you about them. Learn from me. Don't take a Disney cruise during hurricane season. Don't get bronchitis just before a Disney trip. Remember to wear pants.

There are a few things I can do well though. I can tell you what it feels like to hug strangers dressed in furry costumes in one-hundred-degree heat, and I can tell you what it feels like to be "That Guy" at the Monsters Inc. Laugh Floor.

Mainly, I'm just a guy with an addiction and a need to get it all down.

4 **Mousejunkies Travel**

ALL THE FAMILIAR ELEMENTS were in place: people shuffling through wallets to find theme park passes, cast members wrangling guests already worn out from a week of traipsing through queues and keeping to schedules, and people trying to put any body part *but* a finger into the biometric scanner at the turnstiles, thus delaying our entry.

And everywhere was the crush of humanity. The smell of sunscreen mixed with impatience. But finally the throng began to move forward. The rope was dropping and we were about to head into the park.

I was standing outside the main gates at Disney's Hollywood Studios, just minutes away from starting another day of our Walt Disney World vacation, and yet something was amiss. A completely unexpected feeling was enveloping me. My Mousejunkie senses were in full-on alarm mode. As we moved closer to the cast member waving people through the gates and into the park beyond, I started to put my finger on it.

I believe the sensation was...cold.

Not a slight chill that might send locals scrambling for warmer gear, but a full-on arctic bite that was sinking its teeth into my obstinate bones.

It was mid-January. The dead of winter. And shockingly, I was freezing. This would not have been unusual back at my home in the Northeast, where ice storms paralyze daily life and gray, gritty slush lines the roadways nine months out of the year. But this was Florida. The Sunshine State. Land of orange groves and palm trees and very strange infomercials about appliances. And yet I was standing there with my Annual Pass clutched in my numb fist, shivering.

I had no one to blame but myself. As we were packing for this particular vacation, Mousejunkie Amy reminded me that since this was actually winter, it might be prudent to prepare. It was going to be cooler in central Florida during our trip, according to the weather forecast.

"Perhaps packing a pair of pants would make sense," she said.

Since I don't wear pants, I declined. Before you recoil in horror, by "I don't wear pants," I mean "I wear shorts." All the time. Every day. Even back home in the depths of one of those aforementioned winters. I'll head out in mid-February to get my newspaper, coffee, and scratch tickets, clad in shorts—I am a born and bred New Englander and this is what we do.

"It's going to be cold in Florida?" I scoffed. "So it'll be what...seventy degrees?"

Oh, how I laughed. I probably made a disparaging remark about being hearty and having much thicker blood than my Floridian counterparts, and then I packed my shorts. The ones I wasn't wearing at the time.

I relived those rather dumb words as I scanned the mass of people around me. Every single guest was bundled up in jackets, in some cases hats and in every case pants. Wonderful, element-deflecting pants. I refused to admit the folly of my ways, primarily because I was a Mousejunkie—a supposed Walt Disney World expert. I don't make mistakes in the confines of my favorite forty-seven square miles. My rime-encrusted Disney ego was telling me otherwise, however. There was also the telltale shade of purple my skin was turning that announced to the world that I was stubborn, dumb, and obviously had no idea what it meant to tour Walt Disney World in the winter.

I started visualizing odd scenarios: Perhaps I could tear the pages out of my first Walt Disney World book and tape them around my chilled appendages in an effort to stave off frostbite. Surely my warm, humorous words would comfort me. Alas, it was not to be. I didn't have any tape.

In a moment of triumphant "I-told-you-so" celebration, Amy suggested I use staples.

It was rather cold in central Florida that winter. On two nights during our ten day vacation the temperatures dipped as low as twenty-four degrees. The weather was the big news every night as citrus farmers fought to save their crops from the biting cold and for the first time ever a dim tourist from New Hampshire actually missed the crushing heat normally associated with a Disney vacation.

As a constant complainer when it comes to the Florida heat, I just assumed that a much cooler January vacation

would be heavenly. On this particular trip, I could not have
been more wrong.

"I Can't Believe How Hot/ Cold/Humid/Rainy It Is"

Ask anyone who has ever traveled to Walt Disney World with
me: I will whine at any given chance about how the Florida
heat can be unforgiving and even dangerous. It can get so
humid that you may be able to swim back to your hotel. The
rain can be relentless and fall sideways. Unexpected freezes
can catch guests completely unprepared.

And that's all in one day.

Chances are you won't encounter all of Florida's extremes
in a twenty-four hour period, but it's not entirely unheard of.

An interesting thing about the weather in central Florida:
Just because it's raining at Disney's Animal Kingdom doesn't
mean it's raining at Epcot. In fact, while it might be soaking
in Frontierland, Tomorrowland may be sunny and dry.

Rain storms are frequent and often fast moving. While
there may be days that are complete washouts, quite often
the rainfall is predictable and temporary. And a prepared
guest can take advantage of this. Grab a poncho and press
onward.

The Straight Dope   *If you have a rain poncho at
home, bring it. The ponchos they sell in the theme parks all
look the same, so it's easy to lose your traveling mates in the
crowd of identical slickers.*

MOUSEJUNKIE DEB Bill and I are climate polar opposites. I remember Bill saying the queue area for Space Mountain was the coldest place on Earth. I almost passed out; I didn't think Bill considered anywhere cold.

Like Mousejunkie Carol, I bring a sweatshirt and roll it up in my bag, constantly pulling it out for every ridiculously air-conditioned building. Hey, instead of raising park pass prices to save money, why doesn't Disney raise the air condition setting from sub arctic to just arctic? I love coming *out* of the buildings to warm up!

Here's a look at the monthly temperature averages, according to Intellicast.com:

Month	Average Temperature
January	72 degrees
February	74 degrees
March	79 degrees
April	83 degrees
May	88 degrees
June	91 degrees
July	92 degrees
August	1 billion degrees (aka 92 degrees and humid)
September	90 degrees
October	85 degrees
November	79 degrees
December	73 degrees

The heat can often be bearable until the summer months when the humidity arrives. Even then, most of the theme park queues are covered by awnings or are inside and air conditioned. While the heat and humidity were a one-time anathema to me, I've come to prefer it over the cold snaps we've experienced in January and February.

The Straight Dope *If you find yourself overheating in the middle of the Magic Kingdom, try Splash Mountain for an instant cool-down. If you're in Animal Kingdom, the Kali River Rapids attraction is guaranteed to submerge you in cool water, providing head-to-toe relief.*

Then there's the rain. It's possible to go an entire vacation without seeing a drop of precipitation. But into every life a little rain must fall.

In the summer you can set your Mickey Mouse watch by the twenty-minute showers every afternoon. In the winter it's a lot dryer. Here's a look at the average rainfall in the Orlando area in inches:

Jan.	Feb.	March	April	May	June
2.3"	3.0"	3.3"	1.8"	3.6"	7.3"

July	Aug.	Sept.	Oct.	Nov.	Dec.
7.3"	6.8"	6.0"	2.4"	2.3"	2.3"

Perhaps the most common question I get as a Mousejunkie, "When should I go?" is best answered with a little vacation quiz:

➤ "Is cost a concern?"
➤ "Is weather a concern?"
➤ "Do you want to experience special events?"
➤ "Do you have issues standing in a fellow guest's armpit? Because the parks can be that crowded.

But rather than duck the question, I'll answer it directly: You'll find me at Walt Disney World two times during the year for sure—late January and October. January will be cooler (sometimes quite chilly) and less crowded, and October offers Halloween festivities and additional food choices at the Epcot International Food and Wine Festival.

Any time after that is cake. I'll take a Disney trip any chance I get. I've topped out at four times in one year. Mousejunkie Randy, on the other hand, went nine separate times in one year. A Florida resident might not be impressed, but since he lives nearly two thousand miles away from the place, I admire his persistence. And his unflagging enthusiasm.

But even he will tell you, after all those trips, just slow down. And above all, open your eyes and ears. It's the small things that make Walt Disney World such an addictive place.

Deciding when to travel to Walt Disney World is obviously a very important aspect of planning your trip. Almost every time of year has its benefits and drawbacks. For every report of walking on to an E-ticket attraction, there's inevitably a woeful tale of protracted wait times. When it gets crowded, it can become uncomfortable and difficult to get around. The bottom line is that no one wants to wait in one.

When I'm outed as a Disney fanatic, the first question is as inevitable as it is predictable: "When should I go?" Which, translated from the common tongue means "When won't I have to wait in line?" But it's not as simple as asking, "When should I go?" There are many details to take into account: not the least among them crowd levels.

When will Walt Disney World be virtually line-free? Probably never.

Actually, as Disney freaks know, there are times when lines will be nonexistent; it's just something that doesn't happen too often. But there is no simple answer to solving the crowd level conundrum. Historically, there were times when there were fewer people in the parks than others. These times have shifted a bit, and let's face it—if crowd levels are down, then Disney is going to do something to fix that. That's where seasonal special events have come in. Autumn was once a great time to visit. It still is. But the once sparse crowds have been replaced by larger groups of people visiting the annual Halloween celebration or the Epcot International Food and Wine Festival.

When the buses are standing-room only and the entry turnstiles are whirring with wave after wave of paying guests, Disney is happy.

The Straight Dope *Be nice. If you happen to be a strong, able person and your bus is standing room only, give up your seat to a parent carrying a sleeping child, an elderly guest or a pregnant woman. It might make for sore legs at the time, but it'll make you feel good later.*

Crowd Levels

According to figures provided by Disney, you'll want to avoid these dates if large crowds make you break out in the happiest hives on Earth:

➤ Presidents' week in February.
➤ Spring Break, (St. Patrick's Day through the end of April.)
➤ Memorial Day weekend.
➤ The summer months: June through Labor Day.
➤ Thanksgiving Day and the two to three days following.
➤ Christmas week through New Year's Day

To some, however, crowd levels are not something to get worked up about. After all, the busiest days of the year— New Year's, the Fourth of July, Christmas—also offer the longest park hours. Navigating the ocean of newly minted Mousejunkies shoehorned into the theme parks on such days is something Mousejunkie Randy has perfected, and actually prefers.

So you're still not convinced. Here are the recommended times of year to visit Walt Disney World when the crowd levels will likely be lighter. The scientists down at Mousejunkie Labs have spared no expense in uncovering these recommended dates:

➤ Mid to late January: Guests staying for the New Year's holiday have gone home, and it'll be too early for students with February school vacations on the horizon. (Avoid New Year's Day, because that's just insane and only crazy

MOUSEJUNKIE RANDY It is true the crowd levels at the parks are at their highest during the holidays, but it is for a good reason. It's not just that everyone has days off from work. There are things to see and do that you can't see or do any other time of the year. Carol and I go often enough that if we don't get a chance to hit some of the rides, its OK. People-watching is our second favorite activity at the parks next to riding attractions, and during these times there are some great people-safari opportunities. But that's not the only reason we battle the crowds. On the Fourth of July there's a fireworks display that's unmatched in its scope and beauty. Christmas time is Disney World dressed in the splendor of a winter wonderland, and on New Years Eve—let's just say six months later I can still feel the concussions from the New Years Eve special finale of IllumiNations: Reflections of Earth at Epcot. And the festive crowds just add to the magic.

people and Mousejunkies Carol and Randy go then.) It stays slow until Presidents' week, at which point it gets very busy again.

⭐ **The Straight Dope** *Pack well when visiting Walt Disney World during the winter months. It can be quite cold during this time. A midafternoon temperature in the eighties can sometimes give way to an overnight chill dipping into the twenties and thirties.*

➤ Late August: Schools in the southern states are back in session.

➤ September: Disney has offered the Free Dining promotion this time of year recently, but all American kids are back in school at this point and the temperatures are still blazing. This keeps a percentage of youngsters away, and the blast furnace-like heat tends to keep the weaker of the species at bay.

➤ From just after Thanksgiving until just before Christmas. Historically, the closer you get to Christmas, the busier it gets.

The Straight Dope *Extra Magic Evening Hours allow resort guests to spend more time in a theme park after normal closing times. Either get to the EMEH park early, or plan to avoid it entirely. The EMEH park will be the most crowded of the four Walt Disney World themeparks that day, but an early start is a great advantage.*

Extra Magic Morning Hours allow resort guest to enter the EMMH park prior to published opening times and before nonresort guests. This is one of the best opportunities to see the shortest lines at your favorite attractions. The downside: you and the entire family need to get up early on your vacation.

There have been times during my ongoing obsession where lines were much shorter, but it didn't occur often, and it wasn't as enjoyable as I would have assumed.

The first came in the fall of 2001. Three weeks after the terrorist attacks of September 11, Amy and I and Mousejunkies Carol and Randy were scheduled to fly to Orlando for a weeklong vacation. Where I considered canceling, Carol and Randy were determined to get back to a normal life as soon as possible. We arrived in early October to a deserted Walt Disney World. The resorts were quiet, the buses were empty and lines in the theme parks were gone. Amy and I were in the Magic Kingdom one day and walked down the ramp to board our boat at It's a Small World (yes, on purpose.) There was no one else on our boat, no one on about eight boats behind us. Every boat in front of us that we could see was completely empty.

Another night we decided to walk through the World Showcase at Epcot. We got to the American Adventure pavilion, located in the very back of the park. I looked left, toward the Japan pavilion, and didn't see a single person. I looked right, down toward Italy and Morocco, and likewise, saw no one.

Was it nice to not have to wait in lines that week? Sure. But there were much scarier things afoot at the time, and the lack of guests around us served to underscore that.

MOUSEJUNKIE AMY Believe it or not, the crowds are part of the fun. You miss the people when they're not there. When you see the look on a little kid's face when a parade passes by, that makes your experience more enjoyable. You're all sharing this great experience.

Even within the ups and downs of the calendar year, there are days where certain parks are busier than others. According to numbers Disney has made available, here are the days of the week and which parks are busiest:

Day	Busiest Theme Park(s)
Sunday	Magic Kingdom; Hollywood Studios
Monday	Animal Kingdom
Tuesday	Animal Kingdom; Epcot
Wednesday	Animal Kingdom, Hollywood Studios
Thursday	Magic Kingdom
Friday	Epcot
Saturday	Magic Kingdom

Another important consideration to take into account when deciding travel dates is what will be going on during your stay. From officially sanctioned events like Star Wars Weekends to unofficial events that still draw larger crowds, like Gay Days in June, there's usually a special event on the horizon.

The Seasons of Disney

Defining an "off-season" for Walt Disney World has gotten fairly tricky in recent years, so deciding on when to go is a question of whether you want to eat too much, drink too much, or sweat too much.

Travel in October and you'll arrive in time for the Epcot International Food and Wine Festival. Spend New Year's at the World and you'll be toasting with more people than at any other time of the year. Go in July for Independence Day, and you'll get to see special fireworks displays, but you may come away charred by the searing heat.

Disney Vacation Club members take advantage of dates in the fall and winter, since the point cost per room is quite low for the months of September and December. The past few years, Disney has offered a free dining period for the month of September to boost attendance.

While the crowds during those times may not rival summer levels, the parks are much busier than in previous years. There are better times to visit. Not necessarily ideal, but certainly better.

Special Events

Disney has a peculiar way of marking time that carries over to almost all of its promotional seasons. Halloween at Walt Disney World starts in early September. Christmas at Walt Disney World starts at the beginning of November. The Year of a Million Dreams promotion was twenty-two months long, but Almost Two Years of a Million Dreams doesn't have quite the same ring to it.

As a guest, this method of scheduling provides plenty of opportunity to enjoy holidays and special events year-round.

Here's a look at the different "seasons" and special events at Walt Disney World

January
New Years Eve: For the bravest and most committed vacationers, New Year's Eve offers a unique experience. The

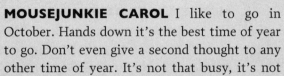

MOUSEJUNKIE CAROL I like to go in October. Hands down it's the best time of year to go. Don't even give a second thought to any other time of year. It's not that busy, it's not that blasted hot and it's usually pretty dry so you won't get rained out every day. Plus, that's when the two best celebrations are taking place: the Food and Wine Festival and Halloween.

parks are packed—often closing the front gates and refusing entrance when they're filled to capacity. Epcot, in particular, provides the most festive and diverse celebrations. Each country in the World Showcase is at its most celebratory, and as a park that serves countless alcoholic offerings, it tends to be the most wild.

Its reputation is now well publicized, with one of the best-known Disney Web sites advising guests: "Arrive early in the morning and be prepared to spend the entire day."

A special version of IllumiNations: Reflections of Earth is presented twice during the night, and Disney's Hollywood Studios features three Fantasmic! performances.

Walt Disney World Marathon: This annual 26.2-mile jaunt held every January brings crazy people—or, "runners" in the athletic parlance—to the resort to race through all four theme parks. A half marathon and 5 k are also included during marathon weekend.

MOUSEJUNKIE RANDY I like to go to Walt Disney World for New Year's, regardless of the crowd levels. I enjoy going to Epcot where there are parties in the streets. There are special fireworks and everyone is living it up all night long. At the same time, it's not like doing the same thing in Times Square where you are forced to freeze with six billion drunks.

It's the busiest night of the year, bar none. But realistically you're not there to ride the attractions. You're there to see the different DJs and dance and see the special New Year's IllumiNations display.

I have a hard enough time speed-waddling from my bus to Soarin' without getting lightheaded and developing blisters, so my hat is off to the people who accomplish such an admirable accomplishment.

Walt Disney World Marathon Weekend is held the first weekend following New Year's every year.

February

Spring Training: The Atlanta Braves hold Spring Training at ESPN's Wide World of Sports complex each February/March.

Previously, I hadn't had much reason to visit ESPN's Wide World of Sports. When I did head over, (begrudgingly, since this was taking away from potential buffet time,) I came away quite impressed. The facilities are top-notch, the grounds are typically eye-catching, and the architecture is pure Disney—classic, huge and utilizing stunning promenades and plazas to blow away any vision of a sports facility I've ever had. Think Big Time Sports mixed with the fast-paced excitement of ESPN run through the Imagineers' filter.

March

The Epcot International Flower and Garden Festival: Epcot blossoms anew every spring during this celebration of creative horticulture. Gardening experts drop in and out through the nearly three-month run. Weekends include free horticulture seminars at the old Wonders of Life pavilion. Make sure you get there early; the word "free"—rarely spoken on-property—attracts crowds.

May

Star Wars Weekends: You'll know things are different when you see a pair of armed Stormtroopers looming over the entry gates at Disney's Hollywood Studios. Guests can meet and greet characters from the *Star Wars* universe on weekends running from May through June. *Star Wars* Weekends, which are essentially a giant *Star Wars* convention, also includes parades, music and interactive experiences.

June

The Expedition Everest Challenge: A road race/obstacle course/scavenger hunt that takes entrants through the exotically themed world of Disney's Animal Kingdom, the Expedition Everest Challenge tests athlete's endurance and smarts. Pre-registration is $209 per two-person team. The fee jumps to $229 in March.

Mousejunkies J and Deb had a chance—and the guts—to participate in the inaugural event.

July

Independence Day: Special fireworks over the Magic Kingdom and dense packs of sweaty tourists mark the American Fourth of July celebration.

MOUSEJUNKIE J I discovered the Expedition Everest Challenge while doing some online research for our upcoming trip. Mousejunkie Deb and I would be staying at Jambo House at the Animal Kingdom Lodge for a few days and then transferring to the Boardwalk. The event coincided with our stay at Jambo House, so the timing was perfect. The race consists of a 5 k run, an obstacle course, and a scavenger hunt.

The Challenge can be run as a solo man, solo woman, man-man, woman-woman, and mixed couple teams. Deb and I would run the race as a couple. The entry fee included a shirt, goody bag, after-party in the Animal Kingdom, and a one day park pass for each person on the team. Not a bad price but paying to exercise always seems wrong. Anyway, we began to train for the race so we would not embarrass ourselves on race day.

We arrived at the Animal Kingdom via Disney's Magical Express on Friday evening. Mousejunkie Deb insisted on getting on the treadmill as a race warm up. I would have opted for drinks at Victoria Falls but as a supportive team member I climbed on the treadmill and ran four miles instead of sipping an apple martini. The next day we awoke and spent some time at the pool relaxing. The race was a nighttime event so we had most of the day to hang out. There would be a special bus that would take us to the Animal Kingdom parking lot where the race was to begin.

We did have to go to Wide World of Sports to register, but Disney had a bus set up to do that as well.

That evening we boarded the bus and headed over to the Animal Kingdom. We began to size up the competition on the ride over and we were beginning to feel confident that we would be among some of the more serious competition. That feeling was reinforced as we queued up in the starting area. The race would go off in waves since there were some 1,500 runners. The mixed couples would go last. As we gazed around the starting area, we noticed the couple next to us wearing cut off jean shorts, boat shoes, and a Yeti t-shirt. Near them was a couple dressed exactly the same wearing large white fur Yeti hats. This tipped me off that there were only a few teams who were actually prepared to run this race. The vast majority were here to say they participated. Winning was not an option for them.

After twenty-five minutes, it was our turn at the starting line. We were in the back of the large parking lot of Animal Kingdom. The gun fired and we were off with the rest of the yahoos around us. The entire wave

(Continued on next page)

sprinted out and began to circle the large parking lot running towards the entrance to park. Deb and I set our pace but found it difficult to actually run well because all the ill prepared people who sprinted out from the starting gate were now walking as they gasped for air and fell to the side, Yeti hats in their hands and clutching their burning chests. Team Cote weaved and bobbed around them and finally got some running room right around the park entrance. The 5 k loop, for the most part, was in the park. We did run on an access road behind Dinosaur for a bit before heading back into the park again. The last part of the run made its way back to the parking lot where we started. I thought it would be neat running in the park but as it turns out I don't remember much of it because I was concentrating on running.

Maybe the people in the Yeti hats had it right.

We finished the 5 k in thirty-two minutes. Not world class but respectable. Immediately we were forced into the obstacle course which consisted of various rope type annoyances. This only took a few minutes and we were handed our clue passport. Now the trek would take us back into the park to search for items. There were four clues and four things to find. At this point we had to decide to either run from clue to clue or take our time and cool down from the run. We weren't going to win so we decided to walk from clue to clue. This took us to several icons within the park: the Tree of Life, the mailbox in Africa, the Jeep on the side of the road in Asia, and finally to the front of Expedition Everest. We then opted to run to the finish line which was in Dinoland, U.S.A. Our final time was just over an hour for all three events.

The winning mixed couple did it in forty-six minutes. Once our answers in the passport were verified to be correct and we were awarded a large bronze compass necklace as a memento. It was now 9:45 P.M. We were sweaty and dehydrated. We hung around for the awards ceremony and then left for the room and showers but not before grabbing a quick ice cream at Dino Bite Snacks to reward ourselves. The park was open until midnight for people to ride Everest and listen to the live music.

September

Night of Joy: Contemporary Christian performers headline an annual concert held throughout the Magic Kingdom. This is a hard-ticket event that runs from 7:30 P.M. to 1 A.M. on two nights. Tickets are $57.95 for one night, and $89.95 for a two night pass.

MOUSEJUNKIE RANDY Disney puts on the best show. When you're looking for Fourth of July fireworks, where else would you go? Even though the parks are a little busy those days, you get to see the greatest spectacle of national pride this side of Washington D.C.

I like to visit the American Adventure at Epcot, and then head over to the Hall of Presidents at the Magic Kingdom, followed by the "Celebrate America Fireworks" also at the Magic Kingdom. Watch from the beach of the Polynesian Resort across the Seven Seas Lagoon. It doesn't get any more patriotic. Besides, at Disney you

(Continued on next page)

can have two Fourth of July celebrations. The Magic Kingdom does the "Celebrate America Fireworks" on both the third and the fourth. So if you want to head over to Epcot on the July Fourth, you can see IllumiNations: Reflections of Earth. It features dazzling special effects, colorful lasers, brilliant fireworks, and fiery torches all choreographed to a musical score, which becomes even more dynamic on the Fourth of July as the normal show is supplemented with a patriotic finale.

Also, Epcot has two characters who appear only on the Fourth of July: Betsy Ross, who tells stories in the American Pavilion; and Ben Franklin, who also makes appearances there.

If Epcot is not your thing, you can go to Disney's Hollywood Studios for a special fireworks show set to a rock'n'roll sound track.

October

Mickey's Not-So-Scary Halloween Party: Trick-or-treat through all the lands of the Magic Kingdom. Guests—many of whom get into the festive atmosphere by donning costumes—are given a candy bag to fill with goodies at spots all over the park. It's a family-fun event that's fine for even the most timid youngster, topped by perhaps the best parade of the year. The Boo to You parade kicks off by with a live headless horseman riding through the streets of the Magic Kingdom, holding a lit jack-o'-lantern high over his head. (Or, more accurately, where his head would be.)

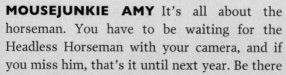 **MOUSEJUNKIE AMY** It's all about the horseman. You have to be waiting for the Headless Horseman with your camera, and if you miss him, that's it until next year. Be there early. When the lights go down get your camera ready. If you're taking a movie, start it early and just let it run. It's something you don't want to miss.

The Boo to You parade is great. Not so much for the floats, but for the performers. The undertaker drill team, with their sparking shovels, is incredible. And the ballroom dancing ghosts recreate a scene from the Haunted Mansion right in front of you.

A special Halloween-themed fireworks display, Happy HalloWishes is also part of the celebration. This hard-ticket event actually kicks off in September, and runs from 7 p.m. to midnight several nights a week through the end of October. Tickets range from $59.95 for adults and $53.95 for children, to a high of $64.95 for Oct. 30 and 31.

Epcot International Food and Wine Festival: Running all through the month of October to Nov. 14, this culinary celebration is a food and wine lover's Super Bowl. Guests can try delicious sample-size foods from countries not normally at the World Showcase. Representative samples and price ranges from past Food and Wine Festivals included the rock shrimp ceviche for $4.75 from Chile or the $5 kielbasa and potato pierogie from Poland, to mealie soup with crabmeat and chili oil for $3.25 from South Africa and the Moroccan tangerine mimosa royale for $6. Snack credits on the Disney Dining Plan can be used to purchase certain items.

The Epcot International Food and Wine Festival is an epicurean orgy of tiny food and many drinks that makes a trip during this time of year a foodie's heaven. The Festival runs during World Showcase hours. You will need a valid park pass to enter. Other than the price of the food samples, there is no additional fee.

The Epcot International Food and Wine Festival is a strong enough event that it's worth planning an entire vacation around. We were going over our schedule for the week during a recent trip when we noticed a fatal flaw in our plans: Not nearly enough Food and Wine Festival. So we called an audible and headed for Epcot.

First task upon entering the World Showcase: dump a margarita down the front of my shirt. Cool and soothing, I'm sure it looked flattering. It happened as we dealt with our first concern, which was getting the kids in our party some food. We stopped off in the Mexico pavilion to grab a few cheese empanadas and a margarita. For me, not the kids.

As I carried the food-laden tray into the new dining area, the raspberry/lime margarita flipped right over and landed across my shirt. An alert and typically incredible cast member ran to this stricken guest and retrieved a new frozen drink. There it was again—top notch service. Luckily, the pink concoction left nary a blotch on my clothing. However, I did smell like tequila for the rest of the day.

Next stop, with the kids in mind: The Gran Fiesta Tour inside the Mexico pavilion. Meanwhile, next stop, with Mousejunkie Barry and I in mind: La Cava del Tequila, the tequila bar also located inside the pavilion proper. I ordered up a tequila flight, and Mousejunkie Barry had a margarita.

Our server told us the brand of tequila was "Scorpion." Why? "Because there's a dead scorpion in the bottom of the bottle."

Of course.

Kids fed, chest bathed in icy tequila and with our stomachs now grumbling, we dove into the food portion of the festival. The first offering came from the Poland contingency. The booth was tucked between Mexico and Norway, so I stepped up and sampled the pierogi with kielbasa, caramelized onions and sour cream. It was certainly good, but a tad bland and not really different from anything we get back home.

We were now on our way. We tackled each booth as we came across it during our clockwise tour of the World Showcase.

The South Korea booth, next in line, threw me for a loop initially. Nothing really jumped off the menu, so I went for the lettuce wraps with roast pork and Kimchi slaw. This sample-sized treat was amazing. It had a little crunch in the lettuce, strong flavors in the pork, and some real spice in the Kimchi.

Next up: China. This was easy—the pork pot stickers. They were soft, tangy and delicious. The booths seemed to be coming up on us fast at this point, so rather than stuff ourselves we stopped off at the Outpost for a short respite before heading off to the South Africa booth. How could I pass up seared beef tenderloin with sweet potato puree and mango barbecue sauce? I could not, obviously.

At this point it struck me that whatever I ate last was becoming my favorite. Everything tasted great and the prices were reasonable (in Disney terms). Each item cost between $3.50 and $5, making it possible to sample quite a few offerings during our day-long trek.

Oktoberfest beckoned to us in Germany, which brought with it some fine German brews. Mousejunkie Barry sampled and raved about the Nurenberger sausage in a pretzel roll.

In Italy, which had its own booth off to one side of its permanent World Showcase pavilion, I went for the baked cheese ravioli in a creamy bolognese sauce. The ravioli was huge. The cheese covering it all was gooey and delicious and the bolognese was creamy and thick. Yet again, the latest sample rose to the top of the list. It was served piping hot, and it was already crushingly humid. A beverage was necessary to keep things in check.

Our entire group took a break by catching the Voices of Liberty in the American Adventure—always a favorite. We followed up with dinner (mainly to get the kids something familiar) at Via Napoli. This new pizza restaurant is fun, the service is fantastic, but the place is incredibly loud. We had a hard time hearing the chef advising us on what to order for our daughter, who has food allergies.

Now it was time to complete the second important task of the day at the Epcot Food and Wine Festival: Dump pizza sauce down the front of my shirt. I thought it matched with the tequila spill nicely. Note to self: Look into "Mousejunkie" branded bibs.

We walked out of Italy and made a beeline to the Japan booth, where I got the spicy tuna rolls. They were, not surprisingly, slightly spicy. I may lack the palate to properly tell the difference, but it didn't seem that different from the sushi trays available at the grocery store back home. I would've preferred the beef sukiyaki rolls served in years past.

Day two of our attack on the Food and Wine Festival was just supposed to be a quick trip to cover the small part of the World Showcase we didn't have a chance to cover previously. It was supposed to be a few light snacks and then back to the pool.

But we immediately came across "15 Beers For 15 Years," a bar between Future World and the World Showcase offering half-size samples of, well, fifteen beers. All plans of a quick morning at Epcot immediately went out the window. A sample pint of Abita Purple Haze and I suddenly felt adventurous.

Mousejunkies Carol and Randy had joined us, and at this point we had evolved from a small group of curious guests to a ravenous gang. An eating, drinking gang intent on grabbing the Food and Wine Festival by the throat and making it say 'uncle.' This is what happens when you open the day at "15 Beers For 15 Years."

We pointed our motley crew in the general direction of Canada and started walking. For about two steps. Because then I spotted the New Zealand booth. I had heard good things about the lamb slider with tomato chutney and I wanted one.

The bread was soft and fresh. The lamb, which I had never tried before, was delicious. It wasn't gamey or strange in any way. And the tomato chutney riding high atop the slider lent just the right amount of beefy acidity. I sensed I may have already come across a finalist for Food and Wine winner.

A few of our group hit the Greece booth, while I made a beeline for Canada. Normally I'd grab a cup of cheddar cheese soup, but this time I went for the chicken chipotle sausage with sweet corn polenta.

The sausage had just enough chipotle bite, while the polenta added a creamy flavor that worked in symphony with the sweet caramelized onions topping it all off. I had been wowed by the lettuce wrap in South Korea on our first day. The lamb slider started us off strong today. But already two booths in, I knew I had discovered the jewel of the World Showcase. I certainly didn't stop sampling, but this offering from Canada was the best thing I tasted anywhere on property, period.

Woozy with the chipotle still dancing on my palate, I jumped in line at the Ireland booth to grab Amy a warm chocolate lava cake with Baileys Irish Cream ganache, while others in our group ordered the lobster and scallop fisherman's pie paired with some Bunratty Meade honey wine.

The lava cake was gooey and rich with a warm center, while the lobster and scallop fisherman's pie yielded sweet seafood hidden in a potato bunker. The meade was sweet and light. Left to my own devices, I'd likely order up a jug and a straw.

Our gang regrouped and we wandered across the International Gateway Bridge into France, where frozen Cosmopolitan slush awaited us.

Sweet-Tooth-Amy struck again in Belgium, where she took down an intimidating Belgian waffle with berry compote. Meanwhile, I took down a less-imposing pint of Leffe Belgian beer.

The food and drinks were coming fast now, so a minor rest period was called. As Japan came into sight, however, any such foolhardy thoughts were banished. Within minutes I had a plate full of wahu ribettes to attend to.

Thus far I'd been overwhelmed with the delicious choices available from every booth we'd stopped at. Now it was time to be disappointed. Someone in our group said the ribettes looked like cat food, and it was all down hill from there. While the meat was tender, there wasn't much flavor. Bland was the word most everyone associated with this item.

Next stop: The Hops and Barley stand in the American Adventure pavilion. Curious as to how lobster rolls might be done in Florida, I ordered one up. The buttered roll was fine, the lobster was fine, but the overall flavor was just fair. You can't really mess up a lobster roll unless you really try, but this version was making an effort.

We had just endured two strikes in a row along the back side of the World Showcase. This called for a Radenberger Pilsner and a plate of spaetzle gratin with ham and cheese.

Mousejunkie Barry described it as being somewhat like mac and cheese—an accurate description. I liked it, but for the third time in a row I was left a bit flat. The pilsner, however, was rather magical. Golden, on the light side and refreshing, it left both Barry and I uplifted.

We were now overlapping some of what we had tried on day one, so we made a beeline to South Korea, where the lettuce wrap yet again beckoned to us. Spicy and tangy, we were not disappointed by this second helping. Several in our group agreed that this was among the better tasting samples in this year's Food and Wine Festival.

A quick sprint to China brought about a needless overindulgence on the pot stickers (no curiosity here—they're just good.) A tequila-fueled tractor beam seemed to be drawing us into La Cava del Tequila, so our now-sated gang gave in to the temptation, while the youngsters in our group queued up for a spin on the Maelstrom attraction in the Norway pavilion.

I was feeling brave, and with the memory of the scorpion in the bottom of the bottle, I asked if I could eat it. I figured if I was ever going to eat a poisonous arachnid, it might as well be now. Our waitress told me she'd be right back with it, and suggested I "don't eat the pincers." She said they were too hard to chew.

I manned up and was totally prepared, only to be disappointed that they didn't have one available. Another guest had beaten me to the questionable tasting.

Mousejunkie Barry had a few suggestions:

"Can you just catch a palmetto bug outside, drown it and give it to him?"

"Is there a mouse you can just stick in a shot glass?"

"Can you pour a shot over a dog and let him lick the fur?"

None of these things came to pass. Regardless, we left the Mexico pavilion very happy with our experience.

The last stop on our second day at the Epcot International Food and Wine Festival would be Puerto Rico. And it was here that the chipotle chicken sausage of Canada would meet up with a worthy contender: the medianoche sandwich of Puerto Rico.

I'm going to have to be honest here. We had just come from a tequila bar. So I'm not exactly sure what was in this sandwich. I believe it's very close to a Cuban sandwich: ham, turkey, pickles, mustard and mayo on toasted bread. The combination was heavenly.

By now the sun was going down, and the kids were looking forward to some pool time. We had undertaken an inadvertent bacchanalian feast, and completed the Epcot Food and Wine Festival in style. A few of us were slightly giggly, but completely well-behaved and in control (despite rereading this section and adding up the beverages consumed on our trek.)

After much debate and weighing the pros and cons of each booth sampled over the course of a two-day tour, the winner of the Best of the Fest, Mousejunkie Division is...

The chipotle chicken sausage with sweet corn polenta. My friends to the north, I salute you.

November

Children's Miracle Network Classic: This annual PGA tournament is held at the Magnolia and Palm golf courses.

Disney has added a food element to the tournament— always a plus in my book. The Wine and Dine Walk is located throughout the back nine of Disney's Magnolia Golf Course. Five specialty locations will offer guests pieces of a progressive menu. Each station is positioned on key holes, where guests can complete the menu as they follow the flow of the tournament.

Festival of the Masters: More than two-hundred award-winning artists showcase their wares throughout Downtown Disney. The three-day festival, held in mid-November, features sculpture, jewelry, photography, and painting, among other mediums. There is no cost to attend the outdoor event.

December

Candlelight Processional: First performed at Disneyland in 1958, the Candlelight Processional and Massed Choir is a nightly event that runs from late November through New Years Eve. More than four hundred performers take the stage to perform classic Christmas music and to back a celebrity guest narrator who reads the story of the Nativity. It is a moving and powerful performance and a can't-miss during the holiday season.

The orchestra is made up of fifty-one musicians, while hundreds of choir members dress in colored robes to create a visual Christmas tree on a multi-tiered stage. Performers in red and black make up the base of the tree, while cast members from all departments dress in green to make up the tree itself. One performer, stationed at the top, is dressed to be the star atop the tree.

At the beginning of the show, the lights are dimmed and members of the choir file in holding candles. As they take their place, trumpeters herald the arrival of the guest narrator (Edward James Olmos is a perennial favorite) and the performance begins.

The celebrity narrator reads passages from the Christmas story, punctuated by traditional Christmas music. It all culminates with "One Solitary Life," by Dr. James A. Francis:

He was born in an obscure village, the child of a peasant woman. He grew up in still another village, where he worked in a carpenter shop until he was thirty. Then for three years he was an itinerant preacher.

He never wrote a book. He never held an office. He never had a family or owned a house. He didn't go to college.

He never visited a big city. He never traveled two hundred miles from the place where he was born. He did none of the things one usually associates with greatness. He had no credentials but himself.

He was only thirty-three when the tide of public opinion turned against him. His friends ran away. He was turned over to his enemies and went through the mockery of a trial.

He was nailed to a cross between two thieves. While he was dying, his executioners gambled for his clothing, the only property he had on earth.

When he was dead, he was laid in a borrowed grave through the pity of a friend.

Nineteen centuries have come and gone, and today he is the central figure of the human race and the leader of mankind's progress.

All the armies that ever marched, all the navies that ever sailed, all the parliaments that ever sat, all the kings that ever reigned, put together, have not affected the life of man on this earth as much as that One Solitary Life.

The power of the music and the depth of the story is inspirational and moving.

Guests wishing to see the Candlelight Processional must arrive quite early, or purchase a Candlelight Dinner Package guaranteeing a seat in the America Gardens Theatre. The show runs about forty minutes, with three performances nightly.

Each pavilion in the World Showcase in Epcot also celebrates **Holidays Around the World**. Storytellers in each country tell tales of holiday celebrations, often acting out fantastic skits that illustrate cultural observances.

TEEN MOUSEJUNKIE RYAN I was really moved by the story and the atmosphere. It was very deep, and probably the most moving experience I had during any Christmas trip to Walt Disney World. (Even though halfway through I started counting how many performers were fainting and being carried off-stage. Don't worry, they're fine. I think it's a combination of the heat and cutting off blood flow by standing on stage so long with their legs straight.)

Mickey's Very Merry Christmas Party: Christmas—on the extended Disney calendar—runs from the beginning of November through New Year's. Guests take part in a festive extravaganza, sipping hot chocolate and munching cookies as snow falls gently onto Main Street USA. A special parade (Mickey's Once Upon a Christmastime Parade) steps off twice nightly, and a Holiday Wishes: Celebrate the Spirit of the Season fireworks display is featured each night of the party. Guests must purchase a separate entrance ticket for the event. (The party runs from 7 p.m. to midnight, $59.95 for adults, $53.95 for children.)

My so-called Mousejunkie Hubby was far too tired after Fantasmic! and stumbled his way out of the park along with the throngs, while Mousejunkie Carol and I made our way to the lights. We spent a good amount of time hunting down hidden Mickey's in the lights; I think we counted almost forty.

MOUSEJUNKIE AMY The Christmas tradition that is a don't-miss for me is the Osborne Family Festival of Dancing Lights at Disney's Hollywood Studios. It's a display of literally millions of Christmas lights and decorations strung up and down the Streets of America. It's a massive and breathtaking thing to see. When the majority of the people are watching Fantasmic!, make your way to the Streets of America to experience the incredible Christmas light show. The music is choreographed with the lights, the faux snow puts you in the mood, and hot chocolate is plentiful as you wander around.

Even though the park was closing, cast members weren't quick to boot us out. It was so relaxing and peaceful, and it really puts you in the Christmas spirit.

Cost Concerns

Another consideration when deciding on travel dates is how much it's going to cost. Different times of the year are more expensive than others, and a sharp-eyed traveler will know when to plunk down the cash to confirm a reservation.

Disney divides the calendar up into their own five seasons: **Adventure**, **Choice**, **Dream**, **Magic**, and **Premier**. In the King's English, those terms don't really mean much. They're fairly interchangeable and they don't signify any kind of cost increase or decrease. But naming them

"Expensive, More Expensive, Wicked Expensive, You're Joking and **Left Arm"** doesn't carry the same sense of fun. The easiest way to look at it is this: Adventure Season is the cheapest time of the year to visit, while Premier is the most expensive.

A room at a value-level resort, Pop Century, during Adventure Season will cost $82 a night during the week, and $92 for weekend nights. That same room during Premier Season will cost $129 a night during the week and $139 for weekends.

On the other end of the spectrum, a garden view, deluxe-level room at the Polynesian will cost $365 a night during Adventure Season, and $580 nightly during Premier Season. (Prices vary depending on the room's specific view and size.)

The seasons are divided up based on historical crowd size. The busier it is, the more expensive it is.

Here's a look at the most up-to-date seasonal categories:

➤ Adventure Season: The months of January and September, and December 1 to 14.

➤ Choice Season: The month of October and November 1 to 23, November 27 to 30 and December 15 to 23.

➤ Dream Season: February 1 to 15, the month of May, June 1 to 10 and August 16 to 31.

➤ Magic Season: February 16 to 28, March 1 to 27, April 11 to 30, June 11 to 30, the month of July, August 1 to 15 and November 24 to 26.

➤ Premier Season: March 28 to 31, April 1 to 10 (Spring Break) and December 24 to 31 (Christmas).

Disney on the Cheap

TEEN MOUSEJUNKIE RYAN I'm a college student, and a Mousejunkie. How can I get my fix without adding to my college debts? Let's go on a hypothetical vacation together to see how to do Disney on a budget.

You're going to have to look at five main elements: Flight, getting to your resort, which resort to stay at, food, and park passes. While we're looking at options and prices, we'll assume you're traveling with a friend.

Flight: Booking early is always cheaper than trying to book the day before you leave. There are budget airlines like Jetblue or Southwest that normally offer fairly reasonable rates, but it depends entirely on where you're leaving from. Flying to Orlando from the northeast, I can usually find flights for a maximum of $150 each way, and sometimes as low as $59 each way. It's a matter of keeping a sharp eye out. **Price: $300** (a rough estimate on the pricier side).

Getting to the resort: Take advantage of Disney's Magical Express. If you're staying at a Disney resort, it's free. The Disney buses (with the sparkly floors) pick you up at the airport and bring you to your resort. When you're leaving, they pick you up at your resort and bring you to the airport with plenty of time before your flight. I did this during my last trip when I was flying by myself, and it was wonderful and easy. There is a special area in the Orlando airport for Disney's Magical Express where they scan your ticket (they mail it to you in advance, then you just hang out and wait for the bus to come pick you up. They take care of your luggage for you. It's delivered to your room some time after your arrival. The service is wonderful and virtually foolproof. **Price: $0**.

Resort: Disney has a value season, so let's choose one of those for our hypothetical vacation. One of the value seasons is in early January, but that's too cold for me, so the next best is in the August/September range. For 2010, the value season for the All Star Music Resort was August 15 to September 30. During that time, you could stay at the All Star Music Resort for $82 per night on weekdays, and $92 on weekends. Price: for five nights, $410; split with your traveling partner, **$205**.

This brings me to my next point: Stay at a value resort. They're the cheapest resorts on Disney property, you still get all of the perks of staying on site, and really, you're only there to sleep. There's no need to empty your wallet on a bedroom.

Park passes: The longer you stay, the cheaper the Disney's Magic Your Way ticket packages get. Don't bother getting the park hopper option. While it is nice to have that flexibility, it gets expensive. Refer to 'Mousejunkies Travel' in chapter 3 for package prices. It's difficult to get a break on park passes. The first two days carry the bulk of the cost, whereas days three, four and five (for the sake of our purposes) increase only a few dollars a day. **Price: $228**.

(Continued on next page)

Food: Sometimes Disney offers a Free Dining Plan. If it's available, take advantage of it. For the past few fall seasons, Disney offered a Free Disney Quick Service Dining Plan if you stay at a value resort starting August 15 through December 21. Luckily, this is during value season, and our hypothetical vacation fits right in.

The Quick Service Dining Plan allows you two quick service meals, two snacks, and one refillable drink mug (which you can refill at your home resort) per person per night of your stay. Basically that comes down to lunch and dinner, and two snacks (breakfast). It's a really great value.

One quick service meal includes an entrée, a dessert, and one non-alcoholic beverage. The snack credits can be used for one of most any of the snacks that you see throughout the parks. Everything is very clearly marked, so you'll never really be confused about where you can use your meal credits. **Price: $0.**

Now, if you're like me, it's really difficult to go to Disney and not get some souvenirs. You can occasionally find some items that have been marked down—check the back of stores for the cheaper stuff, but other than that, I just set aside some money for shopping.

Excluding swag, the price of the entire trip—six days and five nights—is **$733**. It can be done on a college student's budget. That price, to my way of thinking, certainly competes well with those cheapo, eight-people-to-a-room trips to Cabo or the Dominican Republic.

Also, Disney offers various specials throughout the year. They range from not really worth it, to something you'd want to jump on immediately.

So there you have it, our Hypothetical Disney Vacation on a Budget. Keep in mind, prices are subject to change, and of course not everyone can plan to travel during a value season, so make sure to do plenty of research during your planning process to find the best prices for everything.

Getting In the Door

You've chosen when you're going and where to stay. Now, you'll need park passes so you can actually do something other than use your refillable mug.

There are theme parks, water parks, and shows to consider. Then there are all the options you can pile onto your park pass that allow different levels of access and flexibility.

The base passes are called Magic Your Way tickets, ostensibly because you can buy a base pass, or you can add any number of special options to your ticket. See? Your way.

Prices listed below are based on Disney-provided information as of press time.

The Magic Your Way base ticket allows entrance to one of the four Walt Disney World theme parks. It's the basic "get me in the door" pass.

Magic Your Way Base Ticket		
Days	Adults, 10 or older	Children 3–9
1-Day	$82	$74
2-Day	$162 ($81 per day)	$146 ($73 per day)
3-Day	$224 ($74.67 per day)	$202 ($67.33 per day)
4-Day	$232 ($58 per day)	$209 ($52.25 per day)
5-Day	$237 ($47.40 per day)	$214 ($42.80 per day)
6-Day	$242 ($40.33 per day)	$219 ($36.50 per day)
7-Day	$247 ($35.29 per day)	$224 ($32 per day)

Note that the longer you stay, the cheaper it gets (an excuse I use with the family CFO to extend our stays for as long as possible). For example, the difference between a six-day and a seven-day pass is just $5.

If you add the **Park Hopper** option for an additional fee, you can leave one park and go to another any time you want. Jump between all four theme parks all day long with no worries—outside heat stroke, exhaustion, and an over-dose of awesomeness.

The Park Hopper option can be extremely useful. I'm a big believer in being flexible, and the ability to run from one park to another—whether it's to avoid large crowds, make dinner reservations, or to see a specific parade or show—can be invaluable.

If you find yourself standing in the shadow of the Tree of Life in Animal Kingdom and you've made a dinner reservation for the Biergarten in Epcot's Germany pavilion, you're going to need that park hopping option to get there. Add $54 for the Park Hopper option.

Base ticket prices, with Park Hopper option added		
Days	Adults, 10 or older	Children 3–9
1-Day	$136	$128
2-Day	$216	$200
3-Day	$278	$256
4-Day	$286	$263
5-Day	$291	$268
6-Day	$296	$273
7-Day	$301	$278

Add the **Water Park Fun and More** option, and you can hit the Typhoon Lagoon or Blizzard Beach water parks, DisneyQuest, or the Wide World of Sports complex. If you're big on water parks or interested in the virtual games at DisneyQuest, it might be worth it. But I've never known anyone to pick this option so they could visit ESPN's Wide World of Sports complex—where many youth sports tournaments are held—unless they had a child competing there.

One thing to note if you're considering adding this option to visit DisneyQuest at Downtown Disney: DisneyQuest is essentially a large video game arcade. There are several interactive games such as the Virtual Jungle Cruise, where guests board a raft and paddle for their lives, or Pirates of the Caribbean: Battle for Buccaneer Gold, where you fire cannons from the deck of a pirate ship to capture treasure, that are billed as state-of-the-art experiences. I'd agree if this was the 1999 edition of "Mousejunkies." Since it isn't, I feel comfortable saying that most of DisneyQuest feels like it belongs ten years in the past. On the other hand, DisneyQuest still has a dose of Disney's storytelling touch. You enter through a Ventureport (a gussied-up elevator) that dumps you out into a hub where you choose your next destination: the Explore Zone, the Create Zone, the Score Zone or the Replay Zone. It's a great place to spend a few hours on a rainy day, but I would not recommend adding the Water Park Fun and More Option just to visit this five-story arcade.

MOUSEJUNKIE WALT That is something I would not do again. I thought everything in DisneyQuest seemed a little dated. Maybe it was neat five or ten years ago, but it's not state of the art now. Not even close. If it was raining and I was with some kids that wanted to see it, then maybe. But even then I might find something else to do.

Base ticket, with Water Park Fun and More option added		
Days	**Adults, 10 or older**	**Children 3–9**
1-Day	$136	$128
2-Day	$216	$200
3-Day	$278	$256
4-Day	$286	$263
5-Day	$291	$268
6-Day	$296	$273
7-Day	$301	$278

Add the **No Expiration** option, and unused days on your tickets never expire. If you purchase a seven-day pass and only go to the parks for four days, you can hold on to those tickets and use them on your next visit. Because let's face it, if you're reading this book, there will be a next visit.

Base ticket, with No Expiration option added		
Days	**Adults, 10 or older**	**Children 3–9**
1-Day	N/A	N/A
2-Day	$184	$168
3-Day	$252	$230
4-Day	$299	$276
5-Day	$332	$309
6-Day	$348	$325
7-Day	$389	$366

Being Mousejunkies, however, we tend to opt for the Annual Pass. This accomplishes two things: It allows us to park hop and not worry about the number of days we should buy tickets for, and it ensures we'll return to Walt Disney World at least one more time in the calendar year.

An Annual Pass costs $499 for adults, and $450 for children. (Disney Vacation Club members enjoy a $100 Annual Pass discount.) You can purchase the Annual Pass at any time before your trip, and activate it when you get to a theme park. From that moment, you have one calendar year to come and go as you please. The rule of thumb is this: if you're going to be going to theme parks for eleven days or more in one year, it makes financial sense to get an Annual Pass.

It also allows special access to sneak previews and special events held throughout the year. Annual Passholders often get to check out new attractions before other visitors. It gives Disney a chance to soft launch something new, and offers a little extra value to Annual Passholders.

Passholders can also take advantage of discounted room rates, which vary from resort to resort, and have limited availability. Annual-Pass-room discount rates are usually ferreted out and posted online by sharp-eyed Mousejunkies, giving you a bit of a head start on getting that cheaper room. Also, calling 407-WDISNEY can put you in touch with someone who can provide availability information. Rates and dates often change.

Moving Forward

Once you're there, you may want to take advantage of a system Disney has in place to cut down on wait times in lines. Disney's **Fastpass** is a virtual queuing system wherein guests insert their park tickets into a kiosk that then distributes a small ticket with a return time stamped on it. Guests return to that specific attraction at the prescribed time, thus bypassing the sometimes lengthy standby line. Guests

MOUSEJUNKIE JOHN If you visit Disney when it's busy, Fastpass is a must. You're going to stand in some long lines—no way around it. But Fastpass is like standing in two lines at once. Look at your park map. Pick two rides you want to go on. Fastpass one, and stand in line for the other. That way, when you exit the first ride, the wait will be much shorter for the second one in the Fastpass line. For example: The Tower of Terror and the Rock'n'roller Coaster are a short walk apart. You can easily check the wait times for both in under five minutes. Fastpass the one with the longer line and wait in the stand-by line for the other. Once you get the timing down, you'll be using it left and right. I like to Fastpass a ride right before a meal. After I'm done eating, I basically can get right on with little or no wait. (Avoid Space Ranger Spin directly after a double cheeseburger.)

Warning: If you're in charge of getting everyone in your group a Fastpass, don't leave anyone's park ticket in the machine. I went from Great Dad/Husband Who Takes Us to Disney Every Year to Knucklehead of the Week in the blink of an eye. Luckily, Disney cast members are extremely helpful and understanding and my shame was short-lived.

are allowed to have only one Fastpass per park ticket at one time. Once the time on that Fastpass has expired, guests are free to get another one.

For example: A guest inserts a park ticket into the Fastpass machine at Peter Pan's Flight and receives a return time for 1 P.M. He then immediately walks to Mickey's PhilharMagic and attempts to get a second Fastpass using that same park ticket. Instead of issuing a second Fastpass to the guest, the kiosk will spit out a ticket with information explaining when that guest can obtain a second Fastpass—usually when the original start time has passed or two hours after the original Fastpass was distributed, whichever is earliest.

Fastpasses can be a great timesaver, and it certainly results in less time spent standing in line, but it can also mean crisscrossing the park in an inefficient manner just to hit designated Fastpass return times.

The Straight Dope   *Here is where you can burn a little of the extra energy your teenager might have. Make them the official trip Fastpass runner. When you get to your park of choice for the day and everyone has entered the park, have your teen run the group's park passes to that must-see attraction to get the earliest possible return times. This will give them a chance to spend a little alone time and provide you a chance to reminisce about when you could run like that.*

A Few Questions that Come up from Time to Time

How do I buy a Fastpass? Fastpasses are not part of the ticket price structure. They cannot be purchased. They are free, but availability is limited. On very busy days, or at particularly popular attractions (Soarin' at Epcot and Toy Story Midway Mania at Disney's Hollywood Studios), Fastpasses can, and often do, run out.

Can I save money by purchasing discounted Magic Your Way tickets? If you take one piece of advice from this book, it is this: try the extra-spicy bloody Mary at the ESPN Club at the Boardwalk.

If you take a second piece of advice, it's this: Do not, under any circumstances, buy Walt Disney World park passes from Ebay, Craigslist, or roadside shacks.

Stories of families arriving at the theme park gate with counterfeit, expired, or used-up tickets are legion, and there is no recourse. Don't buy partially used tickets. Stick to reliable ticket brokers like Undercover Tourist or the Kissimmee Wal-Mart (4444 W. Vine, Kissimmee), which offers slightly discounted passes. They won't mail them to you, so if you want to take advantage of the discount you'll have to show up in person. They also don't have every ticket option at all times. While the ticket you want may not be available, a trip to neighboring Kissimmee might be worth it to save a few dollars.

Discounts can also be had for active or retired military, AAA members, Florida residents, and Disney Vacation Club members.

"The best part about all the parks, after you've done them all so often, isn't seeing Philharmagic again, or riding Tower of Terror again," Mousejunkie Deb offers. "Although they're fun, the best part is taking in all the theming details and nuances of the Imagineers. Disney World is a creative, innovative, marketing marvel. The entire operation is nothing less than impressive."

Travel Checklist

Before You Leave Home

- ☐ Advanced Dining Reservations made (407-WDW-DINE) Online airline check-in twenty-four hours ahead (if applicable)
- ☐ Park passes bought and packed
- ☐ Digital camera
- ☐ Sun block
- ☐ Bodyglide
- ☐ Chargers for cell phone/laptop/iPad/various gadgets
- ☐ Comfortable shoes
- ☐ Sunglasses
- ☐ Stroller

Before you leave the room

- ☐ Park passes in-hand
- ☐ Sun block applied

- ☐ Bodyglide applied
- ☐ Weather checked (poncho in hand if necessary)
- ☐ Room key/Key to the World in-hand
- ☐ Advanced Dining Reservation confirmation numbers in hand
- ☐ Digital camera with charged batteries
- ☐ Fully charged cell phone
- ☐ Cash and/or credit cards
- ☐ Fanny pack ready to go

 MOUSEJUNKIE AMY I don't care what the reputation of the fanny pack is. It's the most useful way that I've found to carry your money, park tickets, and a small camera. My mom is always toting her giant pocketbook around, lugging it along in the parks. I like the hands-free approach, and the fanny pack is the best option for that.

I know many people prefer a backpack, but after a few hours in the sun, my shoulders are aching and the last thing I want is to be carrying everyone's extra stuff they don't want to carry. With my tried-and-true fanny pack (it's got three different zipper pockets-all with broken zippers at this point,) I feel safe knowing my ID, cash and park tickets are within quick reach.

If you feel shame to be seen with a fanny pack slung in front around your waist, you can always unclip it and sling it over your shoulder as well. I like that it's small, but also has enough room to fit a digital camera. I've had the same fanny pack for every trip, and its a little worse for wear, but I'm always hunting for a new one. I have yet to find one that fits the bill.

Yes, I did say fanny pack. That waist-enhancing fashion mistake has been part of our touring kit from the beginning. As Amy clips that pleather beauty on just before we leave our resort room every morning, I just look the other way and pretend I'm somewhere else.

5 Mousejunkies Sleep

I ONCE STAYED OFF-SITE on a Walt Disney World vacation.

I also stepped on a piece of glass once ended up needing about thirty stitches. I am in no hurry to do either again.

I'm not exactly equating staying off-site to the searing pain that rips through you after having a shard of glass plunged into your foot.

Actually, yes I am. That's exactly what it's like.

This is where a lot of people will question my judgment. I'll admit that there are plenty of fine off-site resorts in the Orlando area. However, there are also a number of less-than-desirable accommodations. I found one of them. It was an experience that helped create an on-site adherent.

I'm nothing if not irrational about certain things. As a Mousejunkie, I want to be completely immersed in all-things Disney from the moment I step off the plane at Orlando International Airport. Bright colors, Disney music, exceptional service, and unparalleled convenience get me whistling *Zip-a-Dee-Doo-Dah* out of my navel and making jazz-hands as I prance from attraction to attraction—both of which are deeply disturbing visual images. But when I'm in the depths of my fix, I don't care. Staying on-site allows that to happen. (I don't really prance. It's more of a hobble by midweek.)

Secondly, I'm really strange when it comes to Florida's unfamiliar fauna. Where I live, there aren't too many things that want to bite you. Yet in my vacation destination of choice, I'm told there are plenty. Someone told me there are things known as fire ants in Florida. To an unstable tourist, this conjures horrific visual images of an insect shooting flames out of its eyeballs at anyone with a northern accent. This doesn't seem to bother the people who live there. But when I'm told to assume there are alligators wherever you find a body of water, my irrational side emerges. This is where I began my—up to this point—lifelong fear of the legendary Orlando Jumping Snake.

I had the opportunity to stay for several nights at an assumedly snake-fire ant-biting critter—free International Drive hotel during a business conference. The room was fine, but I noticed light streaming into the room from the gap between the bottom of the door and the ground. Daylight clearly shone through. And if sunlight could get in, then snakes could get in. I was convinced that if I drifted off to sleep, I would be attacked by one of the famous Jumping Snakes of Orlando during the night. (Jumping, because that's how they'd get up on the bed to bite me. Also, this is a breed of my own creation, since I am nothing less than irrational when it comes to snakes, as well.)

I stuffed a towel under the door (because what do snakes fear more than a freshly laundered bath towel?) and spent much of the night listening for snakes. Which begs the question: how does one listen for snakes?

Regardless, I was convinced that if I was laying my head in a Disney resort not five minutes away, the Jumping Snakes of Orlando would not be a concern.

There are also quite a few not-so-irrational reasons for staying on-site. Among them:

➤ **Location:** Midday naps (otherwise known as "let's watch Stacey on the in-room channel and get out of this heat" time) can be a life saver.

➤ **Theming:** Remain immersed in the magic 24/7. You're an addict. Start acting like one.

➤ **Kids' stuff:** All on-site resorts offer in-room child care for ages six months to twelve years in partnership with independent childcare provider Kids Nite Out. Add the kiddie pools and playgrounds and we're set.

➤ **Online check-in:** Save a step during check-in.

➤ **Concierge:** Need tickets? ADRs? Tee times? Stop by the concierge desk in the lobby for some of that legendary Disney customer service.

➤ **Key to the World:** It's a hotel room key. It's a credit card. It's your park pass. It's a way for me to purchase more Disney stuff without drawing too much attention from our family's CFO until the bill arrives. Be careful who you grant charging access to—it's as good as cash.

➤ **Merchandise delivery:** Purchases at shops throughout Walt Disney World Resort can be delivered to the guest's resort at no charge. Got your eye on an oversized Big Figure but don't want to lug it around all day? No problem. Just have it sent to your resort. Try that at an off-site hotel.

➤ **Free parking at the theme parks:** Don't underestimate the value of reducing this hidden expense.

➤ **Refillable mugs:** Guests can buy a mug they can continually refill with sweet, sweet, life-giving soda at their resort during the length of their stay.

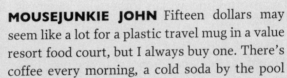 **MOUSEJUNKIE JOHN** Fifteen dollars may seem like a lot for a plastic travel mug in a value resort food court, but I always buy one. There's coffee every morning, a cold soda by the pool during a midday break, and another cold drink upon returning to the resort at the end of a hot day. And it's all free during your stay with the purchase of the mug. You could easily spend $15 on beverages in two days if you bought them individually. And you can bring the mugs home. They are much more durable and dishwasher-safe than those fancy aluminum ones you see in the gift shops. I've gone to work every morning for about ten years with my coffee in a Disney resort mug. At one point, we had so many in the kitchen cabinet that we had to throw some away. They're nearly indestructible.

➤ **Preferred tee times:** On-site guests get preferred tee times at Disney's four championship golf courses.

➤ **Transportation to the tees:** On-site guests get complimentary door-to-door transportation between their resort and Disney's four golf courses.

The bottom line: choose your hotel wisely. I've stayed at each level of Disney's hotels, from Pop Century to

The Boardwalk Resort. Each person's needs and requirements are different, which makes a blanket recommendation
impossible.

While the deluxe resorts are certainly top-notch in every
respect, the amount of time you spend in your room may not
equal the amount of money you might spend for the little
extras. The rooms in Disney's value resorts—Pop Century
and the All Star Movies, Music, and Sports Resorts—are a
bit smaller, but the hotels retain the characteristic Disney
theming, cleanliness, and service.

MOUSEJUNKIE JENNA Since I'm single and
tend to want to spend my time and money in
the theme parks, I always picked a value resort.
I couldn't see the need to spend more money
on my resort and room because I wasn't going to spend
much time there. Instead, I put my vacation budget
toward things like spa visits and tours.

Even after dozens of trips I still find myself back at a
value-level resort from time to time, and I never find myself
grousing about it. That said, there are a few hard-and-fast
rules that apply universally: the more you pay, the more
you get.

The biggest perk associated with the costlier resorts is
location. Something on the monorail line—Contemporary
Resort, Polynesian Resort, or Grand Floridian—will set you
back several hundred dollars a night, but offers easily the
best access to the Magic Kingdom.

★ **Awesome/Stupid Disney Idea** *A monorail dining car. Think about it: a high-priced dining option where
guests could enjoy dinner while circling the Magic Kingdom
resort route. A cast member could ride along while guests
order from one of the restaurants along the route. The
attendant would see to the guests' needs. Mousejunkie
Randy has mocked this concept, pointing out two very obvious shortcomings: the goat smell that seems to permeate
every monorail car and the fact that the monorail is running
at full capacity most of the time. Pulling an entire car out
of rotation would make the crush even worse. Randy's probably right.*

The Boardwalk, Disney's Beach Club Resort, and the
Yacht Club Resort all offer walking-distance access to
Epcot's International Gateway (the back door into the park).
Disney's Hollywood Studios is also a quick boat ride away
from the Epcot area resorts. Crazy people like Mousejunkie
Amy prefer to walk from the Boardwalk area resorts to
Disney's Hollywood Studios. I'd rather wait for a Friendship.

★ **Mousejunkie U** *Friendships are Disney's flotilla of
boats used to ferry guests to and from Epcot area resorts,
Epcot, and Disney's Hollywood Studios. They were built in
the shops behind the Magic Kingdom and are the ninth largest fleet of boats in the world.*

As you might guess, Disney's Animal Kingdom Lodge offers
the most convenient access to Disney's Animal Kingdom, but

MOUSEJUNKIE AMY It's not a long walk at all, and it's beautiful along the water. Depending on where the boats are in their route, you can get to the park more quickly by just walking.

don't be fooled into thinking you can walk there. Transport to the theme park still requires a quick bus ride.

If money is an issue, stay at the value-level resorts off-season. Annual passholders enjoy more savings, as do AAA members.

⭐ **The Straight Dope** *As soon as you know the dates of your vacation, call Disney central reservations (407-WDISNEY) and request the AAA room-only rate. Depending on season and class of resort, you can expect a 10 to 20 percent discount on rooms as a AAA member. When the vacation date gets closer, deeper discounts sometimes crop up. Annual Passholders sometimes also enjoy additional discounts. Using every edge, guests can sometimes score up to forty-five percent off rack rate, so the savings can be fantastic. However, the discounts fluctuate and aren't always available. Persistence is the key.*

Sometimes, however, saving a little extra money doesn't matter.

One way Disney categorizes its resorts is by location: Magic Kingdom area resorts, Epcot area resorts, Disney's

MOUSEJUNKIE WALT Beyond trying to save Disney Vacation Club points (a time share—like lodging option where guests purchase a real estate interest), I don't really care about saving money. I'm not very good at trying to save money anyway. When I go, I want to go as big as I can while still being able to afford it. Sometimes people will ask, Why do you splurge on the Boardwalk view when it costs so much more than a normal view room? The answer is because I like it! I say if you like it, go for it.

Hollywood Studios area resorts, Animal Kingdom area resorts, and Downtown Disney resorts.

Here's a closer look at each resort, by location:

Magic Kingdom Area Resorts

The Contemporary Resort
Theming: Sleek and modern
Facts: One of Walt Disney World's originals, this deluxe-level resort has 655 rooms and suites and a concierge floor in a fourteen-story, A-frame structure. The resort is divided into two sections: the tower and the garden wing. It's located between the Seven Seas Lagoon and Bay Lake, and is within sight of the Magic Kingdom. Great views and an enviable location on the monorail line are two of the primary reasons to consider this resort.

Mousejunkie U *The Contemporary Resort was built using some of the most forward-thinking techniques of the time. Individual rooms were built off-site—including all the plumbing and electrical work, carpeting, doors, and windows—and then lifted by crane into the A-frame structure. This was one of the first major builds to use modular construction.*

The rooms could theoretically be replaced the same way, if it wasn't for the naturally swampy Florida ground beneath it. The entire resort has settled a bit since construction, locking all the rooms in place for good.

Feed me: Table service restaurants include the California Grill, the Wave, the Contempo Café and Chef Mickey's—a character buffet. Contempo Café is the new deluxe version of counter service at the resort. There are also three lounges, two snack bars and, as always, room service.

Feels like: Classic Walt Disney World. The Grand Canyon Concourse, with monorails silently gliding by the massive art installation by Mary Blair, remains both nostalgic and forward-looking.

You should also know: Guests can enjoy water sports such as boat rentals, waterskiing and parasailing, and other recreation options: volleyball, a playground and two swimming pools. There are gift shops, a game room, laundry service, child-care and a health club for those who think they just haven't walked quite enough on their vacation. For the lanyard-wearing types, the resort features 90,000 square feet of meeting space, including a 44,300-square-foot grand ballroom.

Getting to the parks: Buses to all the resorts and attractions except for the Magic Kingdom; walk to Magic Kingdom; monorail to Magic Kingdom; boats to the Magic Kingdom. Guests can also take the monorail to the Ticket and Transportation Center and catch another monorail to Epcot.

How much? As a deluxe resort, The Contemporary can be pricey. Garden wing rates range from $285 a night to $1,400 a night, depending on room size and season. Tower room rates range from $400 to $880 a night.

Mousejunkie U *President Richard Nixon delivered his "I am not a crook" speech during a gathering of Associated Press editors at the Contemporary Resort in November of 1973.*

BayLake Tower at Disney's Contemporary Resort

Theming: Ultramodern

Facts: Connected to the Contemporary Resort by a sky-bridge, this Disney Vacation Club resort has 295 units, including studio, one-and two-bedroom villas, and Magic Kingdom-view three-bedroom Grand Villas. The decor is modern, with striking artwork, flat-screen TVs, full kitchens complete with granite countertops and modern appliances and laundry facilities.

Feed me: The sixteenth floor Top of the World Lounge provides guests with some of the most dramatic views available anywhere at Walt Disney World Resort. Light appetizers and drinks are served.

Feels like: Minimalist, futuristic, quiet. Disney after the robot revolution.

You should also know: This resort is a Disney Vacation Club resort, but rooms can be reserved for paying customers if any are available. Access to the Top of the World Lounge is available only to DVC members staying at the resort using points.

Getting to the parks: Bay Lake Tower offers the same transportation options as the Contemporary Resort: buses to all the resorts and attractions except the Magic Kingdom; walk to Magic Kingdom; monorail to Magic Kingdom; boats to the Magic Kingdom. Guests can also take the monorail to the Ticket and Transportation Center and catch another monorail to Epcot.

How much? Studios range from $385 to $635 (for Magic Kingdom View during Holiday season); one-bedroom suites range from $520 to $775 a night, season and view depending; two-bedroom suites range from $645 to $1,200 a night, and a three-bedroom Grand Villa will run you $1,650 to $2,500 a night if you want to drift off while gazing at Cinderella Castle.

Grand Floridian Resort and Spa

Theming: Turn-of-the-century Victorian

Facts: Disney's jewel on the monorail line has 867 rooms and suites, including 181 concierge accommodations. This ultra-swanky resort opened in 1988. Inspired by turn-of-the-century east coast Florida resorts, its Victorian look is modeled after the Hotel del Coronado in San Diego—complete with sparkling whites and an eye-catching gabled red roof. The marble floor in the lobby was recently redone and features stylish representations of Disney characters. The cavernous five-story open lobby is dotted with invitingly soft chairs and couches, overlooked by a bird cage elevator. Live music throughout the day and into the night adds atmosphere to the extravagant surroundings.

Feed me: Dining options include Cítricos (expensive), Victoria & Albert's (really expensive), Gasparilla Grill and Games, Grand Floridian Café, 1900 Park Fare (a character buffet), Narcoossee's (expensive), and two lounges.

Feels like: Money.

You should also know: Boat rentals, including the Grand 1 fifty-two-foot *Sea Ray* yacht, are available. Guests can also swim, visit the playground, health club, and game room. There is also shopping, child care, and laundry facilities. There is also a meeting facility with nearly 40,000 square feet of meeting and convention space.

Getting to the parks: The Grand Floridian is on the Magic Kingdom monorail line. Watercraft transport is also available to the Magic Kingdom. Other parks and attractions are accessible by Disney's bus system. Guests can also take the monorail to the Ticket and Transportation Center and catch a connecting monorail to Epcot.

How much? Hoo boy. (Which translates to $410 to $2,350 a night, depending on season and view.)

Polynesian Resort

Theming: South Pacific Isles

Facts: Set on the shores of the Seven Seas Lagoon, the Polynesian has 847 rooms, suites, and concierge service designed to transport you to the Hawaiian islands. A massive atrium overflowing with greenery and waterfalls, greets guests in the Great Ceremonial House (Tahitian for "lobby"). Just outside the Great Ceremonial House is the Nanea Volcano Theme Pool—identifiable by the large volcano rising up out of its waters.

The entire resort is set on beautiful white sand beaches facing the Magic Kingdom. Grab a lounge chair and you've scored one of the best spots for viewing the Wishes nighttime fireworks display this side of the Main Street Hub.

Feed me: Dining options include 'Ohana (a ton of food served family style) which also has a character dining experience for breakfast. Kona Café, Captain Cook's, the "Spirit of Aloha" dinner show, The Tambu Lounge, and room service.

Feels like: Hawaii.

You should also know: Recreation and amenities include swimming, boating (rent several kinds of boats at the Mikala Canoe Club Marina), a playground, a game room, shopping, child care, and laundry facilities.

Getting to the parks: The Poly is on the Magic Kingdom monorail line, but guests can also use watercraft transportation to get across the lagoon. Other parks and attractions are accessible via Disney's bus transportation system. Guests can also take the monorail to the Ticket and Transportation Center to catch a connecting monorail to Epcot.

How much? Rooms in this deluxe resort range from $365 to $990 a night depending on season and view (garden view, lagoon view or magic kingdom view), and suites range from $630 to $3,000 a night.

The Straight Dope *Watch the nightly Wishes fireworks display and the Electrical Water Pageant from the beach at the Polynesian. The music accompanying each show is piped-in, and there's plenty of room to spread out and even lie down.*

Wilderness Lodge

Theming: National park lodges of the Pacific Northwest

Facts: Designed to feel like the Old Faithful Inn at Yellowstone National Park, this impeccably themed resort boasts 727 guestrooms. A jaw-dropping six-story lobby, finished with teepee-topped chandeliers, Disney-themed, hand-carved totem poles and an eighty-two-foot-tall stone fireplace, leaves many first-time visitors gazing upward. A hot spring bubbles up from the ground inside the lobby and flows outside and down toward a geothermal geyser that erupts hourly—thanks to Disney magic. Chairs and couches placed strategically throughout the lobby allow visitors to take in the overwhelming surroundings.

Feed me: Dining options include Artist Point (fancy), Whispering Canyon Café (loud), Roaring Fork Snacks (listen for music by Bela Fleck and the Flecktones), Territory Lounge, a pool bar, and room service.

Feels like: The biggest, most opulent log cabin ever.

You should also know: A Disney Vacation Club resort— the Villas at Wilderness Lodge—is located through the lobby, right next door. For business travelers, there is one 750-square-foot boardroom/meeting room. Guests can rent bikes and boats, swim, visit the playground or take advantage of the laundry room, game room, or on-site child care.

Getting to the parks: By boat to the Magic Kingdom and bus to all other parks and attractions.

How much? $240 to $525 depending on view and season.

MOUSEJUNKIE BARRY The Wilderness Lodge will always hold a place in my heart. It was our resort of choice on the first Walt Disney World vacation we took with our daughters and it made such an impression on us that it served as home base for the return trip some fourteen months later. I'm a sucker for tall pines, rustic log cabins, mountain air, geysers, honking geese—the works.

(Continued on next page)

The Wilderness Lodge is as close as you'll get to a visit to Yosemite without actually being there, down to its own Old Faithful. Yeah, it's man-made—Old Fakeful. I still love it. You get the Old Fakeful show every hour on the hour and my girls made sure to attend each and every eruption they could. When they weren't riding Small World of course.

What else did I love? There's the boat launch at the edge of Bay Lake which offers quick trips to either Fort Wilderness or, best of all, the Magic Kingdom. There are two table-service restaurants on-site, including one of my favorites, Whispering Canyon Café. The lobby is phenomenal. Six stories of pine and stone edifaces, carvings, Mission-style lighting fixtures. When we visited the first time, we were there for the Christmas season so we got to enjoy the huge Christmas tree that stands dead-center in the lobby. There's the bubbling brook running from the elevator area leading outside to falls and into the main pool. There's the pool itself, in which the resident ducks like to take a dip now and then. Those same ducks will often visit you when you're eating your breakfast out by the pool and aren't averse to sampling your croissant, if you feel like sharing.

Fort Wilderness Resort and Campground

Theming: Wilderness camping

Facts: 799 camp sites and 409 Wilderness Cabins all set in a relaxed 700-acre wilderness setting. The camp sites are level, paved pads with electric, water, and sewer hookups, and have charcoal grills and picnic tables. All camp sites have close access to air-conditioned comfort stations with private showers, coin-laundry facility, vending machines, and telephones. There are also sites where guests can pitch a tent.

The Wilderness Cabins are air-conditioned accommodations that sleep up to six guests and feature vaulted ceilings, fully equipped kitchens, full bathrooms, TVs, DVD and/or VCR player, outdoor grills, picnic tables, and a private patio deck. Wilderness Cabins also come equipped with hair dryers, foldaway cribs, ironing equipment, with daily housekeeping offered.

Feed me: Dining options include Crockett's Tavern, Mickey's Backyard BBQ, Trail's End Restaurant, and Hoop-Dee-Doo Musical Revue nightly dinner show at Pioneer Hall. Also offered is a campfire and marshmallow roast with Disney characters and a Disney movie.

Feels like: F-Troop come to life. (Kids, ask your parents.)

You should also know: Amenities include watercraft, a beach, fishing, tennis courts, two heated swimming pools, an arcade game room, laundry facilities, and kennels. Groceries and camping supplies at Meadow and Settlement Trading Posts. Unique to Fort Wilderness is the Wilderness Back Trail Adventure Segway Tour. Guests can explore the campground and Wilderness Lodge area via off-road Segways.

Getting to the parks: Buses link Fort Wilderness with all Walt Disney World parks and attractions. Boats will take guests to the Magic Kingdom.

How much? Camp sites range from $44 to $120 depending on season. Cabins range from $270 to $475 a night.

MOUSEJUNKIE JENNA I have spent three vacations camping at Fort with my parents, and have loved every minute of them. Now, when I say "camping," I mean "camping in an RV."

While I have nothing against tents, when it comes to camping at Walt Disney World, I'm with my mother on this one: I want air conditioning, a refrigerator, and something more than nylon between me and the alligators (or armadillos, or turkeys, or lizards).

The Fort is ideally suited to whatever kind of camping you choose. I've seen families with tents, pop-up campers, and the kind of luxury motorhomes the most spoiled rock star would crave. Campsites range from small sites suitable for a tiny teardrop trailer to large pull-through sites for the big diesel pusher coaches. All sites feature a concrete pad for parking or a rig, and a picnic table, charcoal grill, water, and electricity; and all sites, except for Premium sites, feature a sand pad suitable for a tent. Preferred and Premium sites also offer sewer and cable hook-ups. The Premium sites are designed for the longer rigs and don't have a sand pad for tents. The one thing missing is campfire pits. Fires at individual sites are absolutely forbidden.

There's even "camping" for people who don't want to camp, at all. The resort part of Fort Wilderness Resort and Campground has more than four hundred Wilderness

Cabins. The cabins sleep six people, with two bedrooms (one with a double bed and one with a bunk bed), and a Murphy bed in the living room. They have full kitchens and dining areas, a bathroom with tub and shower, TV in the living room, and your own deck and charcoal grill. The cabins also feature daily "Mousekeeping," so while you're in accommodations that feel like a snug little cabin in the woods, you also get the benefits of staying in a hotel. The only things you really need to bring are food, bug spray, and a flashlight. Every camper worth his salt needs a good flashlight.

Fort Wilderness is made up of a series of loops that branch off the three main roads, The loops have conveniently located comfort stations, which are very clean and spacious (but you still may want to shower early to avoid a line). Bus stops for Fort Wilderness's internal bus system are also convenient to loops. Campers are discouraged from driving their own vehicles around the campground when not checking in or out of their site. This contributes to the sense of peace and quiet around the campground. The bus system consists of three bus lines—orange, yellow, and purple—which run through different areas of the campground. All busses visit both the Outpost Depot (check-in, bus transportation to theme parks, kennels and trail rides) and the Settlement Depot (Pioneer Hall, the Marina/Boat Launch, Tri-Circle-D Ranch), only the orange and yellow buses go to the Meadow area. The Settlement is where you will find the Hoop-Dee-Doo Musical Revue, Mickey's Backyard BBQ, Trail's End restaurant, carriage rides and anything

(Continued on next page)

to do with a boat (fishing, boat rentals, transportation to the Magic Kingdom).

At the Meadow, you can find the newly refurbished Meadow Swimmin' Pool, featuring slides and a great kiddie pool, and Chip 'n' Dale's Campfire Sing-A-Long. The Campfire Sing-A-Long is one of those hidden treasures of Walt Disney World. It's a free program featuring songs, jokes, and a visit from Chip 'n' Dale. As you might guess, there are two campfires (attended by cast members). Bring your own s'mores, or buy supplies from the chuck wagon. Afterward, stick around for classic or current Disney movies, shown on the big screen. The Meadow is also the home of one of two arcades at the Fort, bike rentals, the Meadow Trading Post grocery store, a Segway tour, and an archery program. There's another arcade and grocery store found at the Settlement.

One feature that makes Fort Wilderness unique among all Walt Disney World resorts is that campers staying in their own air-conditioned trailer or RV can keep their pets with them. Pets are welcome on designated pet loops for an extra $5 per day. On our last trip, we stayed on a pet loop even though we didn't have any pets with us. It was great seeing all of the different dogs out for walks. At the front of each pet loop, there is a post with a container of baggies and a waste bin to encourage owners to clean up after their dogs. Last year, the Fort opened the Waggin' Trails Dog Park for dogs staying at the Fort to enjoy a little time off-leash. For safety, dogs are not permitted in tents or in vehicles without air conditioning.

The one problem I have with Fort Wilderness Resort and Campground is that there's almost too much to do there. I have to confess, I haven't done most of the activities offered at the Fort. When I visit WDW, I am all about the four theme parks, so I miss out on a lot at the Fort. I do know that some devoted Fort fiends can spend a week or more at Fort Wilderness and not visit a single park. That may not be the Mousejunkie way, but I think I'm actually a little jealous. There's something to be said for kicking back and enjoying the more rustic side of Walt Disney World.

Fort Wilderness is so unique as a Walt Disney World resort, it deserves a more detailed look. Mousejunkie Jenna is the veteran Fort enthusiast in our group.

Shades of Green

Facts: Shades of Green is unique among Disney resorts: it is operated as an Armed Forces Recreation Center for the exclusive use of active and retired military personnel and their families. Shades of Green has 586 rooms in a relaxed, country atmosphere overlooking golf courses, gardens, and pools.

Feed me: Full-service dining is available, as are snack bars, a lounge and room service.

You should also know: Guests can take advantage of tennis facilities, swimming, a fitness center, and a game room.

Walt Disney World maintains golf operations on the two PGA championship eighteen-hole golf courses and a nine-hole walking course adjacent to Shades of Green.

Getting to the parks: Buses link to all Walt Disney World parks and attractions.

Epcot Area Resorts

Pop Century Resort

Theming: Twentieth century pop culture

Facts: A value-level resort, Pop Century features 2,880 rooms with decor inspired by the 50s, 60s, 70s, 80s, and 90s. Outsized icons from each decade are plopped throughout the resort, including a four-story Rubik's cube, a giant Big Wheel, and 65-foot-high bowling pins.

Feed me: Snacks are available at the Petals Pool Bar, but Pop Century has, hands-down, the best quick-service food court in Disney's resorts.

Feels like: Your weird uncle's attic. Only a lot cleaner.

You should also know: Swim in three pools, enjoy a kiddie pool, and visit the Pop Jet playground and Fast Forward arcade. This resort is conveniently located near the ESPN Wide World of Sports Complex.

Getting to the parks: Buses whisk guests to the parks and attractions from the front of the resort. Only Disney buses can whisk.

How much? $82 to $174 depending on season.

MOUSEJUNKIE AMY I really like Pop Century. It's bright and interesting and welcoming. The food court has a good variety. It's one of the newer resorts and it feels that way. If you're choosing among the value resorts, it would be my first choice.

Caribbean Beach Resort

Theming: The Caribbean isles

Facts: This sprawling resort is divided into six Caribbean-themed resort villages featuring 2,112 rooms located on two hundred acres surrounding a forty-two-acre lake. The six themed villages are Aruba, Barbados, Jamaica, Martinique, Trinidad North, and Trinidad South. There are no elevators in any of the two-story buildings. If you are unable to use the stairs, request a first-floor room. The main building, Old Port Royale, can be quite far from some of the buildings. The Martinique and Trinidad North buildings are closest to Old Port Royale.

Feed me: Dining is available at Shutter's restaurant for table service and the Market Street food court.

Feels like: Pirates of the Caribbean.

You should also know: Pirate-themed rooms (in Trinidad South—the furthest village from the main building) immerses guests in the adventure-filled world of buccaneers. Pirate ship beds and wooden "ship's deck" flooring are among the details added to 384 rooms near a zero-gravity pool themed to resemble an old Spanish fort with cannons guarding the walls. All guestrooms include mini-bars and coffee makers. Also available: boat rentals, swimming, a playground, a game room, cycling, nature walks, a jogging track, laundry facilities and shopping. Each village has its own pool, white sand beach with hammocks and playground, laundry facilities, bus stop (so the distance from the main building may not be an issue), and parking area.

Getting to the parks: Buses are available at several locations throughout the resort. You're never too far from a bus stop, and thus your park or attraction of choice.

How much? The Caribbean Beach Resort is considered a moderate resort. Rooms range from $149 to $304 depending on seson, view, and whether it's a pirate-themed room.

Yacht Club Resort

Theming: Upscale Cape Cod
Facts: The oyster-gray clapboard buildings on the shores of Crescent Lake feature 621 rooms and suites. Brass fittings, nautical hardwood floors and rich millwork welcome guests into the warm lobby. All rooms feature French doors that open onto porches or balconies.

Feed me: The Captain's Grille, Yachtsman Steakhouse and two lounges. Heads-up here: There are no counter-service offerings at this waterfront resort.

Feels like: Kennedy country with Mouse ears. If they could stage the Barnstable vs. Falmouth football game on the croquet lawn, it'd be perfect.

You should also know: Let's talk location: Stay at the Yacht Club and you're within simple walking distance of Epcot's International Gateway (the back door to Epcot) or Disney's Hollywood Studios. Bunking down at the Yacht Club also gives guests easy access to all the amenities of the Boardwalk, just across the lake. A marina lighthouse that stands out on Crescent Lake adds an almost tangible ambience to this elegant but comfortable resort. Centrally located to the Yacht Club and its kissing cousin, the Beach Club, is a 73,000-square-foot convention center that includes a 36,000-square-foot ballroom that can seat as many as 2,800 for dinner.

Getting to the parks: Walk to Epcot or Disney's Hollywood Studios; boat to Epcot or Disney's Hollywood Studios; buses to the other parks and attractions.

How much? A deluxe resort, the rooms at the Yacht Club range from $340 to $1,950 a night, depending on season, view, and size of the room. Suites and concierge level rooms are available.

Beach Club Resort
Theming: New England beach cottages
Facts: Designed to resemble New England beach cottages of the 1860s, the Beach Club has 576 rooms and suites in

sun-washed structures of white stick-style architecture. The welcoming lobby features plenty of white wicker furniture in which to kick back and take in the airy atmosphere, and twenty-four-foot-high ceilings.

Feed me: Beaches and Cream, an old-fashioned ice cream parlor. (Though as the home of the Kitchen Sink, ice cream parlor seems a bit modest. Maybe Citadel of Cream: Where Dessert Warriors Go to do Battle would be more appropriate. More on that in the chapter, Mousejunkies Eat.) Guests can also dine in the Cape May Café (a character dining experience for both breakfast and dinner) and two lounges.

Feels like: Saltwater taffy. Fancy, but a little less stiff than it's neighbor, the Yacht Club. (And I'm still lobbying for a Dunkin' Donuts at the guard shack.)

You should also know: Location, location, location. Guests are so close to Epcot, it often feels as if IllumiNations: Reflections of Earth is going off in the bathroom. (Eat at 'Ohana and it might sound like that anyway.) The Yacht and Beach Club resorts share Stormalong Bay, the best theme pool in all of Walt Disney World. Stormalong Bay features three lagoon areas and a water slide created to look like a shipwreck. Guests can also take advantage of a health club, a marina, child care, a barber shop, and laundry facilities. The Beach Club Resort also includes the Beach Club Villas, a Disney Vacation Club resort.

Getting to the parks: Walk to Epcot or Disney's Hollywood Studios; boat to Epcot or Disney's Hollywood Studios; buses to the other parks and attractions.

How much? As a deluxe resort, the Beach Club can be pricey. Suites, such as the Newport Presidential Stone Harbor Club can run as much as $2,290 a night during the holiday season. Rooms, depending on season, view, and size, run from $340 to $805.

The BoardWalk Inn

Theming: Coney Island and Atlantic City around the turn of the 20th Century

Facts: The charming 372-room BoardWalk Inn is more than a hotel—it's an entertainment and dining district that offers guests a seemingly endless array of merrymaking options. Located on Crescent Lake, across from the Yacht and Beach Club Resorts, the BoardWalk features shopping, a children's activity center, a health club, tennis courts, a themed pool and a 20,000-square-foot conference center. Plenty of places to make merry.

Feed me: Disney's BoardWalk restaurants include Flying Fish Café, Kouzzina by Cat Cora, Big River Grille and Brewing Works, ESPN Club, Atlantic Dance nightclub, Jellyrolls dueling piano bar, and Seashore Sweets Bakery. Like its counterpart, the Yacht Club, there is no counter service.

Feels like: The Great Gatsby. Only with less disillusionment and unfortunate pedestrian accidents.

MOUSEJUNKIE WALT My favorite hotel is the Boardwalk, and the location is a big reason why. It's between my two favorite theme parks—Epcot and Disney's Hollywood Studios. And then there's the atmosphere. During the day it's a beautiful place to relax. At night there's entertainment from one end of the boardwalk to the other. There are jugglers, games of chance, musicians—all of which draw a crowd.

I also like the fact that it is its own little resort. There are restaurants, a piano bar, and a microbrewery there.

Think of it this way: If you went on a vacation there and didn't want to ride any of the attractions, you could just hang out at the Boardwalk Resort, maybe hit the pool and relax during the day. At night you can choose from any of the restaurants nearby, or walk right next door to Epcot and enjoy a different country every night. One night you could be drinking wine in Italy. The next you can be enjoying great French cuisine. If you want a trip where you just relax, it's the perfect place to do it.

Or you can go to the Magic Kingdom and be with all the screaming kids. Whatever floats your boat.

You should also know: Live entertainment keeps the Boardwalk jumping well into the night, as do the restaurants and lounges. It's proximity to the ESPN Club, and that establishment's chicken-wing-and-football-fueled Sundays, is yet another reason this place will forever feel like my home away from home.

The resort's themed pool, Luna Park, features a fantastic water slide—the Keister Coaster—plus there are two quiet pools.

The Boardwalk also shares space with the Disney Vacation Club's Boardwalk Villas. The Villas offer studio, one-and two-bedroom suites, and three-bedroom Grand Villas.

Getting to the parks: Walk to Epcot or Disney's Hollywood Studios; boat to Epcot or Disney's Hollywood Studios; buses to the other parks and attractions.

How much? With accommodations ranging from studio rooms to suites, prices range from $340 to $2,780 a night depending on season, view, and room size. (The high end, of course, being the Steeplechase Presidential Suite Inn Keepers Club during the holiday season.)

Walt Disney World Swan and Walt Disney World Dolphin

Theming: Think pink coral and turquoise waves
Facts: While these striking resorts are on Disney property, they are run by Westin Resorts. This doesn't mean the Swan and Dolphin are any less enjoyable, they just look and feel quite different from what you might find elsewhere on Disney property. The resorts, designed by Michael Graves, offer 2,265 rooms and 254,000 square feet of meeting and exhibition space. The massive statues topping each resort—the swans are forty-six feet tall and the fish fifty-six feet tall—can be seen from all over the Walt Disney World resort.

Feed me: There is a long list of restaurants and lounges between these two resorts, notably: Todd English's Blue Zoo, Il Mulino New York Trattoria, Kimonos, and Shula's Steak House.

Feels like: Floribbean.

You should also know: There are four swimming pools, two health clubs and a wide array of recreational activities. The location is ideal for getting to Epcot, Disney's Hollywood Studios, and the BoardWalk via water and walkway. There is a parking charge for guests at this resort. If you park it yourself, you'll pay $9 per day. Valet parking is $12 per day (and the state of Florida takes its piece, as well.)

Getting to the parks: Guests can either walk or take Friendships to Epcot and Disney's Hollywood Studios. Buses are available to all other parks and attractions.

How much? Rooms start at $229 a night, but members of the military, school teachers, and Florida residents enjoy additional discounts.

Downtown Disney Area

Disney's Saratoga Springs Resort and Spa
Theming: Nineteenth century upstate New York resort
Facts: The spirit of Saratoga Springs, N.Y., with its horse racing history and placid upstate feel, is recreated accurately in the 924-unit fifth Disney Vacation Club resort.

Victorian architecture and gurgling springs evoke a gentler age. Comfortable, overstuffed chairs make the lobby a comfortable place to fall into after a hard day of walking, and its spa offers a relaxing way to get away from the theme parks.

Constructed on the site of the old Disney Institute (and before that the Disney Village,) guests can walk to Downtown Disney, or take a quick ferry across the lake. Rooms facing Downtown Disney have a fantastic view of the nearly twenty-four-hour restaurant, shopping, and night-club district.

Feed me: The Artist's Palette—a counter-service restaurant and market—serves breakfast, lunch, and dinner. The Turf Club is a table-service restaurant where you can get ya meat on (prime rib, angus chuck cheeseburger, grilled New York strip.)

Feels like: Upstate New York. With palm trees.

You should also know: The resort is located across the lake from Downtown Disney and adjacent to Disney's Lake Buena Vista golf course. Also, this place is big.

Getting to the parks: Bus transportation is provided to all the theme parks, water parks, and Downtown Disney.

How much? This is a Disney Vacation Club resort, but accommodations, which range from studio rooms to three-bedroom Grand Villas, range from $285 to $1,645 a night.

The Straight Dope *For a room closest to the check-in desk, request The Springs. For a room closest to Downtown Disney, request a room in Congress Park.*

MOUSEJUNKIE WALT My only criticism of Saratoga Springs, which is my Disney Vacation Club home resort, is that it's so big. You can walk forever just to get to the main building depending on where you stay.

TEEN MOUSEJUNKIE RYAN My favorite resort is actually a tie between Saratoga Springs and All Star Music. I know, I know, those are complete opposites. Let me explain: Saratoga Springs is our home resort, so I've stayed there a lot. And having visited Saratoga Springs, N.Y. twice a year for roughly half of my life, I have a bit of a connection there. Throw in the fact that my dad used to be a jockey, and you can see why I love the fancy racetrack themed resort.

Port Orleans French Quarter

Theming: New Orleans French Quarter

Facts: Storm shutters, spicy Cajun food, garishly colored decor, ornate wrought iron fixtures and a feeling of perpetual Mardi Gras recreates New Orleans' French Quarter in this moderate-level, 1,008 room resort. The shuttered windows and doors along the main thoroughfare recreate perfectly the feel of Bourbon Street, as do the street signs, which are identical to those found in New Orleans.

Feed me: Sassagoula Floatworks food court and pizza delivery.

Feels like: Mardi Gras without the risqué bead-tempting antics.

You should also know: The French Quarter boasts one of the more eye-popping pools, Doubloon Lagoon, which is themed like a Mardi Gras celebration. A large dragon twisting around one end also serves as a water slide, while an all-alligator Dixieland band stands guard nearby. But, as it usually does, it all comes down to the food. Beignets and café au lait, ribs and cornbread make this a food court you will not want to overlook. And that, in itself, might be reason enough to stay at this resort.

Getting to the parks: Bus transportation is provided to all the theme parks, water parks, and Downtown Disney. Boats can take guests to the neighboring Port Orleans Riverside, and to Downtown Disney.

How much? Rooms range from $149 a night to $249 a night depending on season.

Port Orleans Resort Riverside
Theming: The old south
Facts: Accordion and washboard music lilts teasingly from behind bushes throughout this 2,048-room resort. The Sassagoula river winds through both the Magnolia Bend (southern-style mansions) and Alligator Bayou (rustic lodges) sections.

Feed me: Dining includes Riverside Mill food court and Boatwright's Dining Hall.

Feels like: Song of the South. But don't tell anyone. Disney pretty much ignores that film.

You should also know: Recreation includes Ol' Man Island, a 3½-acre old-fashioned swimming hole with slides, rope swings and playgrounds; quiet pools; boat rentals; game room; lounges; and a gift shop. If it wasn't for the ribs at the French Quarter's food court, Riverside would top my list of moderate resorts. Never underestimate the power of barbecue.

Getting to the parks: Bus transportation is provided to all the theme parks, water parks, and Downtown Disney. Guests can also take a riverboat to Downtown Disney and to this resort's neighbor, Port Orleans French Quarter.

How much? Rooms range from $149 a night to $249 a night depending on season and view.

Old Key West Resort

Theming: The most relaxing aspects of the Conch Republic
Facts: The first Disney Vacation Club resort built, this resort offers the laid-back charms of Key West with the service and amenities Disney resorts are known for. There are 549 units, with studios, one-and two-bedroom suites, and three-bedroom, absolutely gargantuan 2,375 square-foot Grand Villas that can sleep the entire defense of the Miami Dolphins (up to twelve, actually).

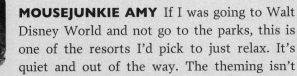

MOUSEJUNKIE AMY If I was going to Walt Disney World and not go to the parks, this is one of the resorts I'd pick to just relax. It's quiet and out of the way. The theming isn't overpowering. The Wilderness Lodge hits you over the head with its log cabin and wooden feel. At Old Key West it doesn't scream "I'm at Disney!" You can just go and hang out by the water and enjoy a drink.

Feed me: Dining includes Olivia's Café, poolside fare at the Gurgling Suitcase, and Good's Food To-Go quick-service restaurant.

Feels like: A take-home version of Key West.

You should also know: Rooms include wet bar, microwave, and small refrigerator, or a full kitchen. There is a health club (for those who think exercising on vacation is a good idea), tennis, swimming pool, sauna, and planned recreation. Guests can use DVC points or book through central reservations. After dark the resort comes alive with festive yet muted lighting, rather successfully recreating the feel of the original location several hundred miles to the south.

Getting to the parks: Bus transportation is provided to all the theme parks, water parks, and Downtown Disney. Guests can also travel to Downtown Disney by boat, which is a much more enjoyable option than the typical bus trip.

How much? Room rates start at the studio level of $295 to $440 a night, and top out at the Grand Villa, $1,690 to $1,725 a night.

Disney's Animal Kingdom Area Resorts

Animal Kingdom Lodge

Theme: African savanna

Facts: This 972-room deluxe level resort is themed to convey the feeling of being transported to an African wildlife reserve. The architecture, plant life, and variety of animals that freely roam the thirty-three-acre savanna just outside the Jambo House lobby contribute to a vivid and convincing atmosphere.

Feed me: The Animal Kingdom Lodge, and the Disney Vacation Club's Kidani Village located just next door, feature two full-service restaurants—Boma: Flavors of Africa and Jiko: The Cooking Place. There's also a counter-service restaurant and two bars: Uzima Springs and Victoria Falls. Kidani Village has its own table-service restaurant, Sanaa.

Feels like: All the beauty of Africa

You should also know: The resort features hand-carved furnishings, African art, and a giant fireplace in a soaring lobby. Guests can stroll along a rock outcropping, Arusha Rock, and enjoy nearly panoramic views of roaming animals and flowing streams. Guests with savanna-view rooms—on the inside of the horseshoe-shaped resort—can view the animals from the comfort of their beautifully themed accommodations.

Animal Kingdom Lodge has Disney Vacation Club rooms, located next to the 449-unit DVC Kidani Village Resort.

Concierge-level guests are offered a safari experience unique to resort guests: the Sunset, or Wanyama, safari. It runs roughly ninety minutes and takes guests on a recreation of an African game drive across the resort's savanna. The safaris conclude with a multi course meal at the hotel's premier restaurant, Jiko.

Here's the real lowdown: The Disney public relations would like you to imagine sitting out on a hotel room balcony in the morning, sipping coffee as a giraffe slowly moves by, grazing on leaves just a few feet away.

In reality, that is *exactly* what it's like to stay at the Animal Kingdom Lodge (assuming you score a savanna-view room.) There's no marketing sleight of hand at work here. It is as beautiful and unique an experience as you'll find without actually traveling to Africa.

More than three hundred animals and birds populate the grounds, which surround the resort on three sides. The animals can be seen from private balconies as well as several public viewing areas.

There's nothing like sharing a caffeine buzz with a zebra first thing in the morning.

Getting to the parks: Bus transportation is provided to all the theme parks, water parks, and Downtown Disney.

How much? Room rates range from $275 to $720 a night, with suites running from $1,245 to $2,260 a night, depending on season and view. This resort is also a Disney Vacation Club resort.

Coronado Springs Resort

Theming: American Southwest.

Facts: Inspired by the American Southwest and regions of Mexico, this 1,917-room resort encircles a fifteen-acre lagoon called Lago Dorado. There are three quiet pools and a five-story Mayan pyramid that serves as the splashy center-piece for a family-fun pool with a water slide.

Feed me: Dining includes the Maya Grill full-service restaurant, the Pepper Market dining court, Rix Lounge, Laguna Bar lounge, Siestas Cantina poolside bar and limited room service.

Feels like: A breezy siesta

You should also know: Special services include in-room coffee makers and ironing equipment, La Vida Health Club, a hair salon, bike rentals, watercraft rentals, an arcade, a sand volleyball court, a kiddie pool, and playground. A 220,000-square-foot convention center includes the 60,214-square-foot Coronado Ballroom. This resort is huge, but a new internal shuttle system helps guests get to and fro.

Getting to the parks: Bus transportation is provided to all the theme parks, water parks, and Downtown Disney.

How much? Rooms range from $154 to $575 a night depending on season, view, and room size. Coronado Springs offers accommodations ranging from studios to junior suites that sleep as many as six people.

All-Star Sports Resort

Theming: Sports

Facts: Colorful, clean, fun, and affordable. This 1,920 room value resort is dotted with buildings surrounded by larger-than-life sports icons representing surfing, basketball, tennis, baseball, and football. My only knock: needs more hockey.

Feed me: Food court, a pool bar, pizza delivery.

Feels like: Tom Brady would stay here.

Wait, who am I kidding? Tom Brady is married to Giselle Bundchen and jets around the world in his own crime-fighting plane. He'd build his own resort with a special wing for his Super Bowl rings and there would be a supermodel stable. But other than that I bet it would look like this.

You should also know: This value-level resort features a commercial center with check-in and guest service facilities, laundry facilities, a gift shop, and game room. There are two swimming pools and a kiddie pool. The design, feel, layout, and style of this resort is virtually identical to the All-Star Movies and All-Star Music resorts, save for the theme-specific decor.

Getting to the parks: Bus transportation is provided to all the theme parks, water parks, and Downtown Disney.

How much? Rooms range from $82 to $174 depending on season and whether it's a standard room or a preferred room (closer to the lobby.)

All-Star Movies Resort

Theming: Disney movies

Facts: This 1,920-room value resort has facilities and amenities that mirror Disney's All-Star Sports Resort. Towering icons from favorite Disney movies adorn the resort, from *101 Dalmatians*, *Toy Story*, and *Fantasia*, to *The Mighty Ducks*, and *The Love Bug*.

Feels like: An animation fan's dream

Getting to the parks: Bus transportation is provided to all the theme parks, water parks, and Downtown Disney.

How much? Rooms range from $82 to $174 depending on season and whether it's a standard room or a preferred room (closer to the lobby.)

All-Star Music Resort

Theming: Fine art. No, I kid, I kid. Music.

Facts: This is the resort that saved my vacation and turned me into a Mousejunkie. Like the other All-Star resorts, it is colorful, clean, and fun. There really is not a lot that feels budget about this value-level resort. It features 1,489 rooms and 215 family suites in buildings with larger-than-life icons representing jazz, rock, Broadway, calypso, and country music. Facilities and amenities are the same as the All-Star Sports and All-Star Movies resorts. The family suites sleep up to six and offer two bedrooms, two full baths, a kitchenette and two twenty-seven-inch flat screen TVs.

Feels like: Disney's rich musical history

TEEN MOUSEJUNKIE RYAN I can't help but love the piano pool, the brightly decorated rooms, and the ridiculously 80s-styled pop stars painted throughout the café. It's just a fun environment, and being a music lover who has stayed there many times, it just seems like home for me.

To reserve a room at a Walt Disney World resort, call 407-WDISNEY (934-7639).

Getting to the parks: Bus transportation is provided to all the theme parks, water parks, and Downtown Disney.

How much? Rooms range from $82 to $174 depending on season and whether it's a standard room or a preferred room (closer to the lobby.) The family suites range from $190 to $355 a night depending on season.

Resorts by the Numbers

According to Walt Disney World figures:

➤ Total number of resorts at Walt Disney World: 34
➤ Number of Disney owned/operated resorts: 24
➤ Number of Disney owned/operated resorts that Mousejunkies J and Deb have stayed at: 24*
➤ Total number of guestrooms at Walt Disney World Resort: more than 28,000
➤ Number of Disney owned/operated guestrooms: more than 21,000

➤ Total number of guestrooms where Mousejunkie Bill took too much cold medicine and stared at the wallpaper for hours: 1*

➤ Number of Disney Vacation Club units: 3,187 (two-bedroom equivalents)

➤ Number of campsites at Disney's Fort Wilderness Resort and Campground: 799

* Figures provided by Mousejunkies researchers.

Nearby Options

There are a number of non-Disney-owned hotels located near Downtown Disney. Many of these offer conference and convention space. Here's a quick rundown of these resorts:

Buena Vista Palace: 1,013 rooms and suites and ninety-thousand square feet of meeting space in a twenty-seven-story, lakeside setting.

Regal Sun Resort: 626-room lakeside resort. Features more than seventeen thousand square feet of meeting space.

Doubletree Guest Suites Resort: 229-room resort consisting entirely of suites with a living room and separate bedroom, refrigerator, microwave, and coffee maker. Dining at Streamers Restaurant.

Holiday Inn: 323-room high-rise hotel featuring in-room coffee makers, four restaurants and lounges, two swimming pools, a fitness center, and a game room.

The Hilton: 814-room resort with seven restaurants and lounges, three swimming pools, and a tropical outdoor spa. Offers more than sixty-one thousand square feet of meeting space.

Hotel Royal Plaza: 394 rooms, conference facilities, on-site dining, and entertainment.

Best Western Lake Buena Vista Resort: 325-room Caribbean-style resort featuring a game room, fitness center, swimming pool, playground, and shopping.

Another benefit of staying on-site is that there's always the option of a midday nap. Midday naps can be valuable. That is, if your kid will nap. Ours usually won't, but a little down time can help. It certainly helps her mother, I'll tell you that. Plus, it gives me time to watch Stacey on the in-room resort TV channel.

No matter where guests stay on-property, from the most exclusive suite at the Grand Floridian Resort to the most affordable studio at Pop Century, there is one element that unites them all, and that is Stacey J. Aswad.

Stacey is the super-friendly, ultra-perky host who guides viewers through the Disney parks on its in-room resort information channels. Love her or hate her, there's no escaping her high-energy welcome. Turn on the TV in any Disney resort, and there she is—colorful, cute, enthusiastic, and ultimately helpful.

There are two guarantees on every Walt Disney World trip: I will start and end each day by watching Stacey for a while, and Amy will roll her eyes every time I do it.

An Interview with Walt Disney World's In-Room Resort Channel Host, Stacey Aswad

To anyone who has stayed on Walt Disney World property in the past five years, she is the face of the vacation kingdom.

Walk into a hotel room at Walt Disney World—any hotel room in any resort—turn on the TV, and there she is. She's perky, enthusiastic, and perhaps most importantly, omnipresent. Guests can't help but feel like they've got a pretty, dark-haired woman traveling along with them.

But just who is that girl?

Stacey J. Aswad is the host of Walt Disney World's in-room resort channel. She'll tell you about the top seven attractions, she'll outline the must-do activities and provide a few insiders' tips along the way. And if you're staying on Disney property, there's no avoiding the infectiously happy tour guide.

"It's starting to hit me, after five years, that I'm seen as this kind of real-life Minnie Mouse," Stacey said from her home in Los Angeles. "I know in Disney culture, I'm 'that' girl and the face of Disney World, but I don't take myself so seriously. I have been called the human exclamation point."

Stacey got the part after auditioning in Atlanta, going through callbacks, meeting the director and then receiving the original twenty-five page script.

"I had four days to learn the script," Stacey said. "I had to have everything memorized. There were no Teleprompters, no ear prompters. I had to learn it word for word. I remember having this moment of, 'Oh my gosh, what have I done?' That was my first real acting/hosting gig. I had been a dancer my whole life, but I hadn't really done any on camera. It was a great baptism."

Stacey hosts two shows that are on a constant loop in the resorts: the thirty-minute *Top Seven Must Sees*, and the newer *Must-Do Disney*.

"When we shot the first time, no one knew who I was," she said of the relative ease with which she moved around the theme parks. "People would look at us and not care. Now people have gone back time after time, and they end up watching me and not getting away from me. People think I live in the park. I get these great emails— 'We were at Disney World and didn't see you.' People think I live in the Cinderella castle."

Over the course of the two shows, Stacey takes viewers on a virtual tour through Walt Disney World. She interacts with characters, walks through the parks and experiences the resort first-hand, including a few of the more hair-raising attractions.

"Some of attractions I had to do multiple times while shooting," she said. "Like Summit Plummet at the Blizzard Beach water park. I had to do that three times in a row."

Her blindingly fast plunge down Summit Plummet— the second tallest and fastest free-fall water slide in

(Continued on next page)

the world—is the perfect example of how the Julliard-trained dancer throws caution to the wind and gives in to her boundless energy.

"I went down, fixed my bathing suit and went right back up," she said. "It was very bizarre. I remember saying to ride operator, 'All I have to do is cross my feet, cross my arms and lean back? Seriously? There's no restraint?' I think I may have said a small prayer, leaned back and off I went. I screamed like crazy."

Which prompts the Binghamton, N.Y. native to explain: "I don't really scream that much in real life."

Stacey flies to Florida to update the shows now and then, and also provides new voice-overs when needed. During the time she's been the inescapable emcee of every Disney resort guest's off-hours TV viewing, she's learned a thing or two about the place. Her number one, top-secret tip?

"Wear comfortable shoes," she laughed.

Surprisingly, someone who is so closely identified with Walt Disney World had very little time in the resort prior to landing the hosting job.

"I had heard about it, but I had a large family so it was like we had our own Disney World at home," she said. "I'd had friends that had gone, but it was this whole mysterious place. So when I first got there I had some expectation of it, but it blew me away—the sheer volume of it. Everything about it is very magical.

"I love challenges, but I had to kind of stop and look around to see exactly what was going on. I was so focused on doing a good job, but I couldn't believe the logistics of it."

The shoot itself is always somewhat of a delicate dance. The timing of each segment is deliberate and mapped out. If a monorail comes by a certain location, they have one chance to get everything right. She often has to board a certain ride car at a certain time, and if they don't get the shot everyone has to wait around for the next timed opportunity.

And as for that famous Stacey energy?

"When I got the first job and we were first shooting it, there was a moment where they said, 'Let's pick it up a little more.' I was like, 'Gosh, really?' I thought I was being over the top.

"I do tend to be free and energetic, but I do have moments of being calm and chilled out."

The segments are updated from time to time, and a few times a year Stacey will find herself back in the parks, raving about one thing or another and enjoying the atmosphere.

"What I find interesting—and the attractions are amazing—is that every time I go back I'm more in tune with the landscaping and architecture," she said. "Don't overlook those things. It's incredible. It's all obviously part of the whole palate of fantasy. Nothing is random, and everything has a meaning or purpose."

Mousejunkies Sleep Checklist

☐ Decide if you'd like to stay on Disney property or have a terrible vacation.

☐ Check your budget/needs to see if you'd like to stay at a value, moderate, deluxe, or home-away-from-home/DVC resort.

☐ Call 1-407-WDISNEY to make your reservation.

☐ If you are an Annual Passholder, see if there are any AP room rates.

☐ If you belong to AAA, see if there are any AAA room rates.

☐ Ask the cast member taking your reservations if they are running any specials (free dining promotion, etc.)

☐ **Disney's value resorts**
All-Star Movies
All-Star Music
All-Star Sports
Pop Century

☐ **Disney's moderate resorts**
Caribbean Beach Resort
Coronado Springs
Fort Wilderness
Port Orleans French Quarter
Port Orleans Riverside

☐ **Disney's deluxe resorts**
Animal Kingdom Lodge
The Beach Club

The BoardWalk Inn
The Contemporary Resort
The Dolphin
The Grand Floridian
The Polynesian Resort
The Swan
The Wilderness Lodge
The Yacht Club

❑ **Disney Vacation Club Resorts/Home Away From Home Resorts**
Animal Kingdom Villas
Bay Lake Tower
Beach Club Villas
BoardWalk Villas
Kidani Village
Old Key West
Saratoga Springs
Treehouse Villas
Villas at Wilderness Lodge

6 Mousejunkies Eat

You've been traipsing around theme parks all day and you're hungry. But you can't decide between escargot with champagne, schnitzel and a beer, or a burger and a Coke.

Don't sweat it—Walt Disney World's got you covered.

Interested in stuffing yourself at a buffet? Be sure to hit

Boma at the Animal Kingdom Lodge. How about a character meal? Chef Mickey's at the Contemporary is your answer. Have you pawned the kids off with your in-laws for a romantic evening out? Narcoossee's at the Grand Floridian should do the trick.

There's something for every taste at Walt Disney World, it just might cost you a bit. (And by "a bit," I mean "a lot.")

Dining at Walt Disney World is expensive. I never fail to experience sticker shock when I see what my meal cost. Yet I don't opt to skip this part of the trip. The service, theming, and quality of Disney's eateries make them just as much a part of the vacation as any theme park attraction.

Of course, there are ways to save a little money, it just takes a little creativity. Just not "Corn People" creative.

MOUSEJUNKIE RANDY Some people find the high-end restaurants at Disney World pricey. But I think they are well worth the value for the money you pay. I have gone to expensive places in Boston and paid twice as much as the high-end places at Disney. You can't beat the quality, the service, or the variety of food choices at Walt Disney World. These places to me are a much better value for your Disney dollars than an $8 cheeseburger at Peco Bill's at the Magic Kingdom. (But how I love that cheeseburger.) I would rather spend $18 for a perfectly cooked steak served with fresh, hot macadamia nut bread and Yukon Gold mashed potatoes at the Kona Café. It's all what value you think you're getting for your dollar. Its vacation live it up a little.

Several years back an early Internet legend tore through the DISBoards—one of the biggest Walt Disney World fan forums online. A family visiting the World thought they'd save a little money by bringing along their own food. Specifically, canned corn.

Said family used a can opener to crack open the golden treats, sat down on a sidewalk on Main Street USA and shoveled those sweet niblets down their gullets with plastic spoons as other guests wandered by.

I'm not one to pass judgment on anyone trying to save a little money at Walt Disney World, but this family, whoever they were, became unknowing celebrities among the Disney fanatic community. These Corn People, as they came to be known, were the topic of conversation for the better part of a year. Every once in a while they'll still be referred to by an old-timer on the boards as an example of slightly odd behavior at Walt Disney World.

The truth is, there are countless restaurants (actually, they are quite countable, but they keep opening new ones and closing older ones and I'm easily confused while under the influence of bread pudding) ranging from affordable to shamelessly expensive. And everyone has a favorite. But there are a few generally accepted rules: Le Cellier is always good, and Tonga Toast is one of the best, if most over-indulgent, breakfast you can get on-property.

Recently there has been a seismic shift in the Disney breakfast hierarchy, however. The mighty Tonga Toast— long the stuff of breakfast legend amongst Walt Disney World guests—may have been knocked from its lofty perch by an unassuming and yet irresistible alternative.

Will there be those who scoff at this subjective proclamation? Surely. But there were those who said man could not reach the moon; that the Red Sox would never win the World Series; that I should probably wear pants in public more often.

And yet I must make this claim: Tonga Toast is dead. Long live the Samoan.

Anyone who has ever eaten breakfast at the Kona Café at Disney's Polynesian Resort has no doubt crossed paths with its signature breakfast dish, Tonga Toast. It's a deep-fried banana-stuffed French toast reportedly brought to the resort by cultural advisor Auntie Kaui. It's bigger than your head and probably has more calories than a footlocker full of Big Macs. But it tastes amazingly good and probably precludes any need for lunch reservations.

And yet it now sits firmly in second place. On the Mount Rushmore of awesome Disney breakfast options, Tonga Toast would be Teddy Roosevelt. Sure, it's up there, but it's kind of looking the other way and you can't really see that he's wearing glasses unless you pay the seventy-five-cents to look through the binoculars and you left all your change back in the car.

Tonga Toast will always remain near and dear to my heart, primarily because that's where my stomach is and it's probably still digesting from the last time I had it in December of 2006. Now, however, I have eyes for another.

It happened rather innocently. I perused the dumbed-down one-page menu (thank you free dining and Disney Dining Plan), and my eyes accidentally tripped down the page past Tonga Toast. It was inadvertent, but the repercussions have become very real. A single word jumped out at me and seared itself into my eyes. Hollandaise. This egg-yolk-and- butter-based sauce has magical properties that turn even the most mundane meal fantastic. So imagine my shock when I saw that the word hollandaise was paired with two other words that render me weak and defenseless: "pulled pork."

The Samoan, in its entirety, is poached eggs with hollandaise sauce served over smoked pulled pork hash.

The Samoan is made up of three elements that are good individually, but collectively reach perfection. Topped with a pile of greens that look like clover but serve to only temporarily obscure the golden glow of the hollandaise, it captured my imagination the minute I saw it.

I tore through the greens, tossing them to the side of my plate as I drilled down to the gooey, aromatic treasure below. I pierced one of the poached eggs and it seeped down onto the pulled pork hash. It was like adding together the vital elements of a potion. Once intermingled, the magic could not be undone. I was enraptured by the visual presentation. But this was nothing compared to when I actually tasted a bite. The Samoan was salty with a hint of sweetness. The pulled pork gave it a tangy bite that tied all the flavors together in a way that I heretofore had not experienced. I temporarily lost the power of speech. My vision grew dim. I swam in a lake of hollandaise buoyed by a raft of pulled pork while egg whites sang a siren song drawing me closer to an island of toast. After a few moments lost in this trip, I heard—distantly— someone calling my name.

I snapped to.

"Daddy, I have to pee," my daughter said.

"Take the kid to the bathroom," I droned to my wife.

I was focused on continuing my journey. I took another bite and jumped back into my eggy rapture. I saw an order of Tonga Toast delivered to the table next to me, and for the slightest moment felt a tinge of sadness. Because I knew that the Samoan had forever chased it from my palate. I would not attack that mountain of deep-fried goodness to feel stuffed ever again.

But it was O.K.. The Samoan had stolen my heart.

There may have been Hawaiian Kona coffee served in a French press pot, but I'm not sure. I marched through the Samoan until it was gone, and then I emerged—sated in every possible way and ready for another.

But this was Kona, not 'Ohana. That over-indulgence would have to wait another day.

★ **The Straight Dope**   *Make your reservations as early as possible, or plan on standing in line at counter service during your stay. Advanced Dining Reservations (ADRs) can be made 180 days out from your trip by calling 407- WDW-DINE (939-3463). You can also make all your ADRs online at disneyworld.disney.go.com/reservations/dining. The interface is incredibly easy to use, and it gives you options if your time or restaurant isn't available.*

Considering the sheer number of dining choices and options, figuring out where to eat has become as important as any other part of our trips to Walt Disney World. Whenever a friend comes home from a visit, the questions invariably go like this: How was the weather, how were the crowds, where did you eat?

We literally plan entire vacations around where we want to eat. Not because we're unusually bacchanalian, but because it can be a hassle to get a reservation.

Here's the key: When you've booked your trip, count 180 days out from your arrival date, and either call 407- WDW-DINE (939-3463) or visit disneyworld.disney.go.com/reservations/dining to make your advanced dining reservations that day. Delay, and you may never know the cool, candle-lit, beefy goodness of Le Cellier or what Fantasyland looks like from *inside* Cinderella Castle.

Can't-Miss Restaurants

Everyone has a favorite Disney eatery, and judging by how difficult it is to get an Advanced Dining Reservation, it must be Le Cellier. The buzz surrounding this restaurant is deafening.

For me, however, if I have a pint of Guinness in my hand and some kind of meat on my plate, I'm pretty happy. Add some great traditional Irish music and I'm in heaven. At **Raglan Road** you get all this. The food revolves around Irish themes, but is much better than anything I've sampled while actually in that section of the world. The Simple Salmon appetizer—smoked salmon served with capers, shallots and creme fraiche—is still a favorite, along with Ger's Bread and Butter Pudding. The music is fantastic, and the Irish step dancer, who performs nightly, is the best you'll find outside of the Emerald Isle.

Nervous about potential changes to some of my favorite restaurants, I thought I'd check my enthuse-o-meter by dropping in on Raglan Road to see if the seemingly property-wide menu alterations had marred my favorite WDW restaurant.

Good news: The torrid love affair between Raglan Road and I continues unabated. At the risk of overplaying the hyperbole card, I'm petitioning the Pope to have chef Kevin

Dundon canonized. There were changes—mainly pertaining to names on the menu. And the entertainment has been slightly altered. But suffice to say when I set foot in the place, I feel like I'm being welcomed home.

We arrived a little ahead of our Advanced Dining Reservations, but found ourselves being led to our table within minutes. We were given "The Bono Seats," situated just under a large painting of the singer's brooding visage. It was there that we were buried beneath an avalanche of great food, great music and fantastic entertainment.

Before I set foot in the place, I knew what I was looking forward to: The Simple Salmon appetizer (the Salmon Swoon in the new parlance) and fish-and-chips, followed by Ger's Bread and Butter Pudding. And about seventeen Guinnesses. But shockingly, we opted to travel a different road this time. The salmon took a back seat to a few alternate choices.

Our server had a basket of bread and a Guinness reduction dipping sauce on the table in seconds, and drinks right behind. The bread is delicious on its own, but dipping it in the reduction added an irresistibly tangy molasses taste that made it all disappear rather quickly.

As a pint of cider chased the bread away, the heady concoction that makes Raglan Road so potent struck me right between the eyes: the food, the drinks, and as if on cue, a song by famed Dubliner Luke Kelly had my head swimming. It was as if the wild-haired, red-bearded troubadour had pulled a chair up at our table to make sure the craic was flowing as readily as the pints.

First, the appetizers: We indulged in the Scallop Forest (sea scallops served atop forks with a lime dipping sauce), the Dalkey Duo (battered cocktail sausages with a Dalkey mustard sauce), and the Heaven on Earth (aptly-named Guinness glazed baby back ribs.) The scallops melted in our mouths—sweet, but with a hint of citrus; the sausages were meaty, salty and addictive, while the ribs (sadly) were gone much too quickly. Paired with a pint of Guinness and the blazing traditional Irish music whipping through the room, the table was set for a look at the new take on its former entertainment.

Trad dancer Danielle Fitzpatrick is now joined by two other performers who trade stomps, jumps and steps between them several times throughout the night. The two women dancers tripped skillfully across the main stage, setting a challenge for the new male dancer who owned the center stage. Between them, a new, faster, wilder, heart-pounding performance cast a dervish-like spell on anyone caught up in the fantastic display of Irish step dancing.

We had just enough time to catch our breath when the entrees arrived. I attacked the Serious Steak (a ten-ounce sirloin with an Irish whiskey marmalade glaze, mashed potatoes and onion strings), while others in our party tried the Raglan Risotto (chicken atop a light shitake mushroom risotto) and the Bangers and Booz (carmelized onions topped the sausage and mash off perfectly.) All of it was fantastic.

Which left only one thing: dessert. It can be only one choice—Ger's Bread and Butter pudding. Bread pudding is found all over Disney property. And in a bare-knuckle pub dust-up, 'Ohana would land a few blows. But by the end, Raglan Road's version would score a clear knockout. It is the best on-property, hands-down. The buttery creation comes in an oversized mug with vanilla and butterscotch sauce. A deliciously crusty exterior gives way to a spongy, flavorful underside that soaks up the sauces hungrily. Do not undertake this dessert lightly. It's a stick-to-your-guts treat that tops everything off with a sweet yet deceivingly potent sock to the appetite. In other words, you're going to be full.

It was at this point I was asked the dumbest question ever. And I mean that with love.

As Ger's Bread and Butter Pudding was brought to the table, Amy asked me a question that had only one obvious answer: "Do you want to split a dessert?"

Amy's a smart girl. She was salutatorian of her high school class and regularly beats me at Jeopardy. So why she would ask such a silly question baffles me. I say it has one 'obvious' answer, but as we learned that night amidst the rollicking music, fantastic entertainment and the incredible atmosphere, there were several other ways to respond to Amy's remarkably silly question.

Here, in order, are the answers I gave her:

➤ "No."
➤ "No, get your own."
➤ "Maybe I could get him to cut it into seven pieces and we could all have a micro-sliver."
➤ "Wait.... I'll ask the waiter if he'll run across the room, flicking it at us as he jogs by."

➤ "I know, see if the waiter will grab a piece of cake, smush it in his hands and punch me in the face with it."

By now, Amy had *that* look on her face—the one that said she got my point, and she was no longer amused by my increasingly annoying answers.

Of course I split it with her. The Bread and Butter pudding at Raglan Road is monstrous, unbelievably rich and unmatched anywhere on Disney property—where bread pudding is evidently a staple. Besides, I had to drive home with her. I'm not crazy.

An Interview with Raglan Road's Danielle Fitzpatrick

Several times every night, a talented Irish step dancer takes the center stage to jump, stomp, tap, and whirl to the driving tunes provided by the top-notch Irish musicians.

That dancer is Danielle Fitzpatrick, a talented young Irish woman from Dublin who enraptures the restaurant's main room nightly. She and her fiancé Colin Farrell, a fiddler in the house band, help make Raglan Road one of the premiere restaurants on Disney property.

"We met in Holland doing a show called *Magical Rhythms of Ireland*," Fitzpatrick said. "I was a dancer and Colin, who hails from Manchester, England was in the band."

"People always think that it's funny having an English man playing in an Irish pub but his mother is from

Galway and his Dad is from Cavan so you don't get more Irish than that. His whole family has been playing Irish music since they were born."

It was Colin who was first approached to make the big move from downtown Dublin to Downtown Disney.

"I danced with *Rhythm of the Dance* for two years before I got the job over here. Colin got the job in Orlando first. One of his friends was approached by the owners of Raglan Road in a bar in Dublin and they asked him if he would like to get a band together for Orlando. He asked Colin to be in the band. So Colin came over in October 2005 while I was still on tour with my dance show. As soon as I got done with my tour the owners asked to meet with me because they were interested in getting an Irish dancer for the restaurant."

Fitzpatrick met with the group, and in the flash of a hard shoe drumming a hornpipe, she found herself in the warmer climes of Orlando in February of 2006.

"I've been here ever since and things couldn't be better," she said. "I love meeting new people everyday. Everybody says how nice Irish people are, but I love American people. I think they are more appreciative of what I do because they don't see Irish dancing that often. It's more of a novelty for them."

Fitzpatrick climbs the stairs to the central stage ten times a night.

"I don't get tired from dancing but if I get carried away at the gym and then have to go to work that's a different story," she laughed.

Then there's the statue.

(Continued on next page)

Mousejunkie U *Outside the restaurant in the Pleasure Island quarter of Downtown Disney is a statue of Irish poet and novelist Patrick Kavanagh (identical to the one located along the Grand Canal in Dublin). Kavanagh wrote the poem—later set to music—"On Raglan Road."*

One night, Kavanagh met Irish singer Luke Kelly, leader of the traditional Irish group The Dubliners, in a Dublin pub called the Bailey. The two talked for a while, and the conversation eventually turned to Kavanagh's poem. By the end of the night, the two had struck an agreement. The result was the wild-haired Kelly recording what many believe to be the definitive version of the song, "On Raglan Road."

To sum up: the statue of the thin, long-legged man sitting on a bench and thinking quietly to himself is not, despite much confusion, Walt Disney.

The next time you pass by, pause and say hello to the man who penned "On Raglan Road," and remember him as the haunting tune calls out from inside the restaurant named for one of his finest works.

On a quiet street where old ghosts meet
I see her walking now
Away from me so hurriedly my reason must allow
That I had loved not as I should
A creature made of clay
When the angel woos the clay
He'll lose his wings at the dawn of day

"There's a sign describing who he is now," Fitzpatrick said of the statue. "So we don't get asked if it's Walt quite so often."

⭐ **The Straight Dope**   *Schedule your dinner for after 8 P.M.—which is when the live entertainment begins at Raglan Road.*

While Raglan Road snares me every time, everyone's got their favorites.

 MOUSEJUNKIE J I've said it before, and I'll say it again: It's all about the food. So here are a few of my favorites:

The Kona Café, located in the Polynesian Resort
I have eaten all three meals there and they were all excellent. It is laid back but the food is great. It's not cheap, but it's reasonable by Disney standards. The fresh bread with the honey-macadamia nut butter is to die for. And let us not forget the best breakfast item in Walt Disney World— Tonga Toast. How can you go wrong deep frying anything and then rolling it in cinnamon sugar? I had a pulled pork sandwich there for lunch and it was very good."

50s Primetime Café at Disney's Hollywood Studios
The place has a fantastic atmosphere and the fare is comfort food at its best—plus there is nothing over $20

(Continued on next page)

on the menu. Just be prepared to play the game with the servers. The pot roast with mashed potatoes is excellent. Just remember to ask for no green beans if you are not going to eat the green beans. Standing in the corner because you did not finish them is a drag. (Yes, seriously.) To top it off, the dessert menu is presented to diners on a ViewMaster. It's the perfect ending to a meal that takes guests back to their youth.

You'll very likely find the place to be crowded and loud—just the way it is intended to be. The Tune-In lounge before the meal is really neat as well. Just like you were transported back in time. Most importantly, they serve Yuengling Lager."

Les Chefs de France in the World Showcase at Epcot

For a really nice meal that makes you feel like you are dining five star but on a budget, eat at Les Chefs de France—*for lunch*. It is a beautiful dining room, the service is very good and the lunch prices are a bargain by Disney standards. They serve fresh French rolls with butter that are mouthwatering. The wine-by-the-glass pricing is reasonable as well. I always get the Bier Kronenbourg 1664. Despite the setting—white linen tablecloths and servers in white dress shirts with black ties—I still felt fine in a polo shirt and shorts. The flatbreads are excellent as well as the stuffed crepes. You can go more expensive and get a dinner-type meal at lunchtime.

Le Cellier in the World Showcase at Epcot

Normally I would put Le Cellier on any list but it can be pricey if you get a drink and a filet mignon. The menu is really a steak menu with a single pasta and seafood choice. Don't get me wrong, I love the place. If I knew the people going had lots of disposable income, I would tell them to go there in an instant.

The Best Places to Pig Out

I have a love/hate relationship with 'Ohana—the family style, Polynesian island themed restaurant in the Polynesian Resort across from the Magic Kingdom. For the normal person, there's nothing to hate about 'Ohana at all. It's a wonderful restaurant where the atmosphere is fun, the entertainment fantastic and the food delicious and plentiful.

And this is where our problem occurs. I'll say it again: the food is plentiful. Normal people know when to stop eating. When a cast member walks by with a skewer of meat and asks, "More steak cousin?" most people would know to say, "No thank you." Especially if they feel nauseous. And especially if the bread pudding has yet to arrive.

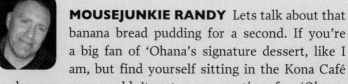

MOUSEJUNKIE RANDY Lets talk about that banana bread pudding for a second. If you're a big fan of 'Ohana's signature dessert, like I am, but find yourself sitting in the Kona Café because you couldn't get a reservation for 'Ohana, remain calm. When they bring the dessert menu, ask for it; Kona and 'Ohana use the same kitchen, and they will be more than happy to get it for you.

In the time-honored contest of me vs. food, there are few restaurants that consistently beat me to an absolutely stuffed pulp and then throw me out on the sidewalk, drunk on an assortment of meats and ready to heave it all into one of the conveniently located trash barrels.

The Straight Dope *If your reservations at 'Ohana are earlier than the nightly Wishes fireworks display, finish up your meal and trudge uncomfortably down to the beach. Stake out a spot in the sand—or if you're extremely lucky, sack out in a hammock—and enjoy the show from there. After Wishes you'll have a front-row seat for the Electrical Water Pageant. The waterborne parade floats across the Seven Seas Lagoon and Bay Lake nightly, weather permitting.*

It's so good: I. Can. Not. Stop.

It's a cry for help I tend to elicit on every trip when we visit 'Ohana. Which is usually every trip. Luckily Mousejunkie Amy will remind me of my history of 'Ohana-induced nausea and throw me a life preserver—which in my peel-and-eat-shrimp-induced haze appears to be made of turkey tips floating in a peanut dipping sauce.

 **MOUSEJUNKIE AMY** He does it every time. He can't resist the phrase "More (insert type of skewered meat here), cousin?" Someone walks by with a pile of food and his brain goes out the window. We certainly get our money's worth.

It's to the point where you can predict the entire evening:

1. We arrive at the Polynesian Resort, check-in at the 'Ohana podium.
2. We order a couple drinks at the Tambu Lounge while we wait to be called.
3. As we are led to our table, the hostess asks, "Have you dined with us before at 'Ohana?" We laugh and laugh. Oh, how we laugh.
4. Before my butt hits the seat I'm shoveling something into my face.
5. As I emerge from the feeding frenzy, I begin complaining loudly about how sick I feel.
6. Stuffed beyond capacity, I waddle down to the lakefront to watch the Wishes fireworks display over the Magic Kingdom.
7. I fervently wish there was such a thing as a Star Trek-type transporter that could just get me to my resort room without all that awful, you know, walking.
8. I swear I will be smarter about dining at 'Ohana next time. (I won't.)

Here's something the Mousejunkies have come up with to ensure your safety in a post-'Ohana splurge coma. Simply cut out the tag, pin it to your shirt before the meal begins and make sure you fall face-up at the end of your rapacious feast.

My name is _____.

I am staying at the _____ resort.

I have just eaten at 'Ohana. I am dangerously engorged and can not speak. Please roll me onto the nearest bus heading for the _____ resort.

There is a Fastpass for Toy Story Midway Mania in my top pocket. Please take it as a token of my thanks.

It's become more and more difficult to get an Advanced Dining Reservation at 'Ohana, and Mousejunkie J, who savors Disney Dining almost more than anyone I know, details why.

MOUSEJUNKIE J "'Ohana means family. But what 'Ohana means to *me* is a homerun. A great meal every time I show up. the food is served family-style, coming to your table in large plates, bowls and skewers. The server will continue to bring said food until you say stop. This is a dangerous proposition for people like myself who just don't know when to stop.

There are four food courses at 'Ohana. The first course is the salad course. A mixed field green salad is served tossed with a honey-lime vinaigrette dressing. The server also brings three dipping sauces to the table: a sweet peanut sauce, chimichurri sauce, and harissa sauce. For you folks who like to avoid fiber or anything green, the 'Ohana welcome bread is good and will hold you over until the appetizer course is delivered.

The appetizer course delivers with a bang. Honey-coriander chicken wings arrive next. I could be happy if I just ate these addictive wings for the meal. I made this fatal mistake once and regretted my decision once dessert arrived. The wings are messy but well worth the effort. Small, hot towels can be brought to help clean your sticky fingers. In addition, pork dumplings are brought as an appetizer. These are standard dumplings you would get a Chinese restaurant.

The third and main course arrives next. Lo mein noodles and stir-fry vegetables hit the table, the prelude to skewers of hot, juicy, and tasty meat that will be arriving shortly. Four skewers consisting of Mesquite turkey breast tips, Asian barbecue pork loin, sirloin steak, and spicy grilled peel-n-eat shrimp arrive hot off the grill. Because there are choices here try one piece of each and then decide which one you want seconds on. As an 'Ohana veteran, I only take the turkey breast tips. They are tasty and juicy and once dipped in the peanut sauce, they are shear heaven.

Dessert is in no way to be an afterthought or overlooked. If you have paced yourself properly, there should be enough room to partake of the decadent 'Ohana bread pudding served with vanilla ice cream and a rich bananas foster sauce. I was never a bread pudding fan until I visited 'Ohana for the first time. Let's face it, anything served hot and a la mode is going to be very good. A little known secret: If you prefer, ask for the pineapple chunks served with a hot caramel dipping sauce. Mousejunkie Deb always asks for, and gets the pineapple and caramel.

(Continued on next page)

'Ohana is one of my favorite dining establishments at Walt Disney World. The food is fantastic, but the atmosphere puts it over the top. The meat is grilled in a huge open fire pit in the middle of the dining room. There is also a lovely Hawaiian woman who walks around playing the ukulele and coaxing children into limbo and coconut rolling contests. 'Ohana means family and this is a top notch, family dining restaurant.

MOUSEJUNKIE JOHN For me, it's all about Le Cellier, the Canadian steak house in Epcot's World Showcase. It's perfection: steak, potatoes, and beer. I love the (fake) candlelit subterranean atmosphere. The food is excellent, and so is the service. The Canadians are always very cordial hosts. If you have a reservation for an early lunch, 11-ish, the staff sings "O, Canada." It feels like you're at a hockey game. Also, I love the hot, fresh pretzel bread. Remember the campfire scene in *Stand By Me* where the question is "if you could only eat one food for the rest of your life..." For me, it would be that pretzel bread. Keep it comin', garçon. Three years of high school French, and that's the best I could muster.

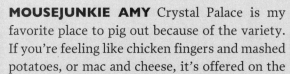

MOUSEJUNKIE AMY Crystal Palace is my favorite place to pig out because of the variety. If you're feeling like chicken fingers and mashed potatoes, or mac and cheese, it's offered on the buffet. But if you want to put in the work of peeling shrimp, you can load up your plate and get your hands dirty. There's a nice array of different salads as well. I'm not a big fan of fish, but there are some great fish choices. My favorites are the prime rib and turkey at the carving station. The turkey is my go to entreé, because it's moist, tasty, and never disappoints.

MOUSEJUNKIE BARRY When you're on vacation it's incredibly easy to allow yourself to go completely nuts with salty, fatty, sugary, and otherwise bad-for-you food. For a Mousejunkie in the throes of a hedonistic Disney World vacation, the diet goes straight out the window. Case in point: Whispering Canyon Café, the table-service restaurant found adjacent to the lobby in the Wilderness Lodge Resort. I always get the skillet—and endless supply of ribs, chicken, mashed potatoes, corn bread and a bottomless ice cream milkshake. It's insane, really. It's ridiculous, painful, shameful, awesome eating. And what do you have to show for it at the end of the meal? A slack-jawed dopey gaze looming over a pile of gnawed-upon rib bones and stained napkins.

MOUSEJUNKIE DEB If it's about stuffing yourself silly, it has to be 'Ohana. There are unlimited amounts of appetizers, entreés, and desserts. You won't ever leave hungry. Nor will you leave with your shorts buttoned. Fashion tip: elastic waistbands or loose-fitting muumuus are recommended.

MOUSEJUNKIE WALT My favorite place to stuff myself has got to be Le Cellier in Epcot. Again, being French Canadian, I love everything about it. I love the bread sticks, I love the cheddar cheese soup, I love the steak, I love the maple crème brûlée. There isn't anything about that place I don't love. I love the cold beer, I love the atmosphere. I could go on all day. And when I do eat there, I order appetizers, entrée, dessert, and plenty of those amazing bread sticks.

MOUSEJUNKIE RANDY I have to say my favorite place for pigging out is Boma in the Animal Kingdom Lodge. It doesn't matter if it's breakfast or dinner—that is *the* place. I can't seem to control myself. I love the variety of foods. My favorite is the authentic South African dish, *bobotie*. This is a baked pork-and-goodness dish, which is served at both breakfast and dinner with a slightly different recipe for each. I think *bobotie* is Afrikaans for "comfort food." If you go to Boma, don't be afraid to take a little taste of everything. Have a food safari. But don't go too crazy, because they have the best dessert buffet on the planet.

Breaking Out of a Comfort Zone

It's not always about volume, however. There are always new dining experiences available.

I'm a creature of habit, so when it comes to dining options when we travel to the World, there are a few must-do restaurants that I return to again and again: Raglan Road, Kona Café, Le Cellier, and the California Grill to name a few.

But every once in a while, I'm forced—kicking and screaming—to maybe skip visiting my cousins at 'Ohana and try something new. This is what prompted my unexpected entrance to the new Paradiso 37 at Downtown Disney.

Why was it unexpected? We had an ADR at the House of Blues, a choice my traveling companions rejected outright. So there we were, standing at the top of the Pleasure Island boat ramp with our stomachs growling and no plan for dinner.

At this point, whatever food was closest to my face would have been my first choice. I looked to my left and saw Raglan Road, one of the aforementioned favorites that I hit on literally every trip to Walt Disney World. The food is amazing, the music is incredible, and the atmosphere is distinctly Irish (if a bit large). However, Mousejunkie Amy, is the type who is interested in trying new things (I know, she's nuts). So any thought of trying to walk into Raglan Road was out of the question.

I looked to my right and saw Paradiso 37. It was close by, and since it was a restaurant, it would likely have foodstuffs to offer our starving troupe.

Before we even set foot inside, Paradiso 37 had a few strikes against it. First, and most importantly, it wasn't Raglan Road. Next, it sits adjacent to the former location of the Adventurer's Club—the greatly missed drinking/dining/ theater experience. And finally, the name of the place told me nothing about what kind of food was served. That may be more a case of ignorance on my part, but it left me with absolutely no expectations as we were quickly ushered inside.

Things started looking up, however, as we were shown to our seats: there was a tequila bar with an entire wall of choices, and the server made a point of letting guests know that they served their beer at an icy twenty-nine degrees, calling it "too cold to hold." I immediately resolved to put that boast to the test. We also learned that the theme of the restaurant was "street food of the Americas." Which was fine, but I still couldn't really grasp what lay ahead. I envisioned my taste buds being seduced by exotic fare from El Salvador or Argentina. Heady spices and unfamiliar textures would woo my appetite and leave me stuffed and happily drinking in these new sensations.

Filled with these enticing thoughts, I eagerly scanned the menu for an appetizer that would transport me to a distant land.

I chose the corn dogs.

They were served with honey Dijon mustard though, and I was pretty sure Dijon is a French word meaning "not ketchup." Amy scoffed at my mundane choice, but I know what I like. And I like corn dogs. Or, as they might call them in the colorfully chaotic streets of mid-carnival Rio de Janiro, *cao de milo.* See? Exotic.

The corn dogs—bite sized and served in a paper cone—
were certainly tasty. The outer coating had a corn-infused
sweetness, while the dog tucked inside was a run-of-the-
mill weenie. I contemplated my choice as I plowed through
the pile of golden brown treats. Exotic? Foreign? Let's just
say their flavorful essence transported me to the unexplored
environs of, well, a county fair midway. They could easily
have been served by some greasy carnie in a faded Winger
t-shirt from the back of a trailer with a fryolator, instead
of our friendly and attentive server on the shores of Village
Lake. I like good food and drink, but I won't pretend to be a
discerning epicurean. A corn dog is a corn dog, and at that
moment they were making me happy.

A perfect pairing would include some of "the world's
coldest draft beer" that the staff at Paradiso 37 seemed to
take so much pride in. I ordered one up and steeled myself
for the shocking chill that would no doubt accompany my
frosty pint. Would my lips bond to the glass? Would I experience brain freeze? Would I have hallucinations brought on
by the impossibly cold concoction?

A thermometer with a digital readout set atop the beer
cooler let everyone know just how cold the brews were. Our
server arrived and set it reverently on the table. So far it
looked as I imagined: amber in color and in a glass. Nothing
screamed 'danger' to me yet. I raised it to my lips and prepared for the shock of a lifetime.

It turns out that cold is pretty much cold and it really
wasn't anything special. Sadly, there would be no hallucinations or brain freeze. Sure, it was refreshing, but the buildup
left the whole experience a little flat.

No matter, the beef would soon be arriving. I went with the bacon and pineapple burger. Served with smoked Gouda and honey-glazed bacon, it was the finest burger I've had on Disney property. The sweet, juicy pineapple worked perfectly with the salty bacon and the gooey cheese. The cold, but not-frigid, beer tamed it, and a toasted roll made it all behave.

Another diner ventured down Mexico way and ordered the Quatro Tacos: four soft tacos stuffed with your choice of grilled chicken, roasted pork, grilled steak, blackened mahi mahi, or roasted mushrooms. The whole thing was served with black beans and cilantro rice. When I put everything on my plate away, no one is surprised. However, our traveling partner in this case was quite slight, and still had no issues finishing her food. Each taco was a perfect size, piled high with fresh ingredients.

Paradiso 37 offers thirty-seven kinds of tequila, ten signature margaritas, and waterfront dining. As Downtown Disney gets slowly taken over by chain-owned restaurants (the Rainforest Café/T-Rex), Paradiso 37 is a welcome addition.

MOUSEJUNKIE AMY I really liked Paradiso 37 because it had a great variety of choices, and you could get some interesting ethnic-influenced foods without going to Epcot. You could try something completely new, but they also have choices that are familiar.

MOUSEJUNKIE JENNA I'll always love the old favorites of 'Ohana, Raglan Road, and the Brown Derby. But it's nice to venture out to new—and new to me—restaurants, too. On my most recent trip, I found two new favorite restaurants: Jiko and Tutto Italia.

Jiko is a wonderfully elegant choice for dinner. I love Boma for all its African flavors and new discoveries, but sometimes, I just want to eat in a quiet restaurant and have a really great server bring me my food. I got to blend both of those wants at Jiko. The service there is excellent, and the menu is varied and well-designed. With a mix of exotic and familiar flavors, you can be as adventurous as you want to be. For instance, I had the seared ostrich filet as an appetizer, the oak-fired filet mignon with macaroni and cheese for my entreé, and a lemon white chocolate mousse for dessert. The ostrich was new to me and very tasty, the filet mignon was a lovely rendition of my favorite cut, and the macaroni and cheese was sublime. The lemon mousse was just the right size and richness to cap that dinner. Jiko has an extensive wine list and I got to try a varietal created in South Africa, pinotage. I had the Eros tea with dessert, which I had previously seen only at the Grand Floridian's Garden View tearoom.

Tutto Italia was quite different from Jiko in a lot of respects, but shared the same attention to detail and excellent service. I was seated in the main dining room and honestly, I never wanted to leave. The

(Continued on next page)

decor is a great blending of opulent formality and welcoming coziness. I was served a basket of assorted breads, dipping oil, and *giardiniera* (olives, peppers, artichoke, etc.). My appetizer was the bufala mozzarella and tomato. The mozzarella is so fresh and soft, with an outstanding flavor. My entreé was the farfalle with peas, prosciutto, and cream sauce. It was a great combination and I loved it, but people who don't like their pasta chewy should be advised that Tutto's view of al dente might be a little firmer than expected. For dessert, I had one of the most ridiculously extravagant dishes I've eaten at Walt Disney World, *copetta sotto bosco*. It arrived in a goblet and was made up of zabaglione cream, fresh berries, crunchy little amaretti cookies, and a drizzle of delicious chocolate sauce. It's delicious, but it's also the most expensive dessert on the menu. To accompany my dessert, I had a cup of espresso—with a gorgeous crema—and a glass of limoncello. The limoncello had to grow on me, because the scent was unmistakably Lemon Pledge. I left Tutto Italia with a box full of leftovers and a belly so full of delicious Italian food that I decided to skip Illuminations and head back to my room to sleep it off.

Meals with Character

Getting your picture taken with a Disney character at breakfast or dinner is pretty much a rite of passage for guests at the Walt Disney World resort.

As guests are seated, Disney characters, ranging from the most popular to a few fringe personalities depending on the restaurant, tour the room. Guests do not need to chase after the character or stand in a lengthy line. They stop at each table to interact with diners and pose for pictures, so a little patience goes a long way.

Awesome/Stupid Disney Idea *Install seatbelts in the chairs at character meal restaurants. There's nothing like having a clinging kid from the next table over in all your family's photos.*

Have a seat and wait, they will come.

Character meals are either buffets, family-style or pre plated affairs. The food ranges from quite good to merely passable. Cinderella's Royal Table, for example—a princess fan's dream—serves one of the best breakfasts I've had on-property. It's also the most difficult reservation to get, and it is the most expensive character meal.

Chef Mickey's, on the other hand, has decent food, but a great character experience. Mickey and Minnie have a celebrity aura about them that can't be denied.

The Straight Dope *Combine a character meal with the correct timing and you'll have Main Street USA and*

Cinderella Castle to yourself for an incredible photo oppor-
tunity. The park itself may open at 9 A.M., but if you book an
Advanced Dining Reservation for 8 A.M., cast members allow
you to pass. Inside you'll find very few people and an amazing
view up the street toward the castle. Fire up the camera and
strike a pose for a rare opportunity.

When we brought our three-year-old daughter, we went
to a few character meals. It was fun the first time, fun the
second time, but then it got to be "How many of these character meals do we really need?" They're fun, but two seems
to be enough. It all starts to feel repetitive by the seven-
teenth photo op. Of course, your mileage may vary, so book
as many as you think might feed your need.

Here's a list of character meals throughout Walt Disney
World's theme parks, and which characters you'll encounter
during your meal:

Theme Parks

Park	Restaurant	Meal	Characters
Magic Kingdom	Cinderella's Royal Table	Breakfast, Lunch, Dinner	Cinderella, Fairy Godmother, assorted princesses
Magic Kingdom	Crystal Palace	Breakfast, Lunch, Dinner	Winnie the Pooh characters

Park	Restaurant	Meal	Characters
Disney's Hollywood Studios	Hollywood and Vine	Breakfast, Lunch	Jo Jo's Circus and Little Einstein characters
Animal Kingdom	Tusker House	Breakfast	Donald, Goofy, Mickey, Pluto
Epcot	Akershus Royal Banquet Hall	Breakfast, Lunch, Dinner	Belle, Jasmine, Sleeping Beauty, Snow White
Epcot	Garden Grill	Dinner	Chip and Dale, Mickey Mouse

Here's a list of character meals in various resorts around Walt Disney World, and what characters you'll meet at the character dining experience.

Resort	Restaurant	Meal	Characters
Grand Floridian	1900 Park Fare	Breakfast, Dinner	Mary Poppins, Alice, Pooh, Eeyore, Mad Hatter
Beach Club	Cape May Café	Breakfast	Goofy, Pluto, Donald

(Continued on next page)

Resort	Restaurant	Meal	Characters
Contemporary	Chef Mickey's	Breakfast, Lunch, Dinner	Mickey, Minnie, Chip and Dale, Goofy, Donald, Pluto
Polynesian	'Ohana	Breakfast	Mickey, Minnie, Pluto, Lilo and Stitch

Dealing With Food Allergies

One of the more impressive things we've come across is the resort's attentiveness to food allergies and their potential affect on guests' health.

Walt Disney World's restaurants, servers and chefs treat dietary restrictions very seriously. Our daughter, Katie, is allergic to eggs and tree nuts of all kinds. When we make our Advanced Dining Reservations months in advance, we're asked about any food allergies in our party. When we arrive at the podium to check in, we're asked. When our server comes to take our order, she asks. And when it's been triple-checked, the head chef comes out, sits down with us at our table, and makes specific notes about Katie's allergies. He talks to us about what she can have, what she can't have, and on more than one occasion she's had a special dish created just for her. It helps us feel more comfortable, it keeps her safe, and it makes her feel special.

One of our first experiences after finding out about Katie's allergies was at 'Ohana, where the head chef came out to talk to us.

As he leaned over to ask Amy a question, my eyes were drawn to his name tag. I'm always interested in seeing where cast members are from, so I always make sure to steal a glance.

My eyes grew wide, I pointed at him and let loose with an involuntary torrent of geeky excitement.

"I know him!" I shouted in barely controlled excitement.

Everyone stopped what they were doing and turned to look at the sputtering weirdo. (That'd be me, having a Disney freakout moment.)

"I know him! Boma!"

The chef stood up straight and laughed as I stuttered incoherent phrases at him.

I slowed down and managed to give a complete explanation to the other people at the table. Chef Tjet Jep, TJ had been the chef at Boma in the Animal Kingdom Lodge. We would make it a point to talk to him on each of our visits. He's very friendly and talkative, but more importantly, he's a very skilled chef. On more than one occasion he gifted us with a special deep-fried Oreo dessert not available on the menu or by request. And if there's one way to this Mousejunkie's heart, it's through his stomach. A deep-fried sneaker would make me your friend for life. You can imagine the influence a gooey Oreo tucked into golden-brown, crunchy batter might have on my affections. Chef TJ is as big a Disney star as Pluto in my eyes.

Only now TJ was miles away from where we were used to seeing him, standing at our table talking about my daughter's food allergies as I started spitting crunchy wontons and praise at him.

"Yes, I work here now," he said as we started snapping pictures and explaining our excitement. He was now creating savory coriander wings and tangy turkey tips nightly instead of pap or fufu (which I mention any time I get the chance since they're so fun to say.)

"Where do you prefer?" he asked. "Boma or 'Ohana?"

I thought for a minute as my pulse began to return to a normal rate.

"Wherever you are!" I answered as he laughed and rolled his eyes.

TJ finished taking notes on Katie's food allergies and headed back to the kitchen with a big wave. It felt like we had run into an old friend—despite the fact he had no idea who we were.

A few minutes later we were reminded why we were so happy to see our old friend. Our server approached with a long white serving tray packed with food not normally associated with 'Ohana. She put it down and a sweet, slightly spicy aroma wafted across the table. TJ was working his magic again. In front of us was a platter of scallops and chicken stir fried in a spicy, creamy sauce and resting on a bed of banana peppers and greens.

He came out of the kitchen a few minutes later to see if we liked his creation (we did). He visited us a third time to build a special dessert for Katie, and to bring us the 'Ohana version of his after-dinner surprise: deep-fried banana

MOUSEJUNKIE AMY Disney goes out of its way to accommodate people with food allergies. They'll come out and ask what she wants, and if it's chicken fingers they'll cook them on a hot plate away from where the other food has been cooked to avoid any cross-contamination. A cautious parent doesn't have to worry. The cast members go out of their way for you. If they don't know what's in the food, they'll go back into the kitchen and read the ingredients. They don't leave the onus strictly on the parent. The last thing you want on your vacation is to end up in the emergency room with anaphylactic shock.

You get spoiled because then you come home and you get some teenager waitress or waiter, and when you ask them about food allergies, you just get a blank stare.

chunks with a chocolate and strawberry sauce on top. It tasted like a warm, soft, deep-fried banana split.

Meanwhile, as we ooh-ed and ahh-ed over the crispy, brown creations, Chef TJ focused all his attention on my daughter. With great aplomb, he unveiled an ice cream dessert that took some degree of skill to construct. With a flash of showmanship, he assembled it in front of her, chasing away any feelings of being left out of the evening's fun because of her allergies. On the contrary, his special treatment made her feel like the star of the show.

Things like this seem to happen often at Walt Disney World. Its part of what keeps us coming back.

Snack Time

Eventually you're going to get a hankering for something sweet. It might be a case of the midday munchies, or flat-out sloth. (You're on vacation: it's O.K.)

Just know there are scores of options for guests to choose from. Disney doesn't just serve belly-busting meals. There are small treats all over the place that become part of the returning guests' tradition. Whether it's a special drink or a sweet reward, it's the unexpected little tastes that help make the experience special.

I'm a fan of spicy food. So every time I visit Walt Disney World, I'm drawn to the ESPN Club on the BoardWalk. Because it's there you'll find the spiciest, most face-melting Bloody Mary on the planet.

The last time we visited, I ordered the drink and asked the server if the bartender could make it "extra spicy." He laughed and said sure.

He came back with a pint glass full of deep red liquid topped with a jalapeño pepper. I took a sip and immediately started hiccupping. I shook my head, unable to speak. The heat given off by this drink immediately rocketed my endorphins through the top of my head. After a minute or so the hiccups stopped and I dared a second sip. Same result. I mouthed "Wow" over and over again as my father-in-law had a good laugh at my obviously pained reaction. Sure, tears may have been streaming down my face and my expression may have read agony, but inside my brain was screaming "More!"

Earlier, I had purchased a pack of antacid at the store down the BoardWalk. I used this opportunity to eat half the pack.

I had discovered the holy grail of spicy Bloody Marys on Disney property. I couldn't tell anyone about it though, since my ability to speak had been melted away by this fiery concoction.

After that experience, the chase was on. Could it be topped? I decided to test bartenders around the property to see if they could meet the challenge: Make me regret ordering a Bloody Mary, while simultaneously putting a smile on my face.

The next attempt came at a rather unexpected time—breakfast.

We had reservations for breakfast at the Kona Cafe in the Polynesian resort. I scanned the menu and saw something that jumped out at me: a breakfast Bloody Mary. I ordered one up, and asked the waitress if it could be made extra spicy. When it was brought to the table, she also placed a small cup of red sauce next to it.

"Chili sauce in case it's not to your liking," she said.

It was not. So I dumped the chili sauce into the drink, stirred it up and took a sip. Now it was perfect. The flavor was completely different from the Bloody Mulligan. It had more of a vegetable aftertaste, like a V-8. It was salty, with strong celery flavors on the back-end. The added chili sauce brought the temperature up nicely, and I left happy. It didn't top the ESPN offering, but I was still pleased with how my quest was progressing.

The Straight Dope *If you drink the breakfast Bloody Mary at the Kona Café and then follow it up with a cup of teeth-jarring Kona coffee, you will suffer from absolutely volcanic heartburn. There is a safety net, however. Directly across from Kona is a shop that sells Tums. Sure, you'll pay a premium, but if you want to survive your own breakfast Bloody Mary/Kona coffee experience, I advise picking one up.*

Over the years I've tried a few others. The Bloody Mary at the Yak & Yeti in the Animal Kingdom theme park was not spicy at all, despite requests to make it so.

The first day on a trip just last year, I returned to the ESPN Club to revisit the scene of my palate-melting joy. I asked the server, "Can I get a Bloody Mulligan, but extra spicy, please?"

Shockingly, I was completely under whelmed. It was not hot. It did not make me weep with regret. I was not pleased. My travel mates were eager to see me brought to my knees, so they urged me to try a second.

This time I ordered the drink as I would from that point on: "This was not hot enough. Can I get another one, but can you ask the bartender to make it so I hate it? Can you make it hot enough that I will regret ever asking for it?"

The second round brought exactly what I had hoped for—a recreation of that first drink. Delicious agony gripped me as I shook my head back and forth, trying to somehow escape the pain while savoring the tangy, peppery tomato flavors.

I would repeat this again on future trips:

On the next trip, I slurped the searing concoction with renewed vigor. The flavors danced across my taste buds wearing tiny golf shoes dipped in molten lava. I was sure I'd be scarred for life. I wasn't, of course, and I strolled the boardwalk afterward as my head swum from the awakening of my senses by this punitive delight.

By now it was becoming routine. Order the drink, ask them to make it so hot that I hate it, and revel in the self-induced pain. I tried to top the Bloody Mulligan at any number of restaurants and bars across Disney property, but I was always drawn back to the ESPN Club to reacquaint myself with my first love. Each time I do, my innards revolt as I splash them with flames throughout the night.

I've put some serious research into my quest for the perfect extra spicy Bloody Mary, but I like to think my quest has yet to come to an end. At this point I'd have to say the Bloody Mulligan at the ESPN Club is in the lead, but there are plenty of other establishments to check off my list before I reach the finish line.

Keep in mind that there's "hot" and then there's "Disney hot," as I was told by a cast member recently. If you intend to engage in self-inflicted cocktail damage, you've got to think beyond "Disney hot." My advice? Try it and report back. Help me along the way before my liver quits and jumps out my ear.

MOUSEJUNKIE RANDY Get me to the Writer's Stop at Disney's Hollywood Studios. That's where you'll find the best snack in all of Walt Disney World. The carrot cake cookie is the sweetest, most amazing confection this side of heaven. It's the perfect combination of a moist carrot cake and thick cream cheese frosting. It's very rich, and I firmly believe it equals two table-service meals in terms of caloric intake.

 MOUSEJUNKIE AMY I never miss the opportunity to get the roasted almonds at Epcot. They have them at Disney's Hollywood Studios too, but I need them at Epcot.

It's the sweet, nutty smell that hits you first. The mixture of cinnamon and the almonds is irresistible. They're warm and served in a paper cone. Once you eat one, it's impossible to stop. There's nothing better than walking around the World Showcase with a warm paper cone of cinnamon-sugar roasted almonds in your hand. I get them every time."

MOUSEJUNKIE JOHN I head straight for Adventureland at the Magic Kingdom—specifically Aloha Isle. That's where I get my Dole Whip—a half pineapple, half vanilla twist with pineapple juice. The way the pineapple juice crystallizes in the ice cream is, well...delightful. Truck drivers don't normally talk this way. They really need to put a stand in Animal Kingdom, as well, so I can get one in two different parks.

MOUSEJUNKIE JENNA I have different favorite snacks depending on where I am at the moment. When I stay at the Animal Kingdom Lodge, I go straight to the Mara for two of my favorite Boma offerings: zebra domes and their red pepper hummus.

When I'm anywhere near Downtown Disney, I develop a hankering for chocolate-dipped pretzel rods from Goofy's Candy Co.

In the Magic Kingdom, I want a Dole Whip. Period.

In the Animal Kingdom, I crave a chocolate-covered frozen banana.

In the Studios, I head to Starring Rolls for a brownie or a cupcake.

In Epcot, I either want a Nutella crepe and a Grey Goose slush, a pretzel *und* beer, or a Habib Daiquiri with or without baklava. When I'm in Epcot, I tend to drink my snacks.

MOUSEJUNKIE DEB I love the hand-made chocolate chip cookie ice cream sandwich at the Main Street Bakery in the Magic Kingdom. And not just because they're bigger than my head. The best part is that it's fresh. You can buy the prepackaged Toll House Cookie Ice Cream Sandwiches at various carts, food courts, and resort gift shop freezer cases around the World, but the ice cream chocolate chip cookie sandwich they make at the Main Street Bakery (and a lesser known fact is they sometimes craft them at food pavilions like the Riverside Mill at Port Orleans) are made to order with fresh Nestle Toll House chocolate chip cookies and smooth vanilla ice cream. The cookies are not too hard, not too soft - the perfect thickness to bite into with ice cream. At around $4, it's got to be one of the best bargains at Walt Disney World.

In the hot Florida weather, they are the perfect snack that satisfies both hunger and mild heatstroke. And if I do suffer from a fatal heatstroke attack, the ice cream chocolate chip cookie sandwich is what I would've picked for my last meal.

TEEN MOUSEJUNKIE RYAN I like the Mickey Premium Bars. I like them because I can get them anywhere I go. It's basically a Klondike bar on a stick with ears, so I know I like it. It's a refreshing snack on a hot day. Of course having it shaped like Mickey's head makes it taste that much better.

MOUSEJUNKIE WALT Whenever I'm in Epcot I have to grab a crepe in France. I'm French, and I grew up with my mother making them for me. We'd get fresh fruit and put blueberries and strawberries on them. I have fond memories of Mom making them for me, and having one at Epcot brings back those feelings.

If I had to pick a close second, I'd stay put right in France. The raspberry turnovers from Boulangerie Patisserie are to die for. On the last day of my trip I always go over to the bakery and buy a dozen to take home.

Picking up the Check

You've eaten to your heart's content, stuffed yourself beyond bursting, and joined the fraternity of Walt Disney World guests who now know the joys of on-site dining. Don't let that euphoric entrée-based haze cloud your judgment, however: if you want to be the hero and reach for the check, that's your choice. But prepare yourself: Disney dining does not come cheap. Try to keep that considerate smile on your face as you stare into the bill and your hair turns gray while your wallet becomes considerably lighter.

That's not to say there aren't ways to save money. There are options, and perhaps the biggest initial decision is figuring out if the Disney Dining Plan is right for you.

The Disney Dining Plan is a way to pre pay for your meals using a voucher system. It's available to guests who purchase a Magic Your Way ticket or book using Disney Vacation Club points. There are varying levels of the plan, with varying costs associated. Depending on which level plan you go with, a certain number of snacks, counter-service meal and/or table-service meal allotments are added to your Key to the World card. Each time you use the plan, a meal is subtracted from your total.

Here is a look at each level of the Disney Dining Plan, and the cost associated with it:

Magic Your Way Plus Quick Service

What you get: Two quick-service meals per day, two snacks per day, one refillable mug.

How much? $31.99 per person, per night of your stay. Children 3 to 9 are $9.99 per person, per night.

You should also know: This will get you two counter- service meals a day (egg sandwiches, breakfast platters, burgers, chicken, tacos, fish, hot dogs), and two snacks a day (a Mickey ice cream bar, a bottle of water, chips, popcorn, soda, fruit).

The Plan in Action: An example of how the Quick Service Dining Plan might work: Breakfast would be in your room or out of pocket, lunch at the Electric Umbrella at Epcot, a snack of a juice bar or a soda by midafternoon, and then dinner at your resort food court.

Magic Your Way Plus Dining Plan

What you get: One counter-service meal, one snack and one table service meal per day. Tip is no longer included.

How much? $41.99 to $47.99 per person, per night (it's more expensive during peak seasons), and $11.99 to $12.99 for children 3 to 9 per person, per night. Tip is not included.

You should also know: A table-service meal on this plan is one entrée (or buffet), one non-alcoholic drink, and one dessert. The children's plan is one appetizer, one entrée, one dessert, and one drink, or a full buffet.

The plan in action: Breakfast would be out-of-pocket, lunch at a counter-service restaurant like Pinocchio's Village Haus, a snack of popcorn for the 3 P.M. parade at the Magic Kingdom, and then dinner at a table service restaurant like the Kona Café.

Magic Your Way Plus Deluxe Dining

What you get: A whole lot of food. You get three meals a day—counter service or table service, your choice-two snacks, one resort refillable mug.

How much? $71.99 per person per night. Children 3 to 9 are $20.99 per person, per night.

You should also know: A table service meal in this plan includes one appetizer, one entrée, one dessert (or full buffet), and one non alcoholic drink.

The plan in action: Get ready to eat. This level of the plan is for those who consider dining at Disney one of the true joys of their vacation. You have the option of eating breakfast, lunch, and dinner at a table-service restaurant, filling in any voids in your stomach with two snacks, and spackling it all in with a refillable mug of whatever non alcoholic beverage you might be able to fit down your gullet. Remember: doggie bags are not normally part of the Disney dining experience, so if you sit down to a meal, chances are you're either going to finish it or leave a lot on your plate.

 MOUSEJUNKIE RANDY The mistake I always see people make on the Dining Plan is that they hoard their snack credits. This sounds like a prudent plan, until they reach the last day of their vacation and are trying to use up twenty-eight snack credits. I tell people to use them up as fast as you can. If you feel like a bottle of water, don't rationalize by trying to get a better value for that snack credit. This way of thinking is what results in twenty-eight snack credits left at the end of the trip. If you're buying a snack and see that little Disney Dining Plan snack symbol next to your choice, use up those snack credits. If you don't heed my warning, you will be making a lot of friends that last day, as you buy everyone within ear shot a Mickey Premium Bar trying to use up all those hoarded credits.

MOUSEJUNKIE JENNA I always wanted to try the deluxe plan because I wanted to be able to eat whatever I wanted without considering the cost. When I dine out, chances are what I want to eat just happens to be the most expensive non lobster choice on the menu. I also like eating three-course meals—even more if I can get it. I'm the kind of person prix fixe and degustation menus are made for. I would rather order three courses of spectacular food and leave half of it on my plate than eat a meager portion of cheap food. A value is only a value if you enjoy the result. But I digress. When it comes to Disney dining, I may be the only person I know who has stashed away a "some-day" plan of a week-long trip on the Deluxe Dining Plan. I know I could easily eat the cost of the Deluxe Dining Plan per night, but it still seems pretty indulgent and something I would only want to do with like-minded traveling partners.

On my last trip, I had a situation with an ideal situation for trying out the Deluxe Dining Plan without going absolutely nuts with food. I was checking into a studio at the Animal Kingdom Lodge Kidani Villas on Wednesday and moving to Old Key West on Friday. For the first two days, I was completely on my own, then I was meeting Mousejunkie Ryan for a day at the Animal Kingdom on Friday. The way it worked it out, I could use my two nights of dining credits over those two-and-a-half days. That's one of those tricky things about Disney's Dining Plan. It's based on the nights

(Continued on next page)

you stay, so if you're there for full days on arrival or departure, you're technically there for up to a full day longer. I ended up having dinner on Wednesday night, a late breakfast and dinner at a signature restaurant on Thursday night, and a character breakfast and dinner on Friday. I used my four snack credits on Thursday's lunch of zebra domes and red pepper hummus from the Mara, and a midafternoon snack of chocolate-covered frozen bananas for me and Ryan at Animal Kingdom. Both breakfasts were buffet, so the three course meal thing was kind of moot. However, my dinners at Tutto Italia and Jiko were enjoyed to the fullest—in every sense of the word.

On the other side of the Deluxe Dining Plan coin, my sister took a vacation with her in-laws last year. Her mother-in-law doesn't do counter service, so the whole trip was Deluxe Dining Plan for six adults and three children. That ended up being far too much food for their group and they ended up skipping 'Ohana because by that night they were 'fooded out.'

I think my conclusion would have to be that three table service meals per day is a bit excessive for most people, but two per day might be perfect for foodies!

Is the Disney Dining Plan for you? It depends on your budget. The quick-service plan is the cheapest, but you miss out on the resort's fantastic table-service restaurants. The Dining Plus Plan gets you a good balance of quick-service and table-service dining, but the cost previously included tip and appetizer, so there's a little disappointment on my part.

MOUSEJUNKIE JOHN When they offer the Disney Dining Plan for free, I almost feel guilty not taking a trip. (Disney occasionally offers a free dining promotion that provides the Dining Plan for free if you pay rack rate for your room.)

If they're doing a free Disney Dining Plan promotion, go! Pick up the phone and make some Advanced Dining Reservations immediately. For me, the food is half the fun of the trip. You're going to be walking five miles a day. And probably doing some swimming. Eat well, my friends.

The wallpaper on my cell phone is a picture of the "Le Cellier" sign. There, I said it.

But even when you do have to pay for the Disney Dining Plan, I think it's worth doing. Food at Disney costs more than at your average fast food joint or local diner. Get used to it. My wife and I sat down one time and did the math, and we figured we were coming out slightly ahead on the dining plan. I don't think it's a huge bargain, but it's definitely convenient.

Here's what we do: Pay cash for breakfast at the resort, which is usually the cheapest meal of the day. Then you really don't need to take out your wallet again until you leave a tip at your sit-down dinner that night. Every time you use your dining plan/room key/park pass card, you get a printout of what you've used and what you have left on the plan. The cast members all know the drill and make it very easy. And I can't stress this enough—Advanced Dining Reservations: make them early and often. There are so many good sit-down restaurants at Walt Disney World. Try a few. You can't eat cheeseburgers three meals a day. Trust me, I've tried.

The Deluxe Dining Plan is for anyone who wants to splurge. I'd love to give it a whirl sometime, but I get the feeling my arteries would likely object.

Look at it objectively: plan where and what you want to eat and then try to figure out if it makes financial sense. Do I spend more than $42 a day dining? Most of the time I do, so the Dining Plus plan would fit my style of touring.

MOUSEJUNKIE JENNA   I absolutely did not find the standard Disney Dining Plan to be too much food, although it came close to that when the table-service meal plan included an appetizer. I never had unused meal credits. For those that did, I chalk that up to poor planning. You need to put some thought into your meals before going to Disney. If you know you're having a huge dinner at 'Ohana, use your counter service credit for breakfast that day and have a snack for lunch. There were occasions that I had a counter service meal credit and a couple of snack credits left on my last day. Those credits purchased a sandwich meal, wrapped to go. So much better than anything the Orlando airport has to offer! And I'm so addicted to the dipped pretzel sticks at Goofy's Candy Co. that it got to the point where I made sure I still had snack credits on the last day.

Now, with all that said, I only recommend the Disney Dining Plan to people who do not have an annual pass and therefore can't get the Tables in Wonderland discount card. And I always ask if they're hearty eaters, because someone who is used to eating less than restaurant portions is going to be overwhelmed.

Still others skip the Disney Dining Plan to create their own experience.

MOUSEJUNKIE J I have never used the Disney Dining Plan. I've always said it was not a good idea for most people. If you are getting it for free as part of a free dining promotion, then you might as well use it (even though these people are the ones clogging up the ADRs at Le Cellier). But paying for it? I say no. There's often too much food and people didn't get a chance to use every credit. There are many stories of people buying a half a suitcase of snacks to take home because they did not use them during the trip. I also heard of a man buying ten lunches at the Earl of Sandwich for strangers on his last day at Walt Disney World because he didn't use his counter-service credits up. After a cinnamon role at Main Street Bakery and a Mickey ice cream here and there, a lot of people find themselves just looking for another snack instead of a double cheeseburger from Cosmic Ray's. This leaves those counter-service credits for the strangers in line on the last day.

If you are a seasoned Walt Disney World traveler or you seek advice from this Mousejunkie, you can save time and consternation by just doing a little planning. Disney does not scrimp on portion size. Deb and I split counter service meals because there's plenty of food. This also leaves you room for a Dole Whip or Plaza sundae after just a few hours. At all counter-service establishments anyone can order off the child menu. They do not ask to

(Continued on next page)

actually see the child eating the meal. Deb will often get the kids meals. They are smaller and cheaper.

Table service is a different story. Since most people are on vacation away from home, doggie bags are out. In my case it makes me eat as much as possible so as to not waste food on my plate. When I know I am going to eat at a table-service place at night, I take it easy on food during the day. If I ate a full counter service and then a full table service each and every day, I would not be happy or healthy. That's just too much food.

Don't get me wrong—it is still all about the food for me. But I make sure I plan it out so I am sampling what Walt Disney World has to offer while not overdoing it. I have overdone it on occasion. For the most part that took place at 'Ohana. All that food and a couple of 'Ohana coladas and I was not hungry again until lunch the following day.

MOUSEJUNKIE DEB With the elimination of the appetizer and gratuity from the standard dining plan, I think the value is close to a wash, at best. How many times do you hear about people who didn't use all their counter service meals and/or snacks and either leave with them on their account, pay for other guests' lunches in line behind them, or stuff their suitcases with nineteen Mickey Mouse Rice Krispy Treats? Nice for the people behind you, but you clearly overpaid for the Disney Dining Plan.

I would recommend people pay for meals on their own without a plan, likely better for your wallet and your waistline. People tend to overorder and overeat on the Disney Dining Plan. Instead, think about splitting an appetizer or skipping a dessert and having a treat later, where you may not end up tipping on its cost if you get a Dole Whip, funnel cake, Wetzel's pretzel, caramel apple, chocolate chip cookie ice cream sandwich, popcorn, or one of a hundred other snacks available.

Florida residents and Annual Passholders have an additional option: the **Tables in Wonderland** card. This card entitles the holder to twenty percent off all food and beverage at participating restaurants. The card costs $75 for Annual Passholders, and $100 for Florida residents who aren't Annual Passholders. The card can be purchased at Guest Services. Tables in Wonderland cardholders also enjoy free valet parking. There are blackout dates, including most major holidays.

Tables in Wonderland cardholders are also offered special dining experiences throughout the year for an additional fee. You just can't get in without the card.

MOUSEJUNKIE DEB The Tables in Wonderland card is expensive, so you need to think through before purchasing. If you're going to use it over two or more trips, it's probably worth it. And the more people that you dine with, the quicker you'll break even.

Mousejunkies Eat Checklist

❑ Call 407-WDW-DINE (939-3463) or visit disney-world.disney.go.com/reservations/dining to make your advanced dining reservations 180 days from the day of your arrival.

❑ Order the Disney Dining Plan. (Or don't.)

❑ If you are an Annual Passholder, order the Tables in Wonderland card. (twenty percent off your bill.)

❑ Plan character meals.

❑ Note any food allergies with the cast member taking your ADR or on the Disney website form.

A List of Walt Disney World Restaurants, by Theme Park, Resort, Water Park and Downtown Disney

(Menu descriptions are samples only. They are not full menus. Fixed-price or buffet table-service restaurant listings include prices and menu samples. Advanced Dining Reservations are recommended for any table-service restaurant.)

Magic Kingdom

Table-Service Restaurants

Cinderella's Royal Table (Cinderella Castle) A fixed-price meal: Scrambled eggs, sausage, bacon, French toast, home fries (*breakfast: adults $47.50, children $31*); pasta, salmon, ham and turkey focaccia (*lunch: adults $51, children $32.50*); lamb chops, pork chops, prime rib, salmon, pasta (*dinner: adults $57, children $35*)

Liberty Tree Tavern (Liberty Square): pot roast, fish, chicken pasta, traditional roast turkey dinner, burgers (*lunch:*

from $11 to $17.99); salad, roast turkey dinner with beef and pork, vegetables, potatoes, and stuffing (*dinner: family-style, $35.99 adults, $15 children*)

The Plaza Restaurant (Main Street USA): Grilled chicken sandwich, steak and cheese, tuna sandwich, burgers, Rueben, club sandwich (*Sandwiches range from $10 to $15*)

Tony's Town Square (Adjacent to City Hall): spaghetti, chicken parmesan, baked ziti (*lunch: $13 to $20*); Chicken parmesan, spinach and ricotta gnocchi, seafood riavoli, shrimp scampi (*dinner: $17 to $30*).

The Crystal Palace (Just off Main Street USA): a character buffet at breakfast, lunch and dinner: scrambled eggs, bacon, sausage, breakfast lasagna (*breakfast: $20.99 adults, children $11.99*); salad bar, macaroni and cheese, pizza, vegetable curry, rotisserie chicken, flank steak, salmon, curry chicken, dessert bar (*lunch: $22.99 adults, $12.99 children*); salad bar, peel and eat shrimp, garlic mashed potatoes, macaroni and cheese, curry mussels, corn spoon bread, cinnamon and lemon rice, prime rib, roasted turkey, roasted pork, dessert bar (*dinner: $32.99 adults, $15.99 children*).

Quick Service Options

Aloha Isle (Adventureland): Dole Whip soft serve, Dole Whip float, ice cream floats

Auntie Gravity's (Tomorrowland): soft-serve ice cream, drinks

Casey's Corner (Main Street USA): hot dogs, French fries, chili, drinks

Columbia Harbour House (Liberty Square): fish and chips, chicken nuggets, clam chowder, tuna sandwich, French fries

Cosmic Ray's Starlight Cafe (Tomorrowland): burgers, chicken and ribs, steak and cheese, turkey wrap, French fries, chicken nuggets

Diamond Horseshoe (Liberty Square): turkey sandwich, tuna sandwich, meatball sub, Caesar salad

El Pirata y el Perico (Adventureland): tacos, burritos, quesadillas (open seasonally, usually during very busy times of the year)

Enchanted Grove (Fantasyland): drinks (lemonade, slushes, coffee, water)

Golden Oak Outpost (Frontierland): French fries, chicken fingers, chicken sandwich

The Lunching Pad (Tomorrowland): turkey leg, cheese-stuffed sweet pretzels, assorted drinks

Main Street Bakery (Main Street USA): breakfast sandwiches, cinnamon rolls, croissants, cereal, fruit, tarts, cakes, coffee

Main Street Curb: Be one of the Corn People. Open a can of corn and eat it with a plastic spoon.

Main Street Ice Cream (Main Street USA): Ice cream sundaes, ice cream cones, ice cream floats.

Mrs. Potts Cupboard (Fantasyland): soft serve ice cream, milkshakes, sundaes, assorted drinks

Pecos Bill Tall Tale Inn and Café (Frontierland): burgers, chicken wrap, taco salad, pork sandwich, chili cheese fries

Pinocchio Village Haus (Fantasyland): chicken nuggets, Caesar salad, pizza, meatball sub, Figaro fries

TEEN MOUSEJUNKIE RYAN The Pinocchio Village Haus saved my life one time. Okay, slight exaggeration. I had been waiting in line for hours, days, weeks to see Ariel with my cousin Katie and Mousejunkie Amy, and it was a bajillion degrees out. I'd been in direct sun the whole time with nothing to eat or drink. I started to get dizzy and black out, so I stepped out of line, stumbled over to the Pinocchio Village Haus, ordered a milkshake and fries, and miraculously I was cured. Here's a tip: if you know that you're going to be standing in a really long line with no shade, get some water and a snack so you don't faint. It really puts a damper on meeting a princess if you're not conscious.

Sleepy Hollow (Liberty Square): funnel cakes, soup, cappuccino, espresso, slush

Terrace Noodle Station (Tomorrowland): beef and broccoli with rice, orange chicken with rice, chicken noodles, veggie noodles, chicken nuggets, tofu

MOUSEJUNKIE RANDY Terrace Noodle Station is also the home of the Wishes Dessert Party. This is a special Advanced Dining Reservation event that runs $21.99 per adult and $11.99 per child. The area is closed off for party guests and the deck is reserved as a special viewing area for the fireworks. The desserts are neverending and are excellent. Carol wasn't that impressed with the exclusive fireworks

(Continued on next page)

> viewing area, but we both successfully ate our money's
> worth of desserts. We did overfill ourselves, but here's a
> tip: don't come straight from a table-service meal.

Turkey leg cart (Adventureland): giant turkey legs

⭐ **Mousejunkie U** *Despite rumors to the contrary—and the frighteningly huge size of Disney's giant turkey leg—they are not emu.*

Epcot
Table Service Restaurants

Akershus Royal Banquet Hall (Norway): Princess Storybook Breakfast: scrambled eggs, bacon, sausage, biscuits, potato casserole, fruit (*$28.99 adults, $17.99 children*); Princess Storybook Lunch: salmon burger, open-face chicken sandwich, chicken breast, stuffed pasta, sausage sandwich, *kjottkake* (*$35 adult, $21 children*); Princess Storybook Dinner: Citrus mahi mahi, pork chop, beef tips, chicken breast, seared salmon, stuffed pasta, *kjottkake* (*$40.50 adults, $22.50 children*)

Biergarten Restaurant (Germany): sausages, brats, spaetzle, pork roast, dumplings (*lunch buffet: $19.99 adult, $10.99 children; dinner: $32.99 adult, $13.99 children*)

Bistro de Paris (France): from the à la carte menu, begin your meal with familiar French appetizers: mussel soup, Mediterranean tuna tartar. Main dishes include double-cut white veal chop, rack of lamb and filet mignon. The silky chocolate soufflé is a favorite dessert option. They also have

MOUSEJUNKIE RANDY If you're ready for one of the best meals on Disney property, try Bistro de Paris. I had the four-course prix fixe, and the selection was excellent, the portions just right, and quality unmatched. The prix fixe was a really good value as gourmet meals go. If you have a group of adults who want to enjoy the finer side of Disney, this is the place to go.

a prix fixe tasting menu consists of four courses, and is available with or without wine pairings. (*Entrees range from $33 to $42. The Three-course menu is $54, and $89 with a wine pairing. Note: There is no children's menu at Bistro de Paris restaurant.*)

Chefs de France (France): broiled salmon, short ribs braised in cabernet, rotisserie chicken, mahi mahi sandwich, onion soup, salmon tartare. There is also a $20 prix fixe three-course option: onion soup or lobster bisque, baked macaroni, quiche Lorraine, or French toast ham-and- cheese sandwich; crème brulée or *profiteroles au chocolat*, puff pastry with vanilla ice cream and chocolate sauce. (*Lunch entrees range from $13 to $20. Dinner entrees range from $25 to $35*).

Coral Reef (The Living Seas): lobster ravioli, grilled mahi mahi, blackened catfish, braised short ribs, tilapia, New York strip steak (lunch); seared Ahi tuna, wild mushroom lasagna, roasted salmon (*Lunch entrees range from $13 to $20. Dinner entrees range from $25 to $30*).

The Garden Grill (The Land): char-grilled strip loin, turkey breast, fish, potatoes (*$34.99 adults, $16.99 children*).

Le Cellier (Canada): prime rib sandwich, steak burger, potato gnocchi, cheddar cheese soup (lunch); Salt-crusted prime rib, king salmon, chicken breast, maple crème brulée, assorted bread sticks (dinner).

Nine Dragons (China): Canton pepper beef, pepper shrimp with noodles, sweet-and-sour pork, honey-sesame chicken (lunch); Kung Pao chicken, shrimp and steak, noodle sampler, fried rice, roasted chicken, veggie and tofu stir fry (dinner).

Restaurant Marrakesh (Morocco): couscous, chicken kebab, lemon chicken, roast lamb *meshoui* (lunch). Also available at lunch: Sultan Sampler: grilled beef or chicken, beef *brewat* roll, chicken *Bastilla*, vegetable couscous for $21.95; Shish kebab (beef), North Atlantic salmon, Mogador fish (dinner). Also available at dinner: Marrakesh Royal Feast: harira soup, lemon chicken, roasted lamb *meshoui*, couscous with vegetables, pastries for $42.95; Berber Feast: roast lamb *meshoui*, chicken kebab, couscous with vegetables, baklava, Jasmine salad for $27.95.

Rose & Crown Pub (U.K.): bangers and mash, shepherd's pie, fish and chips, burgers, corned-beef sandwich (lunch); bangers and mash, Sunday roast, grilled pork, surf and turf, chicken-mushroom pie, cottage pie (dinner).

San Angel Inn (Mexico): *pollo a las rajas, ensalada Mexicana, tampiquena con chilaquiles* (lunch); mole *Poblano, Puntas de filete en salsa guajillo, filete motuleno, pollo a las rajas* (dinner).

Teppan Edo (Japan): Guests can choose from a single: shrimp, scallops, steak, filet mignon, or scallops ($23.95 to $29.95), or a combination: sirloin steak and chicken, sirloin steak and shrimp, or chicken and shrimp ($24.95 to $29.95)

TEEN MOUSEJUNKIE RYAN The San Angel Inn isn't bad, especially if you like authentic Mexican food. Just don't do what I did: I took a picture of the food with the flash on. I only eat pretty food, and what I had ordered was not pretty food. Now I know why the lights are so dim there.

Tokyo Dining (Japan): Tempura and sushi combo, shinjuki gozen, bento box, chicken, strip steak, salmon. Tempura.

Tutto Italia Ristorante (Italy): penne caprese, lasagna, gnocchi *verdi grataniti*, linguine, spaghetti, chicken, salmon (lunch); lasagna, *casareci* (pasta, sweet sausage and tomatoes), Chianti ravioli, *salmone al forno*, veal roast, roasted rack of lamb, filet of sole (dinner).

Quick Service Options

Boulangerie Pâtisserie (France): Fruit tarts, cookies, éclairs, turnovers, ham and cheese croissants, quiche, baguette bread.

Cantina de San Angel (Mexico): tacos, burritos, nachos, and margaritas

Electric Umbrella (Future World); burgers, turkey subs, Caesar salad, chicken nuggets

Fountain View Ice Cream (Future World): ice-cream cones, sundaes, sandwiches, and floats

Fife and Drum (America): popcorn, pretzels, slushes, soft-serve ice cream, frozen lemonade

Kringla Bakeri Og Kafe (Norway): sweet pretzel, *lefse* (potato bread with cinnamon sugar), waffles, custard, Danish, Norwegian club (turkey, ham, and bacon) sandwich, salmon and egg sandwich

Liberty Inn (America): burgers, chicken nuggets, hot roast beef and cheddar sandwich, hot dog, grilled chicken Caesar wrap

Lotus Blossom Cafe (China): pot stickers, orange chicken with rice, veggie stir fry with rice, beef noodle soup, sesame chicken salad

Promenade Refreshments (Future World): pretzel with cheese sauce, pretzel with cinnamon sugar, cookies, hot dog, popcorn

Refreshment Outpost (World Showcase): soft-serve ice cream, soda, frozen lemonade, slushes, coffee, ice cream floats

Refreshment Port (Between Canada and the U.K.): Coffee, latte, chicken sandwich, ice cream sundae, fried shrimp

Sommerfest (Germany): hot dog (known at Sommerfest as a Frankfurter), bratwurst, soft pretzel, apple strudel, German beers

Sunshine Seasons (The Land): eggs, sausage, biscuits, French toast (breakfast); cashew chicken, sweet-and-sour chicken, ginger beef, seared tuna on greens, Caesar salad, ham and salami, turkey sandwich, rotisserie chicken, grilled salmon

Tangierine Café (Morocco): shawarma platters (hummus, tabouleh, couscous salad, bread), lamb wrap, chicken wrap, falafel wrap

Yakitori House (Japan): curry rice, shrimp tempura, California roll, spicy tuna roll, sukiyaki beef roll, teriyaki chicken

Yorkshire County Fish Shop (U.K.): fish and chips, shortbread, Bass ale, Harp lager

Disney's Hollywood Studios

Table Service Restaurants

50s Prime Time Café (Echo Lake): chicken pot pie, pot roast, chicken sandwich, meatloaf, fried chicken (*lunch: $13 to $17*); Pork loin, poached salmon, grilled tuna casserole, fried chicken, meatloaf (*dinner: $16 to $21*).

Hollywood and Vine (Echo Lake): a character breakfast and lunch: scrambled eggs, Mickey waffles, roasted potatoes, biscuits and gravy, fruit, pastries (*breakfast:$26.99 adults, $14.99 children*); salad bar, carved meats, fish, veggies and pasta, fruit, bread, desserts (*lunch: $26.99 adults, $14.99 children*); salad bar, carved meats, fish, fruit, breads, desserts (*dinner buffet: $30.99 adults, $15.99 children*).

Hollywood Brown Derby (Hollywood Boulevard): Cobb salad, rack of lamb, noodle bowl, spice-rubbed grouper, roasted half chicken, filet mignon, salmon with whisky glaze (*lunch $15 to $40. Dinner: $23 to $40*)

Mama Melrose's Ristorante Italiano (Streets of America): *spaghetti fra diavolo*, charred sirloin, chicken parmesan, grilled tuna, flatbreads, *penne alla vodka*, spicy sausage with rigatoni (*lunch: $12 to $20. Dinner: $14 to $22*).

Sci-Fi Dine-In Theater (Commissary Lane): Rueben, smoked ribs, marinated tofu, burgers, turkey sandwich (*lunch: $12 to $22*); Italian grilled chicken sandwich, beef and blue cheese salad, shrimp pasta, butcher steak (*dinner: $14 to $22*).

Quick Service Options

ABC Commissary (Commissary Lane): burgers, fried fish, chicken bleu, chicken curry with rice

Backlot Express (Echo Lake): burgers, hot dogs, chicken nuggets, grilled turkey and cheese, Southwest salad with chicken

Catalina Eddie's (Sunset Boulevard): pizza, Italian cold cut sandwich, Caesar salad

Dinosaur Gertie's (Echo Lake): ice cream shakes, waffle cone, Mickey premium bar, ice cream sandwich, waffle cones

Fairfax Fare (Sunset Boulevard): chili dog, beef brisket, ribs, chicken, Fairfax salad

Pizza Planet (Streets of America): pizza

Rosie's All-American Café (Sunset Boulevard): burgers, veggie burgers, chicken nuggets

Starring Rolls (Sunset Boulevard): pastries, bagels, muffins, croissants, ham sandwich, turkey focaccia, veggie pita

Studio Catering Company (Streets of America): buffalo chicken sandwich, turkey club, Greek salad, chicken Caesar wrap, Tuscan deli sandwich

Toluca Legs Turkey Co. (Sunset Boulevard): turkey legs

Writer's Stop (Commissary Lane): coffee, tea, espresso, latte, cookies, muffins, and pastries

Animal Kingdom
Table Service Restaurants

Rainforest Café (Oasis): an assortment of burgers, fish, pasta, beef, pork and chicken, portobello mushroom burger, salmon, crab cakes, New York strip steak, fried chicken, ribs, sweet-and-sour stir fry, Tuscan chicken

Yak and Yeti (Asia): wonton soup, tempura shrimp, seafood curry, crispy mahi-mahi, seared salmon, dim sum, lettuce cups, pork egg rolls, seared ahi tuna. The Yak and Yeti has a quick service counter in front of the restaurant that has some limited options from the main menu.

Quick Service Options

Dino Bite Snacks (Dinoland): hot fudge sundae, waffle cone, ice cream cookie sandwich.

Dino Diner (Chester and Hester's): hot dogs, popcorn

Flame Tree Barbecue (Discovery Island): ribs, chicken, pork, turkey sandwich, baked beans

MOUSEJUNKIE AMY Flame Tree Barbecue offers you choices that aren't fried. It's not a hot dog, not a hamburger, not chicken fingers. There's barbecue chicken breast and some great ribs. I'd rather gnaw on a drumstick than a burger. You can get a burger anywhere.

★ **The Straight Dope** *The seating at Flame Tree Barbecue is outside, much of it under cover. There are a few tables under the lush trees that dot the area. Do not sit at a table under a tree. Doing so ensures your already seasoned barbecue will have a little extra flavor in the form of bird poo.*

Pizzafari (Discovery Island): scrambled eggs, breakfast pizza, biscuits and gravy, French toast, muffins, Danish, coffee and cereal (breakfast); pizza, Italian sub, Caesar salad (lunch/dinner)

Restaurantosaurus (Dinoland): burgers, hot dogs, chicken nuggets

Tamu Tamu Refreshments (Africa): burgers, Tuna salad, turkey and Swiss

Tusker House (Africa): character breakfast: scrambled eggs, biscuits and gravy, potato wedges, corned beef hash, cheese blintzes, oatmeal, rolls, bread pudding, Danish, croissants, bacon, sausage, quiche (*$24.50 adults, $14 children*); Carved sirloin roast and pork loin with assorted sauces, curry chicken, salmon fillet, tandoori tofu, couscous, corn dog nuggets, rotisserie chicken (*$33 adults, $15 children*)

Resort Dining

All-Star Movies
World Premiere Food Court

All-Star Music
Intermission Food Court

All-Star Sports
End Zone Food Court

Animal Kingdom Lodge

Table Service Restaurants

Boma—Flavors of Africa (Jambo House): breakfast buffet: omelets, bacon, sausage, ham, scrambled eggs, brioche, bobotie, cereal, pastries, West African Frunch (*$18.99 adults, $10.99 children*); dinner buffet: carved meats with assorted sauces, peanut rice, pasta salad, fufu, grilled seafood, chicken tenders, roasted chicken, assorted soups, and couscous (*$31 adults, $15 children*)

Sanaa (Kidani Village): Indian-style bread service with assorted sauces, lamb kefta, burger wrapped in naan bread, tandoori chicken, tandoori shrimp, grilled pork chop (*lunch entrees: $11 to $19. Dinner: $18 to $28*)

Jiko—The Cooking Place (Jambo House): roasted lamb loin, barbecue beef short ribs, spiced crusted tuna, filet mignon, spiced pork loin, grilled salmon, and seared ostrich filet. (*Entrees from $28 to $40*)

Quick Service Options

The Mara (Jambo House): scrambled eggs, potatoes, bacon, sausage, oatmeal, cinnamon roll, bagel, muffin, Danish, and croissants (breakfast); burgers, flatbreads, chicken nuggets, turkey ciabatta, half-chicken dinner (lunch/dinner)

BoardWalk and the BoardWalk Inn and Villas

Table Service Restaurants

Big River Grille & Brewing Works: chicken Alfredo, ribs, grilled meatloaf, hazelnut-crusted mahi-mahi, beer cheese soup, shrimp and scallop penne pasta, chicken marinara (*Lunch: $9 to $22. Dinner: $11 to $30*)

ESPN Club: assorted burgers, a gigantic hot dog, Philly cheesesteak, pulled pork, nachos, chicken dinger sandwich, top sirloin, grilled salmon, ribs (*Lunch and dinner entrees range from $11 to $14*)

Kouzzina: ham-and-cheese omelet, French toast, waffles with mascarpone cheese and honey, blueberry and orange granola pancakes (breakfast); calamari, stuffed grape leaves, pork T-bone, cinnamon stewed chicken, lamb shank, grilled flank steak, and char grilled lamb burger (*Lunch and dinner entrees range from $10.49 to $22.99*)

Flying Fish Café: oak-grilled salmon, oak-grilled Maine scallops, pepper-spiced yellowfin tuna, potato-wrapped red snapper, lamb chops, and New York strip steak (*Lunch and dinner entrees range from $29 to $42*)

Quick Service Options

BoardWalk Bakery: croissants, muffins, parfait, pastries, cereal, ham-and-cheese panini, tuna salad, chicken salad wrap

The Pizza Stop (On the boardwalk in front of Kouzzina), pizza by the slice until midnight

Caribbean Beach Resort
Table Service Restaurants

Shutters at Old Port Royale: New York strip steak, jerk-crusted tuna, Caribbean pork ribs, roasted chicken, pasta with shrimp (*Lunch and dinner entrees range from $16 to $28*)

Quick Service Options

Old Port Royale Food Court: eggs, bacon, sausage, French toast, oatmeal, grits, Mickey waffle, omelets (breakfast); pizza, burgers, ziti, fettucini Alfredo with chicken, meatball sub, hot dog, chicken nuggets, chili dog, buffalo chicken sandwich (lunch/dinner)

Contemporary Resort

Table Service Restaurants

The Wave: ham-and-cheese omelet, smoked salmon, eggs benedict, multigrain pancakes, multigrain French toast, spinach-and-feta scrambled eggs, and for the truly different... "make your own muesli" (breakfast); bacon cheeseburger, tuna salad, grilled chicken sandwich, spice-crusted chicken salad, sustainable fish (lunch); braised lamb shank, chicken pot pie, vegetable stew, cinnamon-rubbed pork tenderloin, grilled beef tenderloin, chili rubbed flatiron steak (*Lunch and dinner entrees range from $9.99 to $28.99*)

Chef Mickey's: character breakfast: scrambled eggs, omelets, Mickey waffles, potatoes, breakfast pizza, pancakes, biscuits and gravy, sausage, bacon, pastries, croissants, muffins, and Danish (*$27 adults, $14 children*); character dinner: beef tips, chicken, fish, pasta, Parmesan mashed potatoes, veggies, macaroni and cheese, pizza, and chicken tenders (*$34 adults, $17 children*)

California Grill: Its borderline criminal to try to summarize the California Grill in anything short of a loving ode composed in rhyming couplet using flowery prose set to a swelling string section, however... assorted flatbreads, sushi, lobster salad, braised lamb shank risotto, Sonoma goat cheese ravioli, grilled pork tenderloin, panko-crusted cod, seared bison, filet mignon (*Lunch and dinner entrees range from $22 to $44*)

★ **The Straight Dope** *When the nightly fireworks extravaganza kicks off, the lights in the restaurant are lowered and the accompanying music is piped in over the sound system. Guests who are not eating at the restaurant can watch the fireworks from an outdoor observation deck adjoining the restaurant.*

Quick Service Options

Contempo Café: waffles, French toast, scrambled eggs, breakfast platters with bacon, eggs, sausage, potatoes and biscuit (breakfast); flatbreads, salads, turkey BLT, spice-crusted mahi mahi, and burgers (lunch); hot open-faced roast beef sandwich, pasta with marinara or cream sauce, beef flat-bread, veggie bake (dinner)

Cove Bar: club sandwich, veggie rolls, Caesar salad, lettuce wraps and assorted frozen drinks, wine, sangria

The Sand Bar: burgers, hot dogs, turkey sandwich, chicken nuggets, Caesar salad

Coronado Springs
Table Service Restaurants

Maya Grill: omelets, eggs benedict, pancakes, sausage, bacon, potatoes, Kobe brunch burger, fruit, English muffin, bagel, toast, and ham (*breakfast entrees from $3.59 to $11.99*); ribeye steak, grouper sandwich, grilled beef shoulder, pork chops, seared scallops, pork empanada (*dinner entrees from $9.99 to $31*)

Quick Service Options

Cafe Rix: smoke salmon tartare, chorizo flatbread, burger pinchos, citrus chicken skewers, sashimi tuna

Pepper Market: eggs any style, omelets, bacon, sausage, hash browns, waffles, fruit, veggie frittata, Mickey waffles, French toast (breakfast); burgers, grilled chicken sandwich, pan-seared salmon, pasta, pizza, barbecue ribs, rotisserie chicken, hot dogs, chicken nuggets, cold sandwiches, nachos, quesadillas (dinner)

Siestas Cantina: burgers, hot dogs, chicken nuggets, buffalo chicken sandwich, Caesar chicken wrap, assorted frozen drinks

Fort Wilderness Resort & Campground
Table Service Restaurants

Trail's End Restaurant: breakfast buffet: scrambled eggs, Mickey waffles, biscuits and gravy, sausage, bacon, grits, cereal, oatmeal, and pastries (*$13.99 adults, $8.99 children*); lunch buffet: pulled pork, salad bar, macaroni and cheese, fried chicken, soup, veggies, chili ice cream sundae bar (*$16.99 adults, $9.99 children*); dinner buffet: ribs, peel-and-eat shrimp, fried chicken, pasta, chili, pizza, veggies, carving station, fish, salad bar (*$22.99 adults, $11.99 children*)

Hoop-Dee-Doo Musical Revue: fried chicken, ribs, mashed potatoes, baked beans, salad, bread and honey butter (horde this, it is amazing), strawberry shortcake, and drinks— including wine and beer (*$62 adults, $32 children for floor seating near the stage; $57 adults, $28 children for seating at the rear of the floor or center balcony; $53 adults, $27 children for left or right hand balcony*)

Quick Service Options

Meadow Snack Bar (seasonal): barbecue pulled pork-smothered hot dog, pulled pork flatbread, turkey sandwich, Caesar salad, pizza, Asian chicken salad, and assorted desserts and drinks.

Mickey's Backyard BBQ (seasonal): Barbecue chicken, pork ribs, burgers, hot dogs, baked beans, mac and cheese, corn on the cob, potato salad, corn bread, and ice cream bars (*$51 adults, $21 children*).

Grand Floridian Resort & Spa
Table Service Restaurants

Grand Floridian Café: Lobster eggs benedict, smoked salmon, steak and eggs, frittata, omelets, citrus pancakes, maple/vanilla French toast, Mickey waffles (breakfast); The Grand Sandwich (open faced turkey, ham, bacon with boursin sauce), Cobb salad, New York strip steak, chicken sandwich, Reuben, Caesar salad, fish, and assorted desserts (lunch); grilled rib-eye, grilled pork chop, shrimp penne pasta, salmon, oven-roasted chicken, Grand Floridian Burger (with lobster, asparagus and horseradish hollandaise), and assorted desserts (*Entrees range from $9.99 to $24.99*).

★ **The Straight Dope** *The Grand Sandwich at the Grand Floridian Café is a criminally well-kept secret. The Grand Sandwich is an open-faced hot turkey, ham, bacon and tomato concoction—and here's the genius of it all—topped with a rich Boursin cheese sauce and fried onion straws. You can top a sneaker with a rich Boursin cheese sauce and fried onion straws and I'll eat it.*

1900 Park Fare: character breakfast: omelets, scrambled eggs, bacon, sausage, Mickey waffles, pancakes, cheese Danish, cheese blintz, bread pudding, yogurt, muffins, pastries, bagels, French toast, biscuits and gravy, grits (*$22.50 adults, $12.75 children*); carving station (prime rib, turkey breast, pork loin), pasta, salmon, curry chicken, raviolis, mussels, lasagna, veggie rolls, salad bar, assorted desserts (*$36 adults, $18 children*)

Cítricos: oak-grilled swordfish, braised veal shank, short ribs, fillet Sicilian, seared tofu, pork tenderloin, roasted chicken, pan-seared black grouper

Narcoossee's: Maine lobster, Alaskan halibut, grilled shrimp, whole snapper, filet mignon, surf and turf, chicken breast, ahi tuna, assorted desserts

Victoria and Albert's: The most upscale restaurant in all of Walt Disney World, the menu at Victoria and Albert's changes daily. Past menus have included king salmon, duck breast, elk carpaccio, assorted caviar, pork tenderloin, Niman Ranch lamb, Kobe beef tenderloin, and assorted insanely rich desserts. (*Fixed price: $125 per person, with an additional $60 for a wine pairing; $200 per person for the Chef's Table and the Queen Victoria Room, with an additional $95 for a wine pairing*).

Quick Service Options

Gasparilla Grill: burgers, hot dogs, chicken nuggets, jerk chicken sandwich, roast beef sandwich, chicken Caesar salad, pizza, Italian sandwich, and tabbouleh wraps

Old Key West

Table Service Restaurants

Olivia's Café: breakfast burrito, pancakes, omelets, banana bread French toast, bacon, sausage, biscuits and gravy, cereal, grits (*breakfast: $10.99 to $12.99*); blackened grouper sandwich, roast beef and blue cheese sandwich, Cuban sandwich, penne pasta with shrimp, Key West salmon salad, turkey club, burgers (lunch); New York strip steak, roasted chicken breast, prime rib, pork chop, fennel-dusted grouper, and mahi mahi (*Lunch and dinner: $12.99 to $27.99*)

Quick Service Options

Good's Food to Go: burgers, hot dogs, chicken nuggets, veggie sandwich, Caesar salad, soup, turkey sandwich, fruit, French fries, onion rings

Polynesian Resort
Table Service Restaurants

Kona Café: Tonga toast, steak and eggs, omelets, pancakes, French toast, Mickey waffles, the Samoan, Kona pressed-pot coffee (*breakfast: $$9.99 to $14.49*); beef teriyaki salad, Asian chicken chop salad, stir-fried noodles, Island chicken sandwich, miso-glazed mahi mahi, Kona club sandwich, kahuna burger, Big Island tacos (lunch); ginger-crusted rib-eye steak, Pan-Asian noodles, coconut-almond chicken, New York strip teriyaki, tuna Oscar, shrimp and scallops (*dinner: $11.49 to $28.99*).

'Ohana Character breakfast: scrambled eggs, potatoes, pork sausage, Mickey waffles, and breakfast breads (*$25 adults, $14 children*); welcome bread, honey-coriander chicken wings, pork dumplings, mesquite turkey tips, pork loin, sirloin steak, peel-and-eat shrimp, noodles, veggies, and bread pudding with bananas and caramel sauce (dinner, served family-style; *$31 adults, $15 children*)

Spirit of Aloha Dinner Show: pineapple/coconut bread, pineapple chunks, ribs, chicken, rice, veggies, drinks included. Specialty cocktails, select beer, and signature drinks are extra (*$62 adults, $32 children for lower level seating closest to the stage; $57 adults, $28 children for lower level* *tables or upper level center; $53 adults, $27 children for upper level or lower level on the left or right)*

Quick Service Options

Capt. Cook's: Mickey waffle, Tonga toast, scrambled eggs, bacon, sausage, egg and bacon sandwich, potatoes, biscuit, assorted muffins, bagels, Danish, pastries (breakfast); burgers, pork sandwich, turkey club, chicken Caesar salad, stir-fried noodles, grilled cheese, pizza

Pop Century
Quick Service Options

Everything Pop: Food court offerings: waffle platter, French toast platter, scrambled eggs breakfast platter, wpotatoes, assorted pastries (breakfast); burgers, chicken nuggets, chili cheese dog, fish sandwich, veggie burger, cheesesteak wrap, assorted flatbreads, assorted soups, lo mein, nachos, assorted pizza (lunch/dinner)

Port Orleans
Table Service Restaurants

Boatwright's: prime rib, voodoo chicken, jambalaya, grilled pork chop, pasta with shrimp, blackened fish fillet, honey-mustard mashed sweet potatoes, corn and crab soup, crawfish bites, spiced shrimp and fried green tomato salad *(Entrees range from $17 to $27)*

Quick Service Options

Riverside Mill: French toast, scrambled eggs, bacon, sausage, freshly-made waffles, omelets, assorted pastries and bagels, grits (breakfast); burgers, grilled chicken sandwich, fish basket, chicken nuggets, assorted pizza, carving station, salads, baked ziti (lunch/dinner)

Sassagoula Floatworks and Food Factory: beignets, Mickey waffles, omelets, pancakes, French toast, sausage, bacon, biscuits and gravy, assorted pastries (breakfast); burgers, hot dogs, cheesesteak sandwich, assorted pizza, grilled chicken sandwich, meatball sub, veggie sandwich, chicken Parmesan, taco salad, chicken quesadilla, chicken Caesar salad (lunch/dinner)

Saratoga Springs Resort & Spa

Table Service Restaurants

The Turf Club: rib-eye steak sandwich, grilled chicken sandwich, Reuben, seared yellowfin tuna, linguine with shrimp, spiced salmon salad, buffalo wings, crab cake, steamed mussels, fried calamari (lunch); grilled tuna, prime rib, mint-crusted lamb chops, pork tenderloin, burgers, and New York strip steak, freshly-made individual apple pie a la mode (dinner) (*Lunch and dinner entrees range from $11 to $28*)

Quick Service Options

The Artist's Palette: breakfast flatbread, egg and croissant sandwich, omelets, Mickey waffles, assorted pastries (breakfast); roast beef and blue cheese sandwich, Asian chicken salad, assorted flatbreads, chicken Caesar salad, chicken cordon bleu panini, peanut butter and jelly sandwich, chicken nuggets, macaroni and cheese (*Lunch and dinner entrees range from $26 to $48*)

Wilderness Lodge
Table Service Restaurants

Whispering Canyon: breakfast skillet (scrambled eggs, red potatoes, bacon, sausage, waffles, biscuits and gravy; *all you can eat for $14.99 per person*), barbecue eggs Benedict, omelets, two eggs any style, bacon, sausage, potatoes, French toast, Belgian waffle, pancakes, assorted pastries (breakfast); canyon skillet (ribs, chicken, pork sausage, baked beans, corn on the cob, coleslaw, mashed potatoes, cornbread; *all you can eat for $17.99 per person*), arugula chicken salad, turkey sandwich, pulled pork sandwich, whiskey maple-glazed trout, grilled chicken sandwich (lunch); canyon skillet (smoked pork ribs, pulled pork, chicken, beef brisket, potatoes, beans, corn on the cob, cole slaw, and cornbread; *all you can eat for $26.99*), grilled rib-eye steak, meatloaf, pot roast, whiskey maple-glazed trout, smoked pork loin (dinner)

⭐ **The Straight Dope** *Want to shake up the dining experience? Make sure to ask for ketchup at the Whispering Canyon Café. Every bottle from surrounding tables will suddenly be transported to your area by boisterous, mischievous servers. If that's not enough, ask for a refill on your soda. A*

*jar the size of a two-liter bottle will be returned to you filled
with whatever sugary beverage you prefer.*

Artist Point: cedar plank wild salmon, pan-seared halibut,
grilled buffalo striploin, white truffle gnocchi, seared scallops, fisherman's stew

The Straight Dope   *Artist Point is known, in particular, for its amazing cedar plank-roasted wild king salmon.*

Quick Service Options

Roaring Forks: scrambled eggs, bacon, potatoes, sausage,
pancakes, biscuits, oatmeal, assorted pastries (breakfast);
ham and cheddar sandwich, salads, turkey and havarti sandwich, tuna sandwich, peanut butter and jelly sandwich,
burgers, chicken breast sandwich, chicken nuggets, assorted
flatbreads (*Lunch and dinner*)

Yacht & Beach Club

Table Service Restaurants

Captain's Grille: crab cake Benedict, eggs Benedict, Mickey
waffle, three-egg omelet, pancakes, steak and eggs, smoked
salmon and bagel, brioche French toast (*breakfast: $9 to
$16*); fish and chips, chicken Caesar salad, burgers, grilled
ahi tuna, sirloin steak salad, roast turkey sandwich, lobster
roll, tomato and mozzarella in ciabatta roll (lunch); Grilled
rib-eye steak, grilled pork chop, New York strip steak, snow

crab legs, wild mushroom and onion tart, crab cakes, roasted chicken breast (*dinner: $16 to $29.00*)

Cape May Café character breakfast: scrambled eggs, omelets, eggs to order, biscuits and gravy, smoked salmon Mickey waffles, bacon, sausage, potatoes, bread pudding, breakfast pizza, and assorted cereals (*$18.99 adults, $10.99 children*); clam bake dinner buffet: clams with garlic butter, peel-and-eat shrimp, snow crab legs, seasonal fish, mussels with roasted tomato butter, barbecue pork ribs, mashed red potatoes, corn on the cob, pasta, clam chowder, tomato bisque, seafood salad (*$26.99 adults, $12.99 children*)

Yachtsman Steakhouse: filet mignon, porterhouse steak, oak-fired rib-eye steak, braised beef ravioli, roasted chicken, pan-seared scallops, prime New York strip steak, roasted rack of lamb, gnocchi, truffle macaroni and cheese (*Only open for dinner. Entrees from $32 to $44*)

Quick Service Options

Beach Club Marketplace: ham and cheese croissant, yogurt parfait, cheese omelet croissant, assorted pastries (breakfast); roast beef and brie on a ciabatta roll, grilled veggie wrap, smoked ham and cheddar sandwich, clam chowder, peanut butter and jelly sandwich, and turkey sandwich (lunch/dinner)

Hurricane Hanna's Grill: burgers, hot dogs, grilled chicken flatbread, turkey sandwich, veggie wrap

Beaches and Cream Soda Shop: burgers, roast beef, hot dogs, turkey sandwich, veggie wrap

Fine, but this place is all about the ice cream, and specifically the Kitchen Sink: Eight scoops of ice cream with every topping you can imagine for $23.99. A hefty tub of icy perfection, the Kitchen Sink can be beaten, but it takes a committed warrior to best this monstrosity. A solid base of peanut butter and chocolate sauce coats the bottom of the bowl. Then comes heaping scoops of chocolate, vanilla, mint chocolate chip, coffee, and strawberry ice cream. The whole thing is dressed with a pile of brownies, Oreos, angel food cake, a Milky Way candy bar, and a can of whipped cream. Yes, the whole can. Still not enough? Toss in a few more brownies, a banana and a few more Oreos. Add a few cherries on top and you've got your dessert of doom.

Individual bowls are distributed so the Sink can be divided. This detail is key, since by the end there's a rather large gray puddle of goo at the bottom.

There are those who claim to have single-handedly consumed the Kitchen Sink. I am dubious of these claims. Although, I'm not above trying it myself.

Water Park Dining

Typhoon Lagoon
Quick Service Options

Leaning Palms: burgers, hot dogs, chicken nuggets, pizza, chicken wrap, chili dog

Typhoon Tilly's: barbecue pork sandwich, fish basket, chicken wrap, chili dog, chicken nuggets, salad, fruit cup, French fries

Blizzard Beach
Quick Service Options

Avalunch: assorted hot dogs (served with coleslaw, banana peppers, tomatoes, onions, chili and cheese), chopped chicken salad, turkey leg

Lottawatta Lodge: burgers, chili dog, chicken nuggets, pizza, deli sandwich, chicken wrap, pizza

The Warming Hut: St. Louis ribs with beans and coleslaw, pulled pork sandwich, barbecue chicken sandwich, chicken wrap

Downtown Disney
Table Service Restaurants

Bongo's Cuban Café: *carzuela de mariscos* (sautéed seafood with Creole sauce, white rice, and plantains), *enchilado de camarones* (sauteed tiger shrimp in a creole sauce served with plantains), *pollo asado* (lemon, garlic, and white wine-marinated chicken served with moro rice and *yucca con mojo*), *ropa vieja* (shredded beef in a tomato sauce with white rice and plantains), surf and turf, fried rice with shrimp, beef, chicken, sweet-and-sour chicken (*Lunch and dinner entrees range from $9 to $29*)

Cap'n Jack's Restaurant: crab cakes, shrimp and penne pasta, pasta Alfredo, Cajun shrimp-and-chicken étouffée, baked salmon, roast chicken, chicken Caesar salad, pot roast, clam chowder, peel-and-eat shrimp, smoked trout and horseradish cream (*Lunch entrees from $12 to $19. Dinner entrees from $18 to $24*)

Fulton's Crab House: linguini with clams, fish and chips, mahi mahi tacos, fried seafood combo, crab club, fried shrimp po' boy, grilled Angus burger, sliders (lunch); Filet mignon, Louie Fulton's crab and lobster experience for two, king crab claws and Australian lobster tail, bone-in rib-eye steak, surf and turf, lobster Narragansett, chilled Florida stone crab claws, striped bass, tuna fillet, Grand Bahama whole yellow tail snapper, and Key West mahi mahi (*Lunch entrees from $11 to $14. Dinner entrees from $27 to $52*)

Paradiso 37: Argentinean skirt steak, Chilean salmon, New York strip steak, surf and turf, *tres* tacos, Baja burritos, chorizo skewers, mac and cheese bites, quesadillas, corn dogs, *queso fundido*, shrimp ceviche (*Lunch and dinner entrees from $10 to $27*)

Planet Hollywood: assorted burgers, cheesesteak sandwich, pulled pork sandwich, turkey club, garlic shrimp, shrimp Alfredo, manicotti, rib-eye steak, fajitas, roasted chicken, blackened mahi mahi, teriyaki salmon, New York strip steak (*Lunch and dinner entrees from $10 to $27*

Rainforest Café: burgers, chicken sandwich, portobello mushroom burger, Caesar salad, clam chowder, New York strip steak, fried chicken, ribs, Tuscan chicken pot roast, crab cakes, coconut shrimp (*Breakfast entrees from $9 to $14. Lunch and dinner entrees from $11 to $40*)

Raglan Road: lobster club, steak sanger, chicken BLT, Guinness meatball sandwich, prosciutto and chicken sandwich, smoked salmon salad, Cashel blue cheese salad, assorted flatbreads, shepherd's pie, Irish stew, fish and chips, Guinness bangers and mash (lunch); Guinness and

onion banger, aujus chicken, beef stew, chicken and mushroom pie, Blue Hill Bay mussels, mixed grill, Kevin's ham,
braised short ribs, meatballs a la Liffey Luv (dinner) (*Lunch
and dinner entrees from $16 to $27*)

T-Rex: assorted burgers (all with hokey dino-themed names
like "Gigantosaurus Burger"), cold cut panini, chicken sandwich, steak and cheese sandwich, rotisserie chicken, barbecue ribs, chicken fried steak, fried shrimp, salmon fillet,
shrimp skewers (*Lunch and dinner entrees from $14 to $27*)

Wolfgang Puck Café: filet mignon, rib-eye steak, steamed
fish, seared salmon, spicy beef goulash, shrimp scampi
risotto, crab cakes, yellowfin tuna tartare, pot stickers, wild
mushroom soup, duck Napoleon, teriyaki beef satay, seared
sea scallops (*Lunch and dinner entrees from $13 to $29*)

Quick Service Options

Cookes of Dublin: fish and chips, Atlantic scallops, fisherman's pie, mini Irish sausages, chicken tenders, Caesar salad,
whiskey and crushed pepper chicken wings, fried candy bars.
Yes, you read that correctly. Perfection.

Earl of Sandwich: A surprisingly reasonable sub shop serving delicious, hot sandwiches: roast beef and cheddar, roast
turkey, meatballs, ham and swiss, mozzarella and tomatoes,
Caribbean jerk chicken, the Hawaiian BBQ, the Earl's club
(roast turkey, smoked bacon, swiss, lettuce and tomato)

★**The Straight Dope**   *The Earl of Sandwich is one of
the best dining values on Disney property. The food is great*

TEEN MOUSEJUNKIE RYAN Best BLT with cheese I've ever had in my entire life. It's really reasonable prices for really good food. You can get a sandwich for $5.

and the prices are comparatively cheap. Just get there early or be prepared to stalk fellow diners for a seat. It gets crowded quickly, and I have to admit I'm not above laying across a row of chairs while Amy fetches my sandwich.

FoodQuest: burgers, hot dogs, chicken nuggets, chili cheese fries, assorted pizza, baked ziti.

Wolfgang Puck Express: Chilean salmon, macadamia nut crusted chicken, chicken fettucini, pumpkin ravioli, barbecue chicken, Cobb salad, assorted sushi

ESPN Wide World of Sports Complex

ESPN Wide World of Sports: All American Hamburger, blackened tilapia sandwich, veggie sandwich pastrami on rye, pulled pork sandwich, chicken nuggets, chicken wings, assorted pizzas, chili nachos

If anyone tells you that eating like this is obnoxiously extravagant, just point out the fact that you'll be walking it all off while traipsing through Disney's vast property. Or simply laugh and tell them they're right.

The way we approach it is to map out your week by theme park destination. Then choose a restaurant either in that park, or convenient to it. Once that's done, it's time to get on the phone with Disney Dining.

The Straight Dope *It's been said before, but it's worth repeating: make your dining reservations early. It is the number one tip most people give. And still many guests don't always heed this advice. Ignoring it can lead to unimaginable heartbreak. Or at the very least grumpy traveling mates and growling stomachs. You can call 180 days out from the day of your arrival to make Advanced Dining Reservations. 407-WDW-DINE.*

The Way of the Mousejunkie

THERE ARE A MILLION WAYS to approach Disney's theme parks, all with different philosophies and goals.

The Commando: This person is intent on doing everything. He or she is up at the crack of stupid and is in a sprinter's stance at the rope drop. This person has a plan, and any diversion from it elicits an outburst of swift, punishing Mouse-Fu.

The Parent: Character meals, character autographs, character photographs, and Dumbo the Flying Elephant. These elements dictate The Parent's touring plans. They can fold and unfold a stroller while boarding and disembarking Disney's buses like a Marine can field-strip a rifle. With boot camp-like discipline, they train by carrying a thirty-pound sack of sand on mile-long hikes. Because at the end of a long day, The Parent must possess the stamina to not only get himself to the bus (always the farthest stop away, it seems), but he must also be able to carry his completely pooped offspring to the finish line.

The Teen: WhatEVER. *eyeroll* The teen loves fast rides, shopping, and independence. They've done the online research, joined several Disney forums and Facebook Groups, and have spoken to (or more likely texted) others of their type about the place. It might be a good idea to listen. They'll usually cite Stitch as their favorite Disney character, and will mock you endlessly for being too scared to ride Expedition Everest even though it's not that you're a chicken, it's that you don't want to get thrown around and go a zillion miles-an-hour backwards first thing in the morning so just leave me alone and stop making fun of me!

The Food Guy: This person builds his touring plans around dinner reservations. He or she knows a thing or two about the finest culinary offerings at Walt Disney World, can tell you where the finest wine can be had, and knows the sous chef at Narcoossee's by name. Sure, he or she will hit the attractions, but SpectroMagic is merely a theory to The Food Guy because it steps off at the same time as the second course at the California Grill.

The Lazy Guy: Hi there. My name is Bill. Can you point me to the closest bench?

The Unprepared: These people are overwhelmed. You'll know them by their stressed expressions. And you'll see them eating at quick service for every meal. They'll ride three attractions and go home and tell everyone that Walt Disney World is overrated. The horror of fleeing Fantasmic!

at the end of the show will haunt their dreams for years to come. The will be treated for PTDSS (Post Traumatic Disney Stress Syndrome.) We won't see them again.

The Completely Reasonable Person Who Doesn't Have to Wait in a Single Line, Never Gets Tired, Never Argues with His or Her Spouse and Sees All There Is To See: This person is a myth.

The Mousejunkie: This person loves Walt Disney World. He or she is a sucker for the entire show: the music, the theatrics, the attractions, the food, and the unexpected emotions it all elicits. He or she has a few must-do things, and considers the rest a bonus. A Mousejunkie enjoys the ambiance, people-watching, and cast member interaction as much as any other part of the vacation.

Of course, a Commando can be a Mousejunkie. A Parent or Teen or Lazy Guy can be a Mousejunkie. Approach it any way you want, just enjoy yourself, be flexible, and be considerate to those around you. I can't stress that enough: everyone paid a decent amount of money to be there, everyone is (very likely) hot and tired. Take a moment to be kind to others. Trust me, it'll enhance your vacation experience.

Taking that a step further, a Mousejunkie goes out of his or her way to be patient, nice, and complimentary to Disney cast members. They work long hours for low pay to make your vacation memorable. They have to put up with inconsiderate guests on a daily basis by putting on a smile and taking the abuse. Thank them for what they do, and if you see a cast member doing something exemplary, stop at Guest Services and report their professionalism. Note the cast member's name, location, and the time. It'll only take a few minutes, and it might help someone who could use a little boost.

 TEEN MOUSEJUNKIE RYAN As a former amusement park employee, I fully agree. It gets hot and people get cranky, and the cast members still have to keep a smile on their faces and deal with it in an amazingly cheery way. It's always nice to feel appreciated by guests.

No matter where you plan to start your vacation, what you want to accomplish, or what you *think* you can accomplish, let this advice guide you: you can't do it all in one trip, so don't try. It'll just leave you frustrated and tired. Walt Disney World is, in a word, huge. It's built to accommodate massive amounts of people, and they've all got ADRs at the restaurant you're trying to get into. Disney holds attendance numbers close to the vest, but according to unofficial tallies, the Magic Kingdom has been averaging around 17 million visitors a year for the past several years. That makes it the most-visited theme park on the planet.

Walking the Walk: Zen and the Art of Not Melting Down

MOUSEJUNKIE JENNA The key to the way I tour is prioritizing attractions. Look over park info, solicit opinions of friends, and then figure out what are your absolute must-sees in each area. Remember that timed shows take longer and are harder to plan around, so try to limit the shows you see. I try to plan no more than two shows per day. Unless you're there on an extended trip or you're there at the absolute least crowded time possible, you can't see everything in one trip. If I'm there on a longer trip and visiting each park multiple times, I like to hit my must-sees on the first day in that park, then revisit my favorites and add in the attractions that were lower priorities on the return day.

MOUSEJUNKIE CAROL Perhaps my own philosophy would suit any Disney traveler. Enjoy what your body will allow you to enjoy. I have talked with many different families that have traveled to Disney. Those that said they had a horrible time felt they had to see everything and tired themselves out. Trying to accomplish that with young children creates a lot of stress. The kids get hot and tired, which in turns creates bad moods and crying. This upsets the parents as they have spent a lot of time

(Continued on next page)

in effort in creating the 'perfect' vacation and all they remember is how cranky the kids were. Does this sound fun?

I completely understand that the park passes are very expensive and that families will feel they need to get fair value for them. Let me add a little perspective to the price of a pass: The majority of the cost of a pass is in the first three days. Adding on days to the pass subsequent to those first three days is a minimal expense. Over the course of a seven day vacation, if you purchased a seven day pass and got four quality days out of the pass, you've gotten your money's worth.

Other families I talked to like to go in large groups. My very first vacation to Walt Disney World was with my family of 15 people, ranging in ages from three to 60. The first day we all tried to stay together and do things as a family. We quickly realized that the older generation did not want to go on Dumbo or see Mickey and that the younger kids did not want the adults to wait an hour to go on Splash Mountain or Big Thunder Mountain Railroad. The answer is simple. Split up! We found that by splitting up the various age groups we all got what we wanted on the vacation. We met everyday for breakfast and met every night for dinner. Other than that we were on our own. It was the best vacation I have ever gone on with the family.

MOUSEJUNKIE DEB I'm not a get-up-at-the-crack-of-dawn person. If I do get up that early, it's to go for a run, so by the time I run for an hour, return to the villa to shower, and get going we're hours behind the opening crowds. We tend to go to the parks that have Extra Magic evening hours so we don't feel rushed. I've heard there are Extra Magic morning hours, but that's just not in my vocabulary, especially on vacation.

I'm married to the Foodjunkie, I mean Food Mousejunkie, so our park touring revolves around where we're eating. If we're having breakfast at the Polynesian, we will probably spend the day at Magic Kingdom. If we're having dinner at an Epcot restaurant, we'll likely be spending our day strolling around the World Showcase.

We don't generally wait in lines longer than 20 minutes. We go during non-peak hours, take advantage of Fastpasses, and are willing to pass on something and check later.

We usually split our week up with park days and resort days, meaning hanging out at the pool, maybe shopping at Downtown Disney, doing a watercraft activity, etc. Even when not storming the parks commando-style, it's a lot of walking and a long day, so we break our week into: park 1, park 2, resort day, park 3, shopping day, etc., depending what our plans are. It's vacation!

We always try to see each of the night shows once during our trips. Even after seeing them all many times, they are so moving and provide an exclamation point to the day.

(Continued on next page)

If someone hasn't been to Walt Disney World in a while, I run down the list of all the new things since they were last there so that they can try to visit those attractions.

Biggest piece of advice: plan. It's vacation and you want to have fun, but without a plan, dining reservations, etc., you can end up wasting a lot of time trying to get around, being disappointed, and getting frustrated. That's something you can largely avoid with some planning.

Remember, you won't be able to do everything, so to try to pick out your top choices.

I do not recommend park hopping. I do it when I have an annual pass, but when I don't, I avoid it. It's an extra expense that's not necessary if you plan your days and dining, and will save you a lot of travel time. Walt Disney World is huge. A bus ride can be twenty-five minutes or longer from one destination to another, so minimizing travel time gets you more park time, more pool time, a more relaxing dining experience, or more sleep!

By the same token, I encourage you to stay on property. It may or may not cost more, but in addition to the total theming immersion and resort perks, you save travel time.

I personally think the night shows are some of the best attractions, so get a later start if that will help you stay up later to see them.

The Fastpass system saves time and will definitely get you into more attractions during the day if you use it smartly.

Also, try to check out the small things. I love Space Mountain just as much as the next person, but I also love reading the Randy Pausch tribute in front of the Mad Tea Party (see below,) looking at all the miniature scenes in the train in Germany, and checking out the celebrity busts in front of what is now the American Idol Experience.

Mousejunkie U *Randy Pausch worked as a Disney Imagineer in virtual reality research. Stricken with pancreatic cancer, Pausch gave a farewell speech at Carnegie-Mellon University known as "The Last Lecture." The speech was a deeply moving, one hour talk on "really achieving your childhood dreams." Pausch succumbed to complications from pancreatic cancer in July of 2008 at the age of 47. Since "The Last Lecture," he has become known as "the dying man who taught others how to live." His lecture was broadened and published, and the speech is widely available for viewing online.*

In 2009, Disney installed a plaque in Pausch's honor in Fantasyland near the Mad Tea Party. It reads: "Be good at something; it makes you valuable...Have something to bring to the table, because that will make you more welcome."

Pulling Back the Curtain

There are a number of specialized tours throughout the parks that provide guests with a behind-the-scenes perspective of how this massive machine works. Among them:

Keys to the Kingdom Tour: A four-and-a-half hour walking tour of the Magic Kingdom divulges some back-stage secrets and tales of Walt Disney's vision and philosophies. Lunch is provided, but regular park admission is necessary in addition to the $70 fee.

The Magic Behind Our Steam Trains: Walt Disney loved steam trains, something that is clearly evident at the Magic Kingdom park, where this tour takes place. Guests can visit the backstage roundhouse and get an intimate look at one of the trains currently in use. The tour costs $49.

Around the World at Epcot on a Segway: This two-hour experience includes a training course and a guided tour through the countries of the World Showcase atop a futuristic Segway. Park admission is not included in the $95 cost, and there is a 250-pound weight limit.

A shorter, less expensive tour called **Simply Segway** is also offered. A one-hour beginner's class, it involves indoor piloting and training for $35.

Divequest: Certified scuba divers can take a thirty-minute exploration among thousands of fish, sea turtles, stingrays, and sharks. 203 feet of visibility comes at a cost of $175. A DVD of your dive can be purchased for $35.

Behind the Seeds at Epcot: An affordable and fascinating (no, seriously) behind-the-scenes look at the Land greenhouses and laboratories. A cast member from the Epcot science team leads this interactive experience that provides a close-up look at everything from pest control to hydroponic farming to fish and alligator farming. The tour costs $16 for adults and $12 for children 3 to 9.

Backstage Safari: Ever want to touch a rhinoceros? The Backstage Safari tour at Disney's Animal Kingdom will give you the chance. This three-hour experience allows guests to observe Disney's animal care facilities, visit the animal housing areas, meet the keepers, and examine the park's veterinary hospital. No photography is permitted, and park admission is not included in this $70 tour.

 MOUSEJUNKIE AMY I loved this tour. The rhino experience, in particular, was memorable. It turns out they're very skittish so you need to be rather sensitive to that. On our tour someone moved a little too quickly for the rhino's liking, and it whirled around much faster than I ever would've imagined an animal that size could have. Our tour guide was great, I learned a lot and I'll never forget it.

Inspiration: Through Walt's Eyes: This new three-hour tour is offered on Sundays, Mondays, and Fridays at Disney's Hollywood Studios. The cast member guide shares historical and personal information about Walt Disney. The tour also provides a look at the Utilidoors at the Magic Kingdom. Park admission is not necessary to take part in this $99 tour.

Backstage Magic: This seven-hour tour spans three theme parks: Magic Kingdom, Epcot, and Disney's Hollywood Studios. All kinds of backstage secrets are revealed, including a look at the intricate American Adventure stage change system, for $224.

MOUSEJUNKIE RANDY The Backstage Magic tour is well worth the money. One of my favorite parts was visiting the Magic Kingdom shops—where everything is custom made for the parks. Every animatronic animal for every Disney park in the world is made there. We got to meet a few veteran animatronic builders who had been at Walt Disney World for thirty years. What they told us is that the job is learned through apprenticeship. It's not like you can go to school to become an animatronic builder. These guys were getting ready to retire and they had found new people who wanted to take the time to apprentice under them.

When we took the tour it was during the preproduction phase of the Pirates of the Caribbean refurb. One of the craftsmen was working on a new parrot that was going to be sitting on the top of the bridge just before the scene with the dog holding the jail cell keys. He showed how this new creation was going to have more moving parts than they had ever put into such a small animatronic.

It really peeled back the skin and showed us all the guts. It was awesome for a Disney freak like me and it also appealed to the engineer in me, as well.

The other great part of the tour is the Christmas warehouse. I've never seen so much Christmas in one place before. This is where every Christmas decoration for every Florida park and resort, and even the DVC resort up in North Carolina, is stored. They have a year-round staff of about fifty people. These people aren't the ones that actually put up the decorations. That department staffs up to about 1,500 people in October to begin getting ready for the holiday seasons. By Thanksgiving they're installing the decorations.

Every five years, every decoration gets some personal treatment or a freshening up. For that staff of fifty full-timers it's just Christmas everyday.

I'd call this tour a bargain for all the history and back-stage magic you get to experience.

Contact 407-WDW-TOUR (407-939-8687) for information about these and other specialized tours.

With a plan in place, park passes in-hand, fanny pack clipped on (and therefore a lack of shame guiding our choices), it's time to unleash these theories on Walt Disney's theme parks.

8 The Magic Kingdom

THE MAGIC KINGDOM is the original. It exudes the magic in its purest and most uncut form. It can seduce with tiny details that sneak up and whisper in your ear, and it can shake you to your core with explosive and moving examples of the fantastic. No matter how many times you visit the Magic Kingdom, it reveals new surprises tucked into cleverly hidden corners you may not have noticed previously. It is the shining, unblemished soul of Walt Disney World, and the most direct path to Walt and Roy's vision.

It's never anything less than pure perfection to be standing on the sparkling clean streets of the Magic Kingdom first thing in the morning. Or to be enveloped in ethereal music wafting from hidden speakers and bathed in the early morning Florida sun.

MOUSEJUNKIE RANDY First thing in the morning the streets are still damp from the steam washing from the night before. A slight morning chill is in the air as the Orlando sun has only been up for about an hour and is still climbing into the sky. Cast members from the Main Street stores

> beckon early morning guests with waves of their Mickey glove-clad hands. It seems as if it's too perfect and can't be real, but it is. And for me, a fellow Mousejunkie, there isn't a better way to start any day.

Every Walt Disney World vacation has to start at the Magic Kingdom.

There are essentially two ways to approach this park:

1. At a leisurely pace, enjoying the details.
2. Go! Go! Go! Go! Eat! Go! Go! Blister! Spend! Argue! Collapse.

First timers are often tempted to take the latter approach. Don't. Now might be a good time for a reading from the Book of Mousejunkies—Bill, verses 19:28

"And a good man shall take his family from this place to another place. And that place shall have sustenance and shelter. And roller coasters. And yet the man will remain vexed for his wife wished to complete every task before returning from whence they had come. The children gnashed their teeth and repeatedly requested gift items and corn of the field, which had been popped.

And Mousejunkie Randy spake unto the good man: "Slow thy pace. For rushing about causes anguish to all. He bade the man lie down with his wife in his moderately priced resort for a nap and allow his children to swim in the pool. For it was wicked awesome."

I'll translate: If you try to do it all, you're going to be tired, broke and you're not going to notice all the details that make the place so special.

The Magic Kingdom sits on 142 acres and is divided into several themed lands: Adventureland; Frontierland; Liberty Square; Fantasyland; and Tomorrowland. Unofficial sections include Get Me Out of This Insane Heat Before I Pass Outland, If That Kid Kicks Me Again I'm Going to Screamland, and I'm Not Waiting In One More Lineland.

The Mousejunkies can help with each of these themed lands.

MOUSEJUNKIE RANDY: My park touring philosophy is this: just keep walking.

I like to go with the flow and try to pass the crowds. The parks are designed like a wheel with spokes. So I pick either a clockwise or counter-clockwise direction and begin. If I get to a ride that has a Fastpass and I really want to make sure I don't miss it, I'll grab a Fastpass.

If it's not a 'I have to do this as soon as possible,' ride just keep walking.

If you continue on with this method, you will eventually get ahead of the crowd. Some might say this approach is touring the park like a newbie. And you might be right in some respects. But where this plan has an advantage over a newbie touring, is that newbies stop at every attraction, wait in the standby line, and then move on to the next one. Since a great number of park visitors are first timers, this plan lets you get ahead of the wave. Just keep walking.

This is also a very relaxed way to tour the park, since you are really not putting any expectations on the next ride or attraction. You should also take advantage of this relaxed, low-pressure pace and just look around as you walk. Most people are attraction obsessed. If you move away from that approach, you'll begin to notice all the little details that Disney has put in the areas away from rides and attractions. These are the little things that make Disney so much more than just another theme park.

Above all, slow down and just enjoy. Enjoy the park, enjoy the rides, enjoy the time you are spending with your family and friends, enjoy watching all the crazy people driving their families around the park like they're leading a cattle drive. Just have fun.

The Straight Dope *If you or someone you are traveling with is celebrating a birthday, stop at City Hall and get a birthday button from guest relations. You'll be greeted by dozens of guests and cast members by name throughout the day, and sometimes it will result in some extra magic.*

A Few General Touring Tips

Fastpasses can be a great timesaver, and certainly result in less time spent standing in line, but it can also mean criss-crossing the park in an inefficient manner just to hit designated Fastpass return times. You have to weigh line standby times against your touring plans, but it can be a lifesaver on a busy day.

Here's a list of attractions where Fastpass is available in the Magic Kingdom:

➤ Big Thunder Mountain Railroad
➤ Jungle Cruise
➤ Peter Pan's Flight
➤ Splash Mountain
➤ Buzz Lightyear's Space Ranger Spin
➤ Mickey's PhilharMagic
➤ Space Mountain
➤ The Many Adventures of Winnie the Pooh
➤ Stitch's Great Escape! (yeah, I don't get it either.)

It All Starts with Main Street U.S.A.

Inspired by Main Street in the town of Marceline, Missouri, where Walt spent part of his boyhood. It's typically buzzing with activity first thing in the morning. The sun is peaking over the rooftops and bathing Cinderella Castle in its very own spotlight, cast members are greeting guests and the park is just coming alive.

Take a moment and look up. Many of the second floor windows along Main Street have names painted on them, which serve as credits for a number of the Imagineers, animators and pioneers who contributed their skills and abilities to the Walt Disney Company. The names appear as part of fictional businesses and quite often refer to a hobby or interest relating to the job or contribution they made to the Walt Disney Company.

Walt Disney's window—the only one facing Cinderella Castle—is located above the ice cream parlor at the end of Main Street. (His name also appears above the Main Street train station and on the Casting Agency door.)

Roy O. Disney's window is on the southeast corner of Main Street: "If We Can Dream It We Can Do It!"—Dreamers & Doers—Roy O. Disney, Chairman."

Mousejunkie U *Roy gets another mention on a Main Street window: "Pseudonym Real Estate Development Company—Roy Davis—President, Bob Price—Vice President, Robert Foster—Travelling Representative." Roy Davis was the pseudonym he used while buying property during the initial phases of Walt Disney World's construction.*

Construction throughout the park utilizes forced perspective to create the illusion of height and size, and it's put to good use in particular on Main Street U.S.A. While the ground-level buildings are normal sized, the second-and-third story levels are progressively smaller. The effect helps complete the illusion of an idealized American thoroughfare from the early part of the 1900s.

The Magic Kingdom was constructed as a two-story structure. When you're standing on Main Street U.S.A., you're actually on the second floor of the park. Nearly a mile and a half of tunnels called "Utilidoors," run below on

TEEN MOUSEJUNKIE RYAN   What kind of teenager doesn't like to shop? Oh, right—boys. The Main Street U.S.A. area has a bunch of really cool shops including the Chapeau Hat Shoppe (Go on, try on some crazy hats!) and the Emporium, which is the biggest souvenir shop...like...ever.

the real ground-floor of the park, allowing cast members to move about without breaking the illusion on-stage, above.

⭐ **The Straight Dope**   *For a look at the Utilidoors in action, take the Keys to the Kingdom tour. ($70 per person)*

Many guides urge guests not to get sidetracked by the shops and characters on Main Street U.S.A. first thing in the morning. I couldn't disagree more. While I don't recommend camping out on a curb for an hour, one of our family traditions is to grab breakfast at the Main Street Bakery. I get a chocolate croissant, and I have no idea what anyone else gets because I'm pretty much delirious with joy at that point. I'm on Main Street U.S.A. with caffeine entering my system, and a light and fluffy croissant dusted with powdered sugar in front of me.

Of course, after the coffee and croissant are gone, my eyes are drawn to the throngs of people moving by the front window of the bakery.

That's when my sense of urgency starts to set in.

Once properly fed and caffeinated, it's time to head for Cinderella Castle.

There's an oft-repeated belief that the Magic Kingdom is constructed in much the way a movie might be presented. The red bricks outside the main gate act as a metaphor for the red carpet. The Main Street train station is the curtain, behind which are posters of coming attractions. The windows along Main Street are the opening credits, and Cinderella Castle represents the start of the movie.

Mousejunkie U *Don't confuse your superlatives: Disneyland is the "Happiest Place on Earth." The Magic Kingdom at Walt Disney World is "The Most Magical Place on Earth."*

Cinderella Castle: This majestic icon of the Magic Kingdom stands 189 feet high with eighteen towers reaching skyward over a moat that holds more than three million gallons of water. But Cinderella Castle is more than an eye-catching structure. It captures the hearts of millions of people every year. It is the gateway to the fantastic world that lies behind and around it, silently watching over Walt and Roy Disney's finest work. Cinderella Castle grabs hold of the imagination of anyone who approaches it and creates dreams. It is the beating heart of Walt Disney World made real in a regal, breathtaking structure built of wonder and magic.

Five mosaics located inside the castle breezeway guide guests through the story of Cinderella. Created by Imagineer Dorothea Redmond and artist Hanns-Joachim Scharff, each mosaic is fifteen feet high and ten feet wide.

⭐ **Mousejunkie U** *Hanns Scharff, one of the peo-*
ple credited with creating the mosaic telling the story of
Cinderella, was a German Luftwaffe interrogator during
World War II. He was renowned and respected for his tech-
niques, which eschewed physical contact, abuse of, or even
raising his voice in the presence of captured prisoners. He
also helped shape U.S. interrogation techniques following the
end of the war. After the war he moved to the United States,
spending the rest of his life working in his medium of choice:
mosaic.

Walk a little further and you'll come across the new
Bibbidi Bobbidi Boutique, a beauty parlor specializing in
making kids over into glamorous princesses or "cool dudes."

A quick aside: The little princesses and mini pop starlets
running around in their dresses, makeup, and hair are ador-
able. And I know Disney is trying to market to younger boys.
But "cool dude," Disney? Seriously?

Fantasyland

A few steps further and guests find themselves in
Fantasyland proper. An idealized world of the playful and
fanciful, Fantasyland offers attractions ideally suited for the
younger set, but also perfect for adults willing to
drop their inhibitions and return to a more inno-
cent time.

It's also boasts the highest concentra-
tion of strollers anywhere on the planet. The
bottleneck between Mickey's Philharmagic

and Pinnochio's Village Haus is nearly impassable on busy days. What's the best way to avoid this sticky congestion? Get through Fantasyland, especially Peter Pan/Small World row, as early as possible. I wouldn't wait in a long line for any of the attractions in Fantasyland if it isn't necessary. And it isn't.

Fantasyland is also set to become the benefactor of the largest expansion in Magic Kingdom history. Concept drawings outline new castle walls, multiple new structures and a new circus-themed area. By 2013, Disney plans to have completed the following:

➤ Guests will be able to visit their favorite Disney princess in her own castle, cottage, or chateau to share a dance with Cinderella, celebrate Sleeping Beauty's birthday, or join Belle in a story performance in the Beast's castle library. (Speculation is that this will replace Story Time with Belle at the Fairytale Garden.)

➤ Dine in one of three enchanted rooms inside the Beast's castle.

➤ Fly with Dumbo above brand new circus grounds, twice the size of the existing attraction with a new interactive, three-ring circus tent.

➤ Journey under the sea with the Little Mermaid, in her very own attraction, identical to the one at Disney's California Adventure in Anaheim.

➤ Meet Tinker Bell and her friends in the magical world of Pixie Hollow.

As the expansion gets underway, attractions adjacent to The Many Adventures of Winnie the Pooh will fall behind the construction wall. This includes Mickey's Toontown Fair, a necessary sacrifice for the new attractions to come.

Here's a look at the attractions found in Fantasyland:

Mickey's PhilharMagic—Donald is actually the star of this impressive 3-D film, which blends classic Disney music, films, characters, and a few unexpected tactile surprises. It all plays out across a 150-foot-wide canvas, one of the largest seamless screens created for such a purpose. Fastpass is available for this attraction, but normally only becomes necessary on very busy days.

Duration: Twelve minutes

Loads: Quickly. The theater empties out, and the next group of guests steps inside.

Prince Charming's Regal Carrousel—This recently re-named carrousel features seventy-two meticulously hand-painted, hard-maple horses spinning under eighteen Cinderella-themed canopy scenes, all around an antique band organ playing Disney favorites.

Duration: Two minutes

Loads: It's slow-loading, but it's a classic in the shadow of Cinderella Castle. It's certainly worth a few minutes of your time, but I'd keep walking if the standby is longer than 20 minutes.

★ **Mousejunkie U**   *Built in 1917, this Fantasyland staple began its life in Detroit. It spent thirty-nine years at Olympic*

MOUSEJUNKIE RANDY Every horse on the carousel has a plastic duplicate. These duplicates are used on the carousel when the real wooden ones are being refurbished. One artist's full time job is to repaint every horse, by hand, one at a time throughout the year. Next time you ride the carousel, see if you can find one of the stand-in horses.

Park in Maplewood, New Jersey. before Disney bought it in 1967 and refurbished it in time for the Magic Kingdom's opening.

Dumbo the Flying Elephant—A pack of sixteen flying pachyderms take guests on a spin around, well, nothing. The staggering popularity of this simple attraction has prompted Disney's Imagineers to create two of these as part of the planned Fantasyland expansion.

Duration: One minute

Loads: Very slowly, so if you plan on taking Dumbo for a spin, get there early or slather on the sunscreen.

It's a Small World—The "happiest cruise that ever sailed the seven seas" takes guests on a tour through different lands populated by 472 dolls who drill that familiar song into your subconscious with "the happiest jackhammer that ever cracked a subconscious."

Duration: Eleven minutes (though for some, seems like three hours.)

Loads: Quickly. You rarely stand still while waiting in line for Small World. It might take a few minutes, but you'll be moving.

Go ahead, mock me, but I never miss this attraction. The whimsical feel and the refurbished Mary Blair design combined with the maddeningly repetitive yet classic song by Robert B. and Richard M. Sherman make this an old-school favorite. I love Small World and I don't care who knows it. Except for maybe Jason Statham. I can only guess that he'd neck-kick me if I mentioned it.

Mousejunkie U *The song that launched a million boat rides is sung in five languages through the attraction: English, Spanish, Japanese, Swedish and Italian.*

Mad Tea Party—If Small World launched a million happy cruises, then the Mad Tea Party launched a million lunches. Giant teacups whirl guests around at a breakneck pace. The chaotic trip around a giant teacup is set to appropriately fast-paced music, resulting in a heaping cup of dizzy for anyone dunked in the oversized china.

Duration: Two minutes

Loads: Medium.

TEEN MOUSEJUNKIE RYAN Spin until you puke during your very own un-birthday party at the Mad Tea Party. Actually, speaking as a former ride operator for a New Hampshire amusement park, please don't puke on the ride. It's disgusting, and no one wants to clean that up. But really, whether you're obsessed with Alice, like me, or you just want to spin around for a few minutes, Mad Tea Party is a blast.

Mousejunkie U *The teacups at the Mad Tea Party can hold 144 gallons of tea.*

The Many Adventures of Winnie the Pooh—Oversized honey pots take guests for a ride through the Hundred Acre Wood in this Fantasyland dark ride. It's amazing how something geared toward youngsters can even affect adults. If Pooh was ever a part of your youth, this attraction will transport you right back to that time. Fastpasses are available for this attraction.

Duration: Five minutes

Loads: Medium. If your young one has his or her heart set on this attraction and the lines are long, which they certainly can be, grab a Fastpass.

Mousejunkie U *This attraction, which opened in 1999 on the spot of the old Mr. Toad's Wild Ride, offers a nod to its former landlord. Just as you go through the first set of doors inside the ride, look back and to your left to see a painting of Mr. Toad handing the deed over to Owl.*

When we first took our then three-year-old to Walt Disney World for the first time, we thought this light-hearted romp through A.A. Milne's world would be perfect for her. No way. Seconds into the attraction she was terrified. From her toddler's point of view, we were heading into a dark tunnel where there was thunder and where Pooh's soul flips up out of his body and floats away. The Heffalumps and Woozles didn't help, either. It took her years to get over what became an irrational fear of the cuddly bear. Now it's her favorite. Go figure.

Peter Pan's Flight—Board your pirate ship and take flight out of the Darling's bedroom, over old London, through Captain Hook's grasp, and into Neverland. Fastpass is available for this attraction.

Duration: Three minutes

Loads: Forget it, just get a Fastpass. The line for this attraction builds very quickly, stretching around the corner and down toward the Columbia Harbor House. It loads deceivingly slowly. However, if you happen to wander by and the standby line is short, jump right in.

Snow White's Scary Adventures—This dark ride guides guests through the classic 1937 film, where they encounter all the characters from the groundbreaking movie, including the Seven Dwarves and Snow White herself.

Duration: Three minutes

Loads: Fairly slowly. However, this attraction is often skipped for newer, sexier options. More often than not, unless the park is jammed, the standby lines for Snow White's Scary Adventures are fairly reasonable.

By now you've worked your way through Fantasyland and you're staring straight down the barrel of the future: Tomorrowland. Or, more accurately, an idealized, fairly schizophrenic—but still eminently seductive—version of the future.

Schizophrenic, you say? Sure. Buzz Lightyear's Space Ranger Spin fits perfectly. Carousel of Progress? That's a stretch. The Indy Speedway? It doesn't exactly scream "future!" to me. Still, Tomorrowland, which was given a complete makeover in 1994 when Disney's Imagineers opted to avoid trying to keep up with ever-changing visions of the future, is home to some of the best-loved attractions in the Magic Kingdom.

Here's a look at the attractions located in Tomorrowland:

Stitch's Great Escape!—You can't see me right now, but I'm crossing my arms and shaking my head. I have a very disapproving look on my face. I'm making that "tsk, tsk" sound that people make when they're disappointed. And now I'm banging my head on my desk.

I'm not going to go any further than that because the head/desk thing kind of hurts and this attraction just isn't worth it.

Set before the events of "Lilo and Stitch," the show focuses on Experiment 626 (Stitch) and his attempts to slip The Man at the Galactic Federation Prisoner Teleport Center.

If your group is in a hurry, if you're claustrophobic, if you have children in your party that might get uncomfortable in the dark, or if you don't like mediocre attractions, consider dropping Stitch's Great Escape from your touring plans. It's consistently panned by guests and ranks lower than most other attractions in its general vicinity. It's a retrofit of the Extra-TERRORestrial Alien Encounter attraction, and retains much of what made that too frightening for children: It's dark, loud, and you're strapped into a seat and can't move.

Duration: Fifteen minutes.

Loads: Quickly. This theater-in-the-round show ends, empties out, and a new batch of people who haven't read this book enter.

Buzz Lightyear's Space Ranger Spin—Join Buzz Lightyear's forces to defend the earth against evil Emperor Zurg. The attraction is essentially a dark ride with some really fun extras—primarily a functioning "laser gun" with which guests shoot at targets. Bulls-eyes trigger movement and audio cues, and participants can even keep score. (I'm not going to say trash-talking is one of the finer points of this attraction, I'll just say that Mousejunkie Amy has yet to best her spouse. But if I keep bringing it up, it's "To the couch! And beyond!") Fastpass is available for this attraction.

Duration: Six minutes

Loads: Medium. The line can get quite long, but since the ride vehicles are constantly loading guests, things tend to move along.

The Straight Dope *To boost your score on Buzz Lightyear's Space Ranger Spin, shoot for smaller, far away targets and anything that moves. Specifically, aim for the back of the robot's left wrist in the first room for a 100,000-point bonus. Target Zurg when you arrive at Planet Z and hit the bottom of his space scooter for another 100,000 points. Also, the volcano at the top of the Zurg room is worth big points.*

Astro Orbiter—Think of this attraction as Dumbo, only higher up. Guests take an elevator up to the boarding area where they pilot their own rockets and spin in circles. That might not sound too gripping, but the Astro Orbiter provides some great views at night and can be visually striking. (Mainly from the ground.)

Duration: Two minutes

Loads: Slowly

Ask most Mousejunkies about the Astro Orbiter and the answer will approximate something along the lines of, "Eh."

Walt Disney's Carousel of Progress—Disney boasts that this musical/comedy stage show "has been seen by more guests than any other theatrical presentation in the history of American Theater since its debut at the 1964 World's Fair."

A showcase for Disney's audio animatronics, the Carousel of Progress follows a family through the years as technology shapes their lives. Guests sit in a dark, cool theater that rotates around the stage, changing scenes and bringing them up-to-date.

Duration: Twenty-two minutes

Loads: Quickly. The theater opens as soon as the previous group has rotated to the next scene in the production.

Call me corny, but I can't miss this attraction. It has Walt Disney's fingerprints all over it. It's classic, and it has that intangible magic that makes the Magic Kingdom so special. It's also relaxing, and who can argue against sitting in a dark, air conditioned theater for a few minutes on a hot day?

Mousejunkie U *The voice cast of Carousel of Progress is quite notable. Jean Shepherd, author and narrator of A Christmas Story, stars as the father, John; his daughter, Patricia, is portrayed by Debi Derryberry, who is primarily known as the voice of Jimmy Neutron on the hit Nickelodeon animated series; the family's grandmother—the video game whiz—is voiced by Janet Waldo, who voiced many cartoon characters including Judy Jetson from The Jetsons and Josie in 'Josie and the Pussycats; finally the great Mel Blanc—Bugs Bunny, Porky Pig, and dozens of other—is the grumpy cousin Orville.*

The Monsters Inc. Laugh Floor—An interactive show based on the Pixar film, guests file into a theater where they watch a standup comedy routine hosted by Mike Wazowski. Several screens placed around the theater show audience members as they interact with the characters on stage. During the show, a camera focuses on someone, usually an adult male audience member, who theretofore is known as "that guy." He becomes the butt of the good-natured jokes for the rest of the show. Yes, I have been "that guy."

 MOUSEJUNKIE AMY   It was funny, because Bill doesn't like to draw attention to himself in any way, but when he was singled out as 'That Guy,' he went with it. He was smiling and waving, and then later in the day people would approach us and say, "Hey, you were That Guy!"

Duration: Fifteen minutes

Loads: Medium. The theater empties out and a new group of guests files in.

During the pre-show, guests are given the opportunity to text jokes for possible use at the end of the show. Shockingly, they've never used my favorite joke. I text it in every time and must deal with crushing rejection on every occasion so far. Experience the genius for yourself:

> Q: "How many surrealists does it take to change a lightbulb?"
> A: "A fish!"

I'm telling you, they're missing out on comedy gold.

Space Mountain—When this classic coaster debuted in 1975, twenty-eight miles per hour may have seemed blindingly fast. Decades later, it still does. Space Mountain still delivers one of the best thrills in all of Walt Disney World.

Sure, it's not as smooth as the Rock'n'Roller Coaster, or as visceral as Expedition Everest, but since it takes place completely in the dark it's got the unknown factor going for it. Dips, turns, and drops fling you around with little-to-no warning. Fastpass is available for this attraction.

Duration: Three minutes

Loads: Slowly. The standby lines tend to build up rather quickly, so Fastpass may be your best option.

Tomorrowland Indy Speedway—Strap yourself into one of these machines and feel the thunder under the hood rattle your teeth. Or, more precisely, feel the lawn mower sized engine buzz contently at about 7.5 miles per hour as you leisurely tour this 0.4 mile track.

Duration: Five minutes

Loads: Slowly, and in the open. Bring sunscreen. I got fairly singed one late morning as we slowly shuffled up the ramp, across the track, and back down to the loading area.

Tomorrowland Transit Authority PeopleMover—A train of five cars using linear induction motors carts guests on a smooth ride through the upper levels of Tomorrowland.

Duration: Ten minutes

Loads: Quickly

As the designated "lazy traveler" in our group, I love the Tomorrowland Transit Authority. It gets you off your feet a bit, it lets you cool down, it provides some great people watching from above, and you get a great view of Cinderella Castle as you pass by the outer edges of Tomorrowland.

Cut back across the Castle Hub and across the wooden bridge to find yourself in Liberty Square.

The cobblestone streets and colonial architecture bring guests back two hundred years. But don't get too comfortable, there are a few minor frights ready to take you by surprise.

Here's a look at the attractions in and around Liberty Square:

The Haunted Mansion—More giggle than scream, guests tip-toe their way through the stretching room where they "drag their bodies to the dead-center of the room" and then move on to their Doom Buggies for a tour through the home to 999 Happy Haunts.

Mousejunkie U *The voice of Paul Frees (Boris Badenov from the Bullwinkle show) is the "Ghost Host" of the Haunted Mansion.*

Duration: Nine minutes

Loads: Medium. Even when the line twists back and forth in front of the mansion façade, it normally keeps moving. The queue is also covered, and once you get close enough to see the front doors you can spend time checking out the cemetery.

Mousejunkie U   *There are five singing busts in the graveyard scene. Despite popular urban legend, Walt Disney is not among them. The farthest one to the left, however, is Thurl Ravenscroft, the soloist on "Grim Grinning Ghosts." (He's was also the voice of Tony the Tiger.)*

Hall of Presidents—Every U.S. president who has ever served is represented in audio animatronic form in this classic Magic Kingdom attraction. A combination film, narrative and truly impressive audio animatronic presentation, it's hard to leave without feeling just a little more patriotic. A refurb has made the show more moving, more informative, and better on every level.

What's new?

➤ Since the 2009 relaunch of the attraction, Abraham Lincoln now recites the Gettysburg address with the original Royal Dano recording directed by Walt for President Lincoln's World's Fair debut.

➤ Barack Obama is one of three presidents programmed to speak in the updated show. The first contemporary president to speak in the show was Bill Clinton. George W. Bush recorded a segment eight years later.

➤ In the new update, George Washington speaks for the first time. He explains the importance of the presidential oath of office and uses portions of a speech he actually gave during his second inauguration.

Duration: Twenty-five minutes.

Loads: Quickly. The theater holds 700 people, and empties out every 25 minutes. No rush to get near the doors, the view is good from anywhere in the theater. Just get inside ten minutes before show time and you'll be all set.

Liberty Square Riverboat—Get on board this steam-powered sternwheeler for a relaxing tour of the Rivers of America. The Liberty Belle takes guests on a half-mile trip around Tom Sawyer Island. Grab a spot along the second-level rail and watch Walt Disney World go by from aboard a steamboat.

Duration: Fifteen minutes

Loads: Quickly

Continue down past the Liberty Tree Tavern and the outlandishly huge turkey leg stand and you'll find yourself in Frontierland.

Here's a look at the attractions located in Frontierland:

Country Bear Jamboree—eighteen audio animatronic bears—and a few other musically-inclined animals—serenade you with an odd collection of funny tunes in Grizzly Hall. Corny? Yes. But it's fun if you've got kids in tow. Big Al is reason enough for me to visit again.

Here's a list of the Bears' greatest hits:

➤ "My Woman Ain't Pretty, but She Don't Swear"
➤ "Mama, Don't Whip Little Buford"

➤ "Tears Will Be the Chaser for My Wine"
➤ "All the Guys That Turn Me On Turn Me Down"
➤ "Blood on the Saddle"
➤ "The Ballad of Davy Crockett"

Duration: Fifteen minutes

Loads: Quickly. This is a typical theater-type load-in. As soon as the show is over, the theater is empty and ready for the next group.

⭐ **The Straight Dope**   *If you attempt to shoehorn yourself into Grizzly Hall just after the 3 P.M. parade, you might find it quite crowded. The parade ends, leaving thousands of guests standing in front of the Country Bear Jamboree looking for the closest attraction. Wait until later in the day for a much more relaxed experience.*

Frontierland Shootin' Arcade—Take a few pot-shots at harmless targets with these light-activated firearms. At twenty-five cents a round it's inexpensive and mildly entertaining, but I played this exact shooting range at Hampton Beach, New Hampshire as a teen. It feels like a cheap, prepackaged attraction you can find anywhere.

Splash Mountain—Now we're talking. Splash Mountain is one of the biggies at the Magic Kingdom—quite literally. The eighty-seven-foot structure towers over Frontierland, daring guests to take a trip into the bayou. Based on *Song of the South*, the Disney film no one talks about, Splash Mountain is a tour through the forests and swamps of Brer Rabbit and friends. It ends with a five-story log flume drop that delivers thrills every time. Fastpass is available for this attraction.

Duration: Ten minutes

Loads: Moderately fast. The queue is capable of handling a massive amount of guests, but standby times aren't normally unbearable, except during the busiest times. In that case, a Fastpass would be the only way.

Mousejunkie U *A Florida State University graduate who worked on Splash Mountain left his mark on the attraction. Just before your log starts the long climb up Chickapin Hill, a small rodent pokes his head out from the ceiling and exclaims, "FSU!"*

Tom Sawyer Island—Run through caves, trails, and hills and explore Fort Langhorn on this island in the middle of the Rivers of America. A playground accessible by raft, there are endless opportunities to relive the days of Tom Sawyer.

The Straight Dope *Try this scavenger hunt: Disney cast members hide between one and five paintbrushes around Tom Sawyer Island every day. If you find one, return it to a cast member for an instant Fastpass to either Splash Mountain or the Big Thunder Mountain Railroad.*

Walt Disney World Railroad—Walt Disney loved steam trains. And his infatuation carried over into his theme parks.

Board one of the Magic Kingdom's authentic steam trains and take a loop around the park. The trains stop at Main Street U.S.A. and Frontierland. When Mickey's Toontown was a bustling borough of the Kingdom, the trains also stopped there. But with the massive construction now underway, Toontown—and its whistle stop—live on only in vacation photos and memories.

Taking a few loops around the Magic Kingdom is a great way to get a quick rest, and if you find yourself near Splash Mountain with a burning need to be at the front of the park, Disney's steam trains are an alternate to hoofing it. It takes about 15 minutes to travel the entire route.

MOUSEJUNKIE RANDY Head to the last train car. If you or your child is lucky, you will get to call the "All Aboard" and get a card as an honorary conductor.

Mousejunkie U *There are four locomotives in the Magic Kingdo—the Roger E. Broggie (an Imagineer and fellow train enthusiast), the Lilly Belle (named for Walt's wife,) the Roy O. Disney, and of course, the Walter E. Disney.*

Big Thunder Mountain Railroad—One of three "mountains" in the Magic Kingdom range, the Big Thunder Mountain Railroad is a roller coaster that takes guests on an out-of-control train ride through the old west. Falling rocks, dry river beds, and an assortment of audio animatronic figures color the red rock caverns that whip by. Fastpass is available for this attraction.

⭐ **Mousejunkie U** *According to the legend of Big Thunder Mountain Railroad, a "rainmaker" was brought to the town of Tumbleweed to break a devastating drought. The audio animatronic snake-oil salesman has a name: Professor Cumulus Isobar. Look for him bailing water out of the back of his wagon.*

Duration: Three minutes

Loads: Medium. This popular attraction can get bogged down in long lines early in the day. Fastpass is the way to go if you want to venture into the Big Thunder Mining Co.

As coasters go, this one is mild. I'm a big chicken when it comes to thrill rides, and this one is just fast enough to give me a slight bump in blood pressure. It's more hairpin turns and jumping over hills than heights or inversions.

⭐ **The Straight Dope** *For a faster feel and a little more tossing and shaking, sit in the caboose.*

There is one final, unexplored land that awaits guests. It is perhaps the most exotically themed, and holds some of the most classic and best-loved attractions.

Here's a look at the attractions in Adventureland:

Enchanted Tiki Room Under New Management—The original characters from the Enchanted Tiki Room are here. It's just that they barely get going before Zazu and Iago (the new management) burst in to take over the show. Three hundred-fourteen figures groove through this musical. While Zazu and Iago may have brought new blood to the attraction, they're version just doesn't have the catchy melody of the original.

Duration: Ten minutes.

Loads: Quickly.

⭐ **The Straight Dope**   *A few of the theatrical lights are pointed into the audience from above, and are absolutely blinding if you're sitting in the wrong spot. Keep one eye on the ceiling as you choose your seat.*

Jungle Cruise—A stand-up comedy routine disguised as a cruise down the Nile, the Amazon, the Congo, and the Mekong rivers is led by some of the best cast members at Walt Disney World. As guests cast off into the jungle, a world of animatronic beasts await around every corner. The skipper keeps things lively, showering adventurers with some incredibly bad (great) jokes and puns throughout the attraction. If it wasn't for these quick-witted, pith-helmeted cast members, the dated look of the animatronics might detract from this now classic attraction. Fastpass is available at this attraction.

Duration: Ten minutes

Loads: Slowly

Magic Carpets of Aladdin—The third iteration of the Dumbo ride in the park, the Magic Carpets of Aladdin lets guests board their own flying carpet and soar over Adventureland, which is great as long as you don't mind going in a circle. This hub-and-spoke ride works essentially the same as Dumbo and the Astro Orbiters. The ride vehicles can be controlled by the rider, tipping it forward or back, and making it rise and dip.

Duration: Ninety seconds.

Loads: Moderate to slowly.

Pirates of the Caribbean—Johnny Depp's Captain Jack Sparrow has infused new life into this well-loved attraction. Guests board small boats and are plunged in the midst of a chaotic scene where a coastal town is being pillaged by a motley crew of scurvy swashbucklers.

An update added Captain Jack, a creepy Davy Jones, and Jack's nemesis Barbossa to the show.

Duration: Nine minutes

Loads: Medium to slowly, but don't let that dissuade you from getting in line. This queue is among the best in all of Walt Disney World. Walk through the caves, look through prison bars, examine cannon and rifles and soak up the exquisite theming. Believe it or not, this line is half the fun.

Mousejunkie U   *One hundred-twenty-five audio animatronics figures harass and entertain guests—sixty-five pirates and townspeople and sixty animals and birds.*

TEEN MOUSEJUNKIE RYAN You can't miss Pirates of the Caribbean. There's just something incredibly exciting about sitting in a boat, listening to pirates sing, and trying to be the first to spot Captain Jack Sparrow.

Mousejunkie U *According to cast members who work at Pirates of the Caribbean, there's an oft-repeated legend centering on a ghost named George. The "George" in this tale worked on the attraction and somehow died inside. Each night cast members must say "Goodnight George" before leaving. If this routine is forgotten or ignored, the ride experiences shutdowns and emergency stops the next morning.*

MOUSEJUNKIE RANDY One December 30th evening, Carol and I were about to board Pirates of the Caribbean, only to notice some strange looking plain-clothes security people appear. It's not uncommon during the Holiday for celebrities to be about the parks, so I wondered "Which Hollywood type would need all this security?"

We boarded our boat and survived our trip to the Caribbean. When we were unloading there was additional plain clothes security, so whoever it was must be somewhere on the ride.

We headed up to the gift shop and Carol and I put on a couple of those new Jack Sparrow hats that have the dreadlocks hanging down. We look up and standing right in front of us is President Jimmy Carter and his wife. In my pirates hat I gave him a hearty "Hello President Carter." He gave me an odd look and said, "Well, hello." You never know who you will run into at Walt Disney World.

Swiss Family Treehouse—Climb through the treetop home of the Swiss Family Robinson. You remember them, don't you? The movie is only fifty years old. Get your butt up into the tree. The home of the aforementioned shipwrecked family is recreated faithfully. Explore at your own pace. Full disclosure: My pace is usually set by the bench outside the attraction's entrance.

 TEEN MOUSEJUNKIE RYAN Everyone has their own likes, dislikes and ways of approaching the Magic Kingdom. I have a pretty simple "teen-centric" approach:

All of the Magic Kingdom Mountains are a must-ride, so don't you dare pass Splash Mountain. The lines might be super long, but it is definitely worth it. Just make sure you keep your eyes open as you hurtle towards the briar patch! (That's where the camera is, and that's where you have a great opportunity to ham it up for the souvenir picture.) Oh, and yes, you will get wet.

While we're on mountains, I once rode Big Thunder Mountain seven times in a row during one of the night-

(Continued on next page)

time parades. 'Twas quite an experience. An awesome experience.

The Haunted Mansion just might be one of my favorite rides in the Magic Kingdom. Being completely obsessed with Halloween might have something to do with that, but even if you're not one for fright night and terror, you will love this ride. From the moment you take your seat in the Doom Buggy and avoid the eyes of the wonderfully creepy hosts patrolling the queue, awesomeness ensues. Whether you choose to shriek at the top of your lungs simply to scare the people behind you, sing along with the busts, or chat with the ghosts riding with you, The Haunted Mansion is a fun, perhaps slightly creepy, but mostly just really cool ride in the dark. Don't forget to look for the hidden Mickeys. Can you find them amidst the waltzing deadies?

That never-ending tune might drive you 'round the bend, absolutely bonkers, and completely mad, (I'll tell you what, all the best people are) but you simply cannot skip out on It's a Small World. It's tradition. You have to stand in line for at least forty-five minutes, wave to the ride operator, then take that everlasting boat-ride through every country imaginable, and finally end up in Dolly Heaven where everyone can live happily together and sing their favorite song for the rest of eternity. Trust me, it just isn't a Disney trip if you don't ride It's a Small World. Of the Mountains, Space is definitely my favorite.

Maybe I just like the dark, but something about zoom-ing along an unseen track is exciting to me. The neon lights definitely help set the mood for the out-of-this-world ride, but take it from me, if your eyes start to adjust to the dark, shut 'em. Space Mountain is way more thrilling if you can't see where you're going. That, or just ride with Mousejunkie Randy, who will shout out each turn before it happens, until he decides he has your trust, and then he'll shout the wrong direction, causing your stomach to lurch, your heart to stop, and your brain to spin.

As far as entertainment goes, any of the parades or fireworks shows are worth stopping to watch. Though if you've seen the parades before, or just don't feel like standing in the crowd listening to the same song play over and over, definitely use that time to go ride some of the rides that usually have intense lines. The rest of the park will be virtually empty during the nighttime parades and fireworks, and it's a great chance to catch up on things you missed earlier. Do me a favor though, don't miss Wishes (fireworks) or the Boo To You Halloween parade during Mickey's Not So Scary Halloween Party. Which, I suppose, brings me to the MNSSHP. It's awesome, and you should do it at least once. You get to dress up in a Halloween costume, go trick-or-treating in the Magic Kingdom, and watch an awesome parade and some great fireworks. It's after the park closes, so the lines aren't nearly as horrific as during the day, and it's a lot of fun. The headless horseman leads the parade, and last time, Captain Barbossa stopped to chat with me because I was dressed like a pirate. Good times, good times.

Also, don't forget: you're never too old to visit your favorite princess or character. It's just not Disney until

(Continued on next page)

I get a hug from Mickey, and I met Jasmine three times during my last trip. You don't have to do the autograph book thing if you don't want, but at least go pose for a picture. You won't regret it.

I tend to whine about the heat and humidity in central Florida any chance I get. ("Bill is hot at 60. Deb is cold at 90."—Mousejunkie Walt, copyright 2010) When things get particularly oppressive, there are places to duck into that will provide some much-needed rest, cooler temps and an inconspicuous place to maybe catch a quick nap.

Disclaimer: I don't nod off on purpose. Sometimes it just happens. Heck, I've seen Mousejunkie Randy with his head back on the Carousel of Progress (his eyes snapped open when I took a photo of him—either that or his lumbago was acting up.) *and* stretched out on Ellen's Energy Adventure at Epcot. And this is a man who will out-tour almost anyone.

If things get too heated, consider these sleep-inducing, comfortable, gloriously air-conditioned oases in the Magic Kingdom:

➤ **The Carousel of Progress**—I've stated earlier that I love this attraction, and that affection is unequivocal. But I have to admit that I've nodded off when John blew the fuse and came-to when he was burning the turkey.

➤ **The Hall of Presidents**—While the new refurb has improved this attraction immensely, sometimes days of constant park touring take their toll. Great story, great attraction, great air conditioning. Just remember: snoring is not patriotic.

➤ **Liberty Square Riverboat**—Most of the seating on this steamboat is located outside along the rail. But I discovered a very soft, comfortable seat on the second, inside level.

➤ **Mickey's Philharmagic**—You have to be really tired to sleep here, with the noise and audience reaction and tactile surprises, but it is dark and cool and therefore not impossible.

MOUSEJUNKIE DEB I do not nap. I have sometimes been known to fall asleep in my hotel bed. That's about it.

I'm going to turn the question around. When it's cold outside (below 80 degrees), my favorite place to warm up is in a rocking chair in front of the fireplace in the Villas at the Wilderness Lodge lobby. The Wilderness Lodge lobby is good, too, but all the rocking chairs are usually taken.

Walt Disney World From Your Butt

It's not always about losing consciousness though. Sometimes just getting off your feet can be just enough to recharge the batteries.

Over the course of a Walt Disney World vacation, there's plenty of walking, running, hurrying, standing in line and jumping out of one attraction and into the next.

I know I'm not the only one that equates Disney vacations with blisters and the need for a second vacation for recovery purposes. Which is why some of my favorite Disney moments have come when I was sitting on my butt.

My name is Bill and I'm a benchaholic.

For anyone who has traveled with me, this will come as no surprise. I love walking the World Showcase at Epcot, but I also love parking it for a while and letting the day go by.

On one trip years ago, Amy and I sat on the benches near the fountains between Futureworld and the World Showcase at Epcot. We watched a few toddlers playing in the water and we wondered aloud if we'd ever be sitting in that exact spot someday, watching our own child play in the water. Fast-forward a few years and there we were: sitting on that same bench, watching our own daughter splash around. Sometimes the time between Disney vacations seems to completely fall away when you return. This was one of those moments. One moment we were there alone, watching someone else's children laugh and play, and the next we were watching our own daughter run around in the unpredictable fountains, laughing.

But let's be honest—most of the time my love for benches doesn't run quite that deep. It's also a place to get off my feet. But given a few minutes to do just that, and one of my favorite Walt Disney World pastimes will begin to occur: People-watching. In fact, put a cool drink in my hand and I could while away an afternoon while kicking back.

All this has led to a strange "favorite" at Walt Disney World. I actually have a favorite bench.

It's located just outside the watch shop on Main Street USA. There are two, actually—small, white and tucked just under the shop window. It's in the little alley near the second-floor window that advertises piano lessons. Sit there long enough and you'll hear those piano lessons, a little tap dancing and maybe some singing.

I've escaped an insane rain storm by ducking under the overhang and sitting around while it eventually passed by. I've called my credit card company in a panic from that bench after learning that someone had stolen my identity and was charging expensive audio/visual equipment. (It was solved rather quickly—something I attribute to the magical properties of that bench.)

I've admired many an ill-advised purchase of yet another new watch on that bench.

I've sat quietly while the Keys to the Kingdom Tour comes by to point out that the window above my head is the one dedicated to Walt Disney's father, Elias. And I've pondered my advancing age (although I'm not that old) as I enjoy a needed rest there.

But it's not the only one. Benches that make it to the 'favorite' list have to have a few key elements about them. One is relative comfort. And that's not what I expected at all when I planted my butt on a stone bench just to the side of Aladdin's Flying Carpets.

They're situated right next to a shop in a small walkway that leads to the restrooms. The backs are just high enough where I can spread my arms out across them and listen to the music floating my way from Adventureland. They're curved, almost like a pub booth, and smooth.

And yet there are new, more excellent benches being created by the skilled minds of Disney's Imagineers every day.

Take, for example, the new bench outside the caramel shop in the Germany pavilion.

Try it out. You've got an amazing view of Spaceship Earth, a great place to watch guests walking by, and a perfect spot to listen to the great German music pumping through the area. But best of all is that smell. Caramel. All around you. How do you say "get me some of that, I'll be right here" in German? All I know is I'm going to have to commit that phrase to memory.

Yet another sits just under a stand of trees at Animal Kingdom. Solid and perfectly placed, it allows for some of the finest people-watching in the park, within sight of the Tree of Life, yet shaded by the lush greenery that adorns the rough-hewn paths.

A shaded place to plant it can be the perfect spot when you've spent a long day trudging around a theme park. Make no mistake, that's exactly what I do: I trudge. I don't skip or jaunt lightly. I'm kind of a big guy, so I either lope or trudge. I do it happily and I wouldn't want to be anywhere else, but I'm not exactly graceful in my travels through the World. So when my legs are screaming at me to stop, my practiced eye darts around the clusters of guests to seek out a bench, one in the shade, and one that affords a nice view of everything that's going on around us.

I can offer one warning, however. I have a particular fondness for Raglan Road at Downtown Disney. Outside of Raglan Road is a great statue of Patrick Kavanaugh—the author of "On Raglan Road" —sitting on a bench.

"What's this?" you say. "A bench located right outside your favorite restaurant? Surely this is heaven."

Not exactly. It's an artistic beauty, but it's got these little jagged edges that'll wreck your night if you catch one. Still, it is the most picturesque bench in the World

So do not underestimate the regenerative powers of sitting on your butt for a while. Besides, when you slow down and take the time to catch all the tiny details around you, Walt Disney World really starts to come to life.

Besides, sometimes it's just good to park your butt.

The Straight Dope *If you arrive at the park during the daily 3 P.M. parade, hop on the train at Main Street Station and take it to Frontierland. You'll miss the crowds and be half-way across the park in minutes.*

Above all, approach the Magic Kingdom slowly. It allows for a more relaxed pace, and the opportunity to notice the details Imagineers created through the years.

Epcot

IN A PERFECT WORLD, I'd spend an entire week at Epcot.

The thing is, Epcot *is* a perfect world. A sprawling, wondrous park filled with idealized dreams of technology, exploration and cultural unity.

Every morning Epcot slowly awakens as the Friendships begin crisscrossing the World Showcase Lagoon, their staccato signals providing the soundtrack to a new day. Guests arrive in the shadow of Spaceship Earth—the eighteen-story geodesic sphere that serves as the icon of Epcot—and are greeted by meticulously groomed grounds, swelling music and the promise of a day-long journey taking them from the very beginnings of written communication to the far-reaches of space, to a showcase of diverse cultures waiting to be discovered.

At the end of every day, guests are sent back to their resorts alternately exhausted by their odyssey and seduced by IllumiNations: Reflections of Earth, a moving display of fireworks, lasers and music that imparts a message of hope and unity.

Or it could be the frozen margarita stand between Mexico and Norway. (A little pricey at $8.99—or $12.99 if you prefer Patron—but very cooling and quite potent.)

But let's not get ahead of ourselves. Epcot doesn't have the number of traditional "ride" type attractions that a park like the Magic Kingdom does. While there are fewer thrillers, they are of the big-bang type, and everyone heads straight for them. You've heard it before, but it's worth saying again: You'll need to get there early if you want to avoid lengthy queues.

Here's a list of attractions that offer Fastpass at Epcot:

➤ Soarin' (The Land pavilion in Future World)
➤ Test Track (behind Innoventions East in Future World)
➤ Mission: Space (behind Innoventions East in Future World)
➤ Maelstrom (in the Norway pavilion in the World Showcase)
➤ Living with the Land (The Land pavilion in Future World)
➤ Captain EO (behind Innoventions West in Future World)

Epcot is separated into two major sections: Future World and the World Showcase. Future World is located at the front of the park, while the World Showcase sits behind it.

TEEN MOUSEJUNKIE RYAN Mouse Gear, located in Future World, is a huge souvenir shop that has everything from apparel to... something that starts with a "z" and everything in between. And while we're talking shopping, I enjoy visiting the little shops in my favorite countries in the World Showcase. What's cooler than a stuffed Tigger from England? Nothing, I tell you. Nothing.

Here's a look at the attractions you'll find in Future World:

Soarin'—Guided through the preshow by "Patrick Your Flight Attendant" (actor Patrick Warburton), guests are launched on a breathtaking journey over the Golden State. The ride vehicle simulates a hang-glider type flight, navigating over the Golden Gate Bridge, national parks, orange groves, and even Disneyland.

★**Mousejunkie U**   *In one scene, guests fly over the PGA West golf course in La Quinta. A golfer drives a ball off the tee, which seems to "fly" right by guests' heads. According to a Walt Disney World exec—who divulged this information to me at great personal risk—the man hitting the golf ball is former Walt Disney Company chief executive Michael Eisner.*

The ride provides a bird's-eye view, and a rather convincing experience. The ride vehicle sways gently, and appropriate scents are piped in during certain scenes.

Soarin' is where you want to be headed as soon as the ropes drop and the park opens. You, and very likely ninety percent of the other guests, will be heading in the same direction. Walk up past Spaceship Earth, bear right, and walk straight through Innoventions toward The Land pavilion. Soarin' is located inside on the first level. Just follow the crowd.

Head inside, go down the stairs, high-five the cast members greeting you with giant, four-fingered Mickey gloves, bear to the right, and get a Fastpass. Then get right in the standby line. This allows you to ride the attraction, exit, and then ride it again at the Fastpass return time if you are so inclined. The Land pavilion is somewhat inconveniently located from the rest of the gate-busters, so once you've hit Soarin' and The Land and maybe had something to eat, you've pretty much exhausted that pavilion.

Duration: Five minutes

Load: Slowly. Either get there early or plan on getting a Fastpass as soon as you enter the park. Fastpasses often run out, so don't put it off too long.

 MOUSEJUNKIE WALT   Soarin' is one of my all-time favorite rides for a very specific reason—it fulfills Walt Disney's original goal. It's a ride I, my grandfather, and my four-year-old nephew all went on together. It's something families can do together, and it's amazing in that respect.

Living with the Land—The natural followup to Soarin', (its load area is right next to Soarin's exit) Living with the Land is part dark ride, part boat ride, part greenhouse tour and all educational.

Wait, I know you probably don't want to be lectured at while on vacation, but trust me—there are alligators. It's actually a really interesting look at agriculture all over the world and the work Epcot is doing to revolutionize farming.

Duration: Fifteen minutes

Load: Quickly

Spaceship Earth—Yes, "the big golf ball" is a ride. Spaceship Earth takes guests on a journey of discovery, examining how communication and technology have changed the world. Audio animatronic figures populate life-size diorama scenes starting in the Stone Age, going through the renaissance, and into the future. It's a slow-moving ride that underwent a refurb not too long ago, allowing for some interactive elements in the second half.

Duration: Fifteen minutes.

Load: Quickly. The attraction's ride vehicles are constantly rotating through and moving people up into the attraction proper.

Since my park touring "type" is Lazy Guy (which basically means I don't like blisters and I covet bench-time,) Spaceship Earth has always been one of my favorites. It's dark, cool, slow-moving and it tells an interesting tale. I park my butt in one of the blue, hard, plastic seats, and for the next fifteen minutes, I'm enthralled. I look for hidden Mickeys and try to pick up subtle details the Imagineers may have hidden among the many scenes.

The Straight Dope *Don't feel like you need to rush to Spaceship Earth right away. Lines can form right after the rope drop, slowing progress. The lines tend to diminish greatly as the day goes on.*

Mission: Space—Experience preflight butterflies, the exhilaration of liftoff, all the G-forces of a slingshot around the moon, and a hair-raising finale that'll have you catching your breath. And potentially losing your lunch.

Guests have, on occasion, complained of motion sickness after experiencing the attraction. The ride compartment sits at the end of a centrifuge, which spins and places a sustained 2.5g on riders. You really don't feel the spinning, but it's absolutely clear that something is going on. The g-force feels amazing, and there's a weightless sequence that's surprisingly effective.

Mission: Space offers guests two ride options: the original and a more mild experience that cuts out the centrifuge element. Upon entering the queue, a cast member will ask which side you'd prefer. He or she will hand you a red card or a green card. Red indicates you prefer the original, more intense ride, while a green card indicates that you answer to the name "Sally." (Any insult to anyone named "Sally" is purely unintentional. It's just an expression. Sally is actually a wonderful name. My grandmother was named Sally. . . No she wasn't.)

I found the milder side to be only slightly less disorienting, since the visual effects are what made me feel queasy.

Duration: Fifteen minutes

Load: Slowly

Test Track—A simulated ride through automobile proving grounds, guests strap-in and run through a number of tests from acceleration and braking to heat and cold resistance. The finale features a crash test that results in a nearly mile-long tear along the exterior of the attraction. Reaching speeds of up to 65 m.p.h., Test Track is one of the fastest Disney theme park attractions ever constructed.

Duration: Twenty minutes

Load: Slowly. Consider Fastpass or taking the single-rider line to speed up the wait.

Mousejunkie U   *The host in the preshow area might look familiar. That's actor John Michael Higgins, who has starred in scores of films and TV shows such as Kath and Kim, A Mighty Wind, Best in Show, Arrested Development, and Community.*

Universe of Energy—Ellen DeGeneres, Jamie Lee Curtis, Alex Trebek and Bill Nye the Science Guy host this journey through time that offers a look at how energy makes the world go around. The attraction starts with a funny preshow that finds Ellen tanking in a game of *Jeopardy!* against her former college roommate, Jamie Lee Curtis. Bill Nye rescues Ellen and takes her on a trip back to the prehistoric age—that's where things pick up.

A massive, moving theater slowly glides through the rest of the show, giving guests a close-up look at some animatronic dinosaurs.

Duration: Forty minutes

Load: Quickly. Head inside and grab a bench along the wall or have a seat on the floor. It's nice and cool, and the preshow keeps things moving.

The Straight Dope *On particularly hot days, be sure to visit the Universe of Energy. It's air conditioned, dark, and lasts about forty minutes. Several of the Mousejunkies have been known to take advantage of these factors to steal a quick nap. Though not all at the same time. That would just be strange.*

Imagination!—Figment, the purple dragon, pops in and out of this dark ride that guests ride through The Imagination Institute. Hosted by Dr. Nigel Channing (Monty Python alum Eric Idle), ride vehicles cart guests through a number of "imagination" experiments where Figment runs rampant, creating both chaos and entertainment. (Author's note: allegedly.)

Figment and I have a tangled history. I'm not a fan of the attraction, which is now in its third incarnation. There are, of course, those who love it and are confounded by my dislike of the cloying dragon. The cheese-meter needle is pinned throughout this ride.

Duration: Six of the longest minutes ever

Load: Quickly

The Seas with Nemo & Friends—Board your "clamobiles" and take a trip down to the Sea Base. Characters from the Pixar film, *Finding Nemo* follow along, somehow swimming alongside fish of the non-animated type inside the main massive aquarium tank.

Once you've arrived at the Sea Base—essentially an aquarium—there are dozens of aquatic exhibits to check out.

The two-story viewing area into the main tank is hypnotic, and provides an amazing view at more than three thousand types of marine life.

Turtle Talk with Crush—This interactive show where the perpetually spaced-out sea turtle from *Finding Nemo* interacts with guests, is a can't-miss. Attendees sit in a small theater with a large screen "looking out into the ocean." Crush swims into view, talks a little about ocean life, and engages youngsters from behind his "tank."

Duration: Fifteen minutes.

Loads: Medium. The theater empties and refills at the completion of each show.

Club Cool—Essentially a store for Coca Cola, its sponsor, this area is located next to the Fountain of Nations behind Spaceship Earth. Guests are given a chance to sample unusually flavored soda from around the world, and/or buy Coca Cola merchandise.

The fun part comes in the sampling, and attempting to trick your friends into trying an awful concoction from Italy called Beverly. It tastes like a mixture of gin and aspirin, and has garnered a reputation, rightfully so, for its nastiness.

Here's a list of soda flavors available in Club Cool:

➤ Beverly (Italy)
➤ Fanta Kolita (Costa Rica)
➤ Kinley Lemon (Israel)
➤ Krest Ginger Ale (Mozambique)
➤ Lift Apple (Mexico)

➤ Mezzo Mix (Germany)
➤ Smart Watermelon (China)
➤ Vegeta Beta (Japan)

Innoventions—At the center of Future World, just behind Spaceship Earth, sit Innoventions East and West. Both buildings house interactive exhibits, examples of new technology and a chance to play some Disney-themed video games.

⭐ **The Straight Dope** *Need to get a few character pictures? The Epcot Character Spot is a fantastic place to do this. There's an entire indoor section adjacent to Innoventions where many Disney biggies are gathered: Mickey, Minnie, Donald, Goofy, Pluto, and Chip and Dale. Line 'em up and shoot away. You can either use your own camera or take advantage of Disney's Photopass photographers.*

Digital pictures taken by Disney's Photopass photographers are linked to a free card containing a barcode and serial number. Guests log on to the Photopass web site using the serial number and can view or purchase the pictures for up to thirty days. The great aspect of Photopass is that every member of the touring party is included in the photo—no one is left holding the camera. On the downside, the photos are exorbitantly expensive. Photopass is available at all four theme parks.

One morning, we worked our way through the Epcot Character Spot when we got to the end and prepared to head back outside. We rounded the corner and who stood in front of us? Belle. All by herself. There wasn't even a character handler in sight. She kneeled down, opened her arms, and my then-three-year-old ran to her. She had nearly five minutes completely alone, just visiting with Belle and comparing outfits and making small talk. It was one of those moments that can't be duplicated or planned for.

A simple approach to Future World would look like this:

1. Get to Soarin' when the park opens. Get a Fastpass and then get in the standby line.
2. Ride The Land while waiting for your Soarin' Fastpass time.
3. Cross through Innoventions and ride Test Track.
4. Head next door and hit Mission: Space.
5. Check out the Universe of Energy.
6. Ride Spaceship Earth.
7. Visit The Living Seas with Nemo & Friends or kick around in Innoventions.

You've now hit the biggies in Future World. If time allows or if you can't think of any reason not to, visit Imagination! on your way to the World Showcase. Or you can skip it and head straight for the World Showcase Lagoon and make your next biggest decision of the day: Clockwise or counter-clockwise?

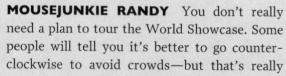 **MOUSEJUNKIE RANDY** You don't really need a plan to tour the World Showcase. Some people will tell you it's better to go counter-clockwise to avoid crowds—but that's really not the case. Just go in and explore every country. Check

out the little corners. That's where you'll find the most rewarding details.

And make sure to catch the street performers throughout the day. They're some of the best free shows in all of Disney World. They're not on any map, but they're all fun and interesting.

Exploring the World Showcase

The World Showcase boasts eleven pavilions representing various countries from around the world. Clockwise, in order, the pavilions are: Mexico, Norway, China, Germany, Italy, the American Adventure, Japan, Morocco, France, the United Kingdom, and Canada. Each country's pavilion is staffed by cast members who are from that particular country. Spending the day strolling through the World Showcase is a great way to get a taste of different cultures—both figuratively and literally.

Spend a little time in each of the countries. Be friendly. Say hello. It's a great opportunity to speak to someone from another culture and to try out what you learned in some of your high school foreign language classes.

Each country's pavilion has a table service restaurant and at least one quick-service option. Several have attractions, all have shopping, and each offers a chance for the adults in your party to grab a beverage. This is just one of the elements that sets it apart from the Magic Kingdom. The Magic Kingdom is a dry park. Epcot, however, is not.

And the benches. Oh, the benches. There are benches everywhere. Glorious, restive, inviting benches designed for camping out and enjoying said adult beverages. The World Showcase promenade runs 1.2 miles—a pittance for Mousejunkies such as Deb, J, or Ryan. But for some it can seem to be an uphill marathon.

If you're traveling with children, take advantage of the World Showcase Kidcot Fun Stops. Kids are presented with a mask which they can color on and decorate at craft areas normally located deep within each of the pavilions. This forces guests to really visit each pavilion, talk to cast members from that country, and it gives kids something to do in an environment that otherwise has little in the way of traditional theme park rides.

The World Tour

Mexico: The Mexican pavilion, constructed to look like a Mesoamerican pyramid, represents perhaps the finest Inside/Outside in all of Walt Disney World.

An Inside/Outside is a design feature when you enter a building but it appears as though you are outside. It's my preferred way of getting outdoors. It's temperature controlled, and the chances of me getting a sunburn in an inside/outside are virtually nil, since I am of Irish ancestry and my translucent skin can become painfully charred by just thinking about the sun.

Entering the pavilion, a Mexican marketplace is spread out in front of you under a starry sky. In the distance a volcano rumbles over a Mayan pyramid as boatloads of guests on the Gran Fiesta Tour starring the Three Caballeros glide silently past diners.

The Gran Fiesta Tour, comes off as a rather slapdash retrofit of the former El Rio del Tiempo. Kids might find the Donald Duck storyline engaging, but it has stripped the attraction of any dignity and seems to run counter to the park's theme. It teaches guests nothing about the diverse people and regions of Mexico.

 TEEN MOUSEJUNKIE RYAN I keep riding the Gran Fiesta Tour starring the Three Caballeros, hoping it will get better. But much like with crème brulée, I continue to be disappointed.

Fairly new to the Mexico pavilion is a tequila bar called La Cava del Tequila, which in the literal translation means "I bet I can kick tequila's butt. Pass me some of those chips."

La Cava del Tequila is a somewhat dark, cozy rest stop offering a vast array of tequilas to sample. It's a comfortable location and it becomes incredibly easy to wile away hours without realizing how off-track your touring plan has become.

Norway: Designed to look like a 10th century Norwegian village, an austere stave church dominates the lagoon-facing portion of the pavilion. A series of shops—where guests can buy staggeringly expensive sweaters, sweets, or plastic Viking helmets—lead back into Norway's attraction, Maelstrom.

A fifteen-minute dark ride where guests board a Viking-style boat, Maelstrom emphasizes Norwegian history, mythology, and fishing traditions. A collection of audio animatronic Norwegian warriors, polar bears, and trolls drop in along the way. The journey ends in a re-creation of a small Norwegian fishing village. Guests are ushered through a theater where a short film about the country is shown. In addition, Norway has the most statuesque and blondest cast members.

A friend of the family is from Norway, and taught me the only Norwegian phrase I believe I will ever need: *"Jaeg snakker ikke Norsk."* (I do not know how to speak Norwegian.)

There are two mandatory tasks that must be accomplished on every visit to the Norway pavilion. I must try on a tiny plastic Viking helmet, and I must try out my single line of Norwegian on a cast member. Some laugh, some stare at me in a confused manner, and Amy usually just stands behind me and shakes her head in embarrassment.

Mousejunkie U *Impress your friends—point out the hidden Mickey in the mural facing the loading area in Maelstrom. He's sitting in the Viking ship with the striped sails.*

China: The brilliantly reconstructed Temple of Heaven hosts the Circle-Vision 360 film, *Reflections of China*. The film showcases sweeping images of the vast country, focusing on seven cities and regions.

Tragically, there are no benches in the theater.

The rest of the pavilion is laid out with ponds, bridges, and a pagoda. Inside, guests can see historic representations of Chinese artifacts such as the famous terra cotta warriors.

Characters from the Disney film, *Mulan* appear here, and the Dragon Legend Acrobats perform daily.

The Straight Dope *The temple in China is acoustically perfect. Stand in the direct center and listen to yourself speak. You'll hear your own voice as others hear you.*

It works amazingly well. If you see a guy looking up at the impossibly ornate ceiling inside the Temple of Heaven and talking to himself, that'd be me.

Germany: Guests are welcomed into an almost impossibly perfect representation of a fairytale German village, complete with a glockenspiel and a statue of St. George slaying a dragon.

A perpetual state of Oktoberfest exists, with brew and German food flowing in equal portions in the Biergarten restaurant in the back of St. George's Platz.

Next to the pavilion is a miniature train and village, a fantastic place to slow the pace and meditate on the incredible handiwork that went into creating the small scale hamlet.

Italy: A mix of beautiful architecture is punctuated with a recreation of St. Mark's campanile. This fully functioning bell tower draws guests inward, past replicas of the Doge's palace in Venice and the exterior of the Sistine Chapel.

The landscaping here includes olive trees and grapevines, adding a seductive and evocative feel to the reproduction of St. Mark's Square. Where Alfredo's once offered solid Italian fare, there's a new, even more expensive restaurant—even by Disney standards—called Tutto Italia in its place.

At the rear of the pavilion is the Neptune Fountain, and the new Via Napoli pizzeria.

 TEEN MOUSEJUNKIE RYAN   Italian boys with Gelato. Need I say more?

The American Adventure: A massive, colonial-style building houses the America pavilion's multimedia presentation, "The American Adventure." Narrated by audio animatronic figures of Benjamin Franklin and Mark Twain, guests are taken on an American history lesson from the earliest settlers up through brief glimpses of the terrorist attacks of 9/11.

The show's theme, "Golden Dream" is part of the sweeping, emotional finale that gives a glimpse of the American experience and what it took to build the country.

The Straight Dope   *Do not miss the Voices of Liberty, an a cappella group, which performs in the rotunda of the American Adventure, an acoustically superior venue. If you visit around Christmas, the Voices of Liberty will perform classic Christmas carols. Check your park map for times.*

Japan: The castle in Japan, visible from the waterfront all around the World Showcase, is a replica of the Shirasagi-Jo, a seventeenth-century fortress considered one of the most well-preserved of its kind. A torii gate stands out in the water in front of the Japanese pavilion, while venturing further back into the pavilion reveals beautiful gardens, and shopping opportunities.

The Straight Dope *Walk all the way to the back of the pavilion, go into the shop and take a left. There you'll find a counter where you can sample several different types of sake. Sip on it while shopping for a relaxing break.*

The Matsuriza, or traditional Taiko drummers, are part of the natural background soundtrack that saturates the fabric of Epcot. The sounds of the drums echoes all the way across the lagoon, mixing with the piercing horns of the Friendships that ferry guests around the World Showcase and to and from the Boardwalk Resort area.

Also, be sure to look for Bijutsu-kan, a collection of Japanese arts: "Spirited Beasts: From Ancient Stories to Anime Stars."

The waterfront along the Japan pavilion is a great place to watch the nightly IllumiNations: Reflections of Earth performance. You get a great view of the floating globe centerpiece, and an easy exit via the International Gateway.

Morocco: One of the most finely detailed of all the World Showcase pavilions, Morocco was designed to evoke the feel of a city from this north African country. A replica of a minaret in Marrakesh stands overlooking the intricately constructed alleyways and back rooms. Nineteen Moroccan artists spent months re-creating the intricate, colorful tile masterpieces of their homeland.

Shops sell everything from musical instruments to clothing to fezzes.

The Treasures of Morocco is a forty-five-minute tour designed to teach guests more about the culture, people, and history of this north African land. This type of tour is unique to the Morocco pavilion.

Plus—belly dancers!

France: Wander through a neighborhood in Paris from La Belle Epoque, complete with shops, fountains and a distant view of the Eiffel Tower. The central Florida version of the city of lights truly comes alive after dark. The bubbling fountain outside Chefs de France is lit up, creating one of the most beautiful spots in a park packed with them.

The film, *Impressions de France*, provides a tour of the country set to stirring classical music.

An amazing chair-balancing-juggling-acrobatic act, Serveur Amusant, is a can't-miss. It is staged just outside the entrance of Chefs de France several times daily.

Mousejunkie U   *The replica Eiffel Tower stands 103 feet tall. The real Eiffel Tower in Paris stands 1,063 feet tall.*

The United Kingdom: A tea shop, authentic phone boxes and a neighborhood pub turn this pavilion into a small slice of the United Kingdom.

Mousejunkie U *If you haven't been to Walt Disney World in a while and you're itching for a little Epcot fix, there's a way you can reach out and touch someone in the theme park. There are payphones (remember those?) in the UK pavilion located in the brightly-painted red phone boxes. Here are the numbers: 407-827-9861, 407-827-9862, 407-827-9863.*

At press time, these numbers are fully functional. In about a half an hour of dialing one afternoon, I:

➤ *Helped a family from Mexico make Advanced Dining Reservations at the Rose and Crown Pub for that evening.*

➤ *Spoke to a Brazilian who promptly hung up when our conversation turned to the World Cup results.*

➤ *Spoke to another Brazilian who said she was staying at All Star Movies, and that it was very hot that day.*

The Rose and Crown Pub is a cozy watering hole, offering a fantastic place to pull up a pint of Guinness and grab a seat. It also serves as the UK's table service restaurant.

The Straight Dope *Photo opportunities with Winnie the Pooh characters are often available in the back of the Toy Soldier shop. It's an out-of-the-way location with very little foot traffic, so the lines are often quite short.*

A picturesque garden tucked in the back of the pavilion is another great spot for a breather. This dad enjoyed one of his beloved benches while Mousejunkie Amy and our seven-year-old wound their way through the hedge maze near the back of a picturesque park. But don't get the impression the UK pavilion is all about relaxation. British Invasion, a Beatles-inspired act, provides toe-tapping renditions of tunes made famous by the Fab Four. They perform several times daily in a gazebo just off a large garden area.

MOUSEJUNKIE JOHN Beatle freaks and especially Beatle freak musicians (like me) have much to take in during a set by the British Invasion. Even if they were just four dudes in jeans and t-shirts playing polished Fab Four covers, it would be enough to please the casual classic rock fan. But these cats really go all out.

They play several shows a day, each focusing on a different era of the Beatles career. You might get the early Cavern Club Beatles, A Hard Days Night/Ed Sullivan Beatles, Sgt. Pepper Beatles, Abbey Road rooftop Beatles, etc. All with the period-appropriate clothes (leather jackets, matching black suits, psychedelic marching band uniforms, for example) and instruments (Hofner, Rickenbacker, Gretsch guitars.) This stuff all goes over my wife's and daughters' heads, but my inner guitar junkie eats it up.

It's usually easy to spot the moptop wigs, but I'll have to pay close attention next time the 1969-era group takes the stage. Will "Paul" apply a fake beard? Will he play lefty?

Canada: But where is Don Cherry? Do they serve Timbits? Where are the hockey rinks? Where is Rush?

Visitors to this World Showcase pavilion will learn it is so much more than those truly Canadian, yet already quite well known cultural exports. Canada's vast wilderness is illustrated by the splashing waterfalls cascading down a mountainside, and its majesty plays out in a towering version of the Chateau Laurier.

Located near the Le Cellier restaurant, the Circle-Vision 360 movie, *O Canada!*, hosted by Martin Short, was updated in 2007 and goes even further to show the many faces of our neighbor to the north. The updated theme from the film revisits the original, which is now sung by Canadian Idol Eva Avila.

Awesome/Stupid Disney Idea   *Give Off Kilter— admittedly a great live act and a favorite of many who visit Epcot's Canada pavilion—a break. They work hard. It's hot out. Get Rush in for a few months. I know it sounds crazy. Just consider it.*

Soused with the Mouse: An Epcot Tradition Exposed

For those drinking around the world: You have reached the finish line (assuming you went clockwise.) Please gather your things and move quietly to the exit. While it does seem like a fun way to travel the World Showcase, I've seen the results. And it's not pretty. In Mexico, it's an exciting start to the day. By Italy it's riotously funny. By the United Kingdom it's just sloppy.

However, in the interest of better serving the reader, the researchers down at Mousejunkie Labs conducted a highly controlled experiment in order to lift the veil of secrecy that surrounds Drinking Around the World. That is, starting at one side of the World Showcase at Epcot, and ordering an alcoholic beverage at each country while traversing the entire loop—from Canada to Mexico.

Drinking Around the World is an activity alternately whispered about in hushed tones or blurted out to no one in particular in slurred torrents of indecipherable yammering. Usually somewhere near the Germany pavilion. Convinced that it could be done without causing a scene and with some dignity (read: still wearing pants by the end), the Mousejunkies huddled and came away with a plan. Consider it a service, as it were. For the betterment of all Disney guests, we would conduct our own Epcot pub crawl.

Drinking Around the World, simply, means partaking of eleven drinks throughout the course of the day. It may not sound like much for the experienced imbiber, but in practice the drinks can start to come quickly. Without proper preparation and focus, it can end poorly. If unsuccessful, draftees can find themselves broke, sick, sunburned and lost—and all joking and hyperbole aside, potentially tossed out of the park. It happens. Cast member harassment is a common side effect when drinking around the world, something that no Mousejunkie would take part in.

As we prepared to embark on our journey, we agreed to adhere to three simple ground rules:

1. An alcoholic beverage must be ordered and consumed at each country's pavilion. The circuit must be completed before the 9 p.m. showing of IllumiNations: Reflections of Earth.
2. Hands-off the cast members. Cast members must be treated with the utmost respect at all times.
3. Also, avoid engaging other guests. Especially the bigger ones with neck tattoos. No matter how bullet-proof we get.

When the call went out for brave souls to take on this challenge, Mousejunkie Walt stepped into the breach. He put all thoughts of his own well-being out of his head. (More room for margaritas that way.) He knew it would be risky. He knew that it could result in a debilitating hangover that could find him with a head the size of Mickey's the next morning. But he also knew that he was working for a something greater than himself. For this reason, Walt signed on and answered the call to act as the stunt liver.

As your humble scribe, my job would be to follow our stunt liver around the World Showcase, taking notes and reporting progress. And if forced, I would join Mousejunkie Walt in sampling the wares, if only to support him in this noble effort. And only under great duress and protest. A journalist must remain completely detached and impartial. Except when he is thirsty. Or when he doesn't feel like it.

Having had some experience in occasional overindulgence, we knew that a proper foundation must be built. We would begin construction at the Kona Café in the Polynesian

Resort. It would be the base upon which the rest of the day would be built. It would be constructed of alcohol-absorbing elements: Eggs, cheese, potatoes, hash, and the most important and magical of elements, hollandaise sauce. This alone would assure a healthy and energetic afternoon. Oh, and a Wasabi Mary (Absolut pepper vodka, wasabi, spices and tomato juice. In my case an extra helping of chili sauce was brought out to kick up the pain.) Yes, I realized this was not the best idea. But who can pass up something called a Wasabi Mary? It was on the breakfast menu, along with a mimosa. Mimosas are what you drink while watching *Glee*. Wasabi Marys are what you drink if your name is Spartacus. Actually, boilermakers are. But I'm not that stupid. As far as you know. Obviously, the testosterone level was high as we prepared for the day's challenge.

Walt chose to gird his innards with the famous Tonga Toast—nearly half a loaf of sourdough, fried and stuffed with bananas. Sitting like a three-pound stone in his stomach, Walt was ready.

We boarded the monorail outside the Polynesian and a short time later found ourselves deposited at the other end into Epcot. With Spaceship Earth looming above and the World Showcase just behind it, our mission was upon us. We wound through Innoventions Plaza, and just as we crossed over into the World Showcase, Walt stopped. He looked left toward Mexico and considered tequila. He looked right toward Canada and took the first step on the journey. We knew at that point there was no turning back.

Except when we got to the Canada pavilion. Because the beer stand was closed.

We wandered around aimlessly for a while, seeking our starting point but finding no such purchase. Thankfully, the Rose and Crown Pub beckoned in the distance. Assured by cast members in Canada that the beer cart would soon be operational, we opted to kick off in the UK pavilion and return to Canada later.

The United Kingdom: Walt ordered a pint of Bass ale for $8. I couldn't necessarily toast our quest with a glass of air, so I had the air replaced with Strongbow Cider for $5.75. We were on our way.

A quick backtrack to Canada found us standing in front of the beer cart. As Walt ordered his Labatt Blue, we started talking to the cast member, who asked what we had planned for the day. We told her our plan to Drink Around the World. She eyed us warily.

"It can get scary," she admitted. "We get these big guys coming through, and if they start in Mexico and end in Canada they can be really drunk. And we have to shut them down if they're visibly intoxicated. I've been physically threatened, yelled at . . . We just call security but it's not fun."

Suddenly, I felt badly. We doubled our vow to treat cast members exceptionally well, and struck out toward France.

We loitered for a brief time as Walt finished his Canadian beer, before winding our way to a shop around back for a glass of merlot, running $5.87.

It seemed as though things were beginning to move rather quickly as we found ourselves standing in the Tangerine

Café in Morocco, each holding a cold Moroccan beer. Walt had consumed four drinks in a relatively short time. It was time to start thinking about pacing ourselves. We grabbed a seat and sipped slowly as we watched the day go by.

It was at this point that this whole experiment started to seem like such a great idea, that if there was an award ceremony for amazing ideas, this one would win first prize. A cool, breezy day in Epcot with a head full of happiness? It could only be improved if we were being transported around the World Showcase in litters borne by supermodels. Really strong ones.

With Morocco now a distant memory, we turned our attention to the East. The Taiko drummers pounded rhythmically as we marched toward the walls of the Japanese fortress in front of us. Like two warriors striding into battle (hey, the whole fortress thing left us feeling like we were in *The Seven Samurai*), we strode into the shop with Bushido leading us.

That bravado was soon replaced with really strange facial expressions and the pursing of lips in a decidedly un-warrior-like manner, since neither of us were really fans of the cold sake.

Here's what we learned so far: Plum wine is also offered at $5.25 a glass. It's got to be better.

After five drinks, we found ourselves at home in the American Adventure. Familiarity embraced us, as we each ordered up a Sam Adams for $6.25. We walked with our brews and struck up a conversation with a woman now known as "the best cast member ever." Friendly, talkative and down-to-earth, she kept us company as we finished our beer in time to catch a showing of *The American Adventure* inside.

Full of patriotism (and not to mention beverages), we passed through Italy (Fumaio wine); Germany (Spaten Oktoberfest); and a Tsing Tao in China.

An $8 Carlsberg is all that stood between us and the finish line: Mexico. Normally, this would be a simple matter of which beer to choose. But there was a wild card facing us that we hadn't really thought about: Tequila.

La Cava del Tequila, a new tequila bar in the bowels of the Mexico pavilion, called out to us. We could not ignore its exotic beacon, and bellied up to the bar.

Walt ordered a Clasica margarita for $12.50, and we grabbed a bench outside the bar to reflect on our findings.

First, a disclaimer: We approached this challenge like a pair of 40-year-olds, not 25-year-olds. What does this mean? Walt ordered and consumed a drink in every country along the way. But there may have been a little left in the glass before we moved on, and I may have lightened his load a bit by sharing at a couple points. Our intent was to complete the spirit of the challenge, not bleurgh all over Epcot.

Second, the final tally for Walt's drinks came in around $150 with tip included. It could easily go much higher if we opted for choices such as the Nuvo sparkling vodka in France ($15), or the Campo Azul Extra Anejo tequila in Mexico for $20 a shot.

He had survived the challenge, and emerged a wizened man. (And, to be honest, not exactly soused. We were in it for the fun, not the chaos.)

MOUSEJUNKIE WALT I will say that it was one of the most fun days that I've had at Epcot. I really enjoyed it. It was such a different way to enjoy the park. Normally, you don't often think about going down there to do that. It was such an adult thing to do. I love the countries anyway; I love Epcot, seeing the different cultures and talking to the cast members and wandering through the pavilions. When you think of Germany though, you think of beer. When you think of France you think of wine. When you think of Mexico, its tequila. I'm not talking about falling down drunk, just about having good time.

We went through the entire World Showcase, taking pictures in every country. We wanted to shoot with something representing the country we were in. So we'd have pictures of us wearing a fez or a sombrero and posting it online. I started getting comments on those pictures immediately. I've had people say they wanted to fly down and take part the next time we plan on drinking around the World. You can go down with a group of people and that's the entire day.

A little advice though: I would always do it the way we did it. I'd always start in Canada and end up in Mexico. Why? I love margaritas. Everywhere else is beer or wine or sake. By time you work your way around to Mexico, you have enough in you to just sit down and relax with a flight of tequilas. Starting with that would've made the day a little rougher.

We finished up just in time for IllumiNations: Reflections of Earth, the fireworks-laser-pyrotechnic show set to music and performed every night over the World Showcase Lagoon. It's viewable from anywhere in the World Showcase, though a few locations are more sought-after than others.

MOUSEJUNKIE WALT IllumiNations is one of my favorite things to do, and I always make sure to watch from the Canada pavilion. Most people say you can see IllumiNations from anywhere, and that is true. But to get the best view, head for Canada—and here's why: First, there are not a lot of trees in the way. More importantly, you're looking across the lagoon at more countries than anywhere else in the park. Why does this matter? During a certain point in the display the countries are lit up by brilliant white lights. So when the white lights come on, you get a much better view. I've watched IllumiNations from all over the park, and when you're on the other side near Japan or Germany, you look across and see Canada and England. That's it. It's not as good. If you're in Canada you can see the American pavilion and everything to the left of it from there.

Just before the show is launched, the lights around the park are dimmed, leaving only the lagoon torches burning. A narrator sets the scene:

Good evening. On behalf of Walt Disney World, the place where dreams come true, we welcome all of you to Epcot and World

Showcase. We've gathered here tonight, around the fire, as people of all lands have gathered for thousands and thousands of years before us; to share the light and to share a story—an amazing story, as old as time itself but still being written. And though each of us has our own individual stories to tell, a true adventure emerges when we bring them all together as one. We hope you enjoy our story tonight; Reflections of Earth.

Low drums begin to sound as a single rocket hurtles through the night sky. When it explodes it sets off a display of fire, sound, fury, and hope in three acts: chaos, order, and celebration. The music, reflecting each act, is alternately wild, introspective, and triumphant.

Between being tossed around by attractions such as Test Track and Mission: Space, walking endlessly through the World Showcase and ultimately being serenaded by an inspiring performance of hope, I have never left Epcot feeling anything less than completely exhausted and happy.

10 Disney's Animal Kingdom

THE PROMISE OF PULSE-POUNDING exotic adventures and heart-racing encounters with a menagerie of beasts might be what lures guests to Disney's Animal Kingdom theme park, but it's the perfectly realized world that captures their imagination.

The world Walt and Roy Disney created, with an army of Imagineers, cast members, and creative types, very likely reached its artistic peak with the opening of Disney's Animal Kingdom. This is not to say that it's the best theme park. The Magic Kingdom has the biggest heart, Epcot's journey is epic and Disney's Hollywood Studios transports guests to another time and place like no other. What it means is there isn't a theme park on the continent that has perfected its theming, atmosphere, its feel, or its soul as completely as Animal Kingdom.

Joe Rohde, executive designer and vice president, creative, as well as lead designer of the park, has created a convincing world where guests feel as if they have been transported to Africa, Asia, and even the prehistoric past.

Hats-off to Rohde, because he and his team have set the bar extremely high. This, of course, benefits Mousejunkies everywhere. Because if Disney's Animal Kingdom is now the standard against which new projects are measured, we can look forward to a future of unmatched artistic achievement.

Disney's Animal Kingdom is divided into seven themed areas: The Oasis; Discovery Island; Camp Minnie-Mickey; Africa; Rafiki's Planet Watch; Asia, and Dinoland U.S.A.

The Oasis is actually the main entrance area leading deeper into the park. While there aren't any rides in the Oasis, don't write it off as a track meet to the more exhilarating attractions like Expedition Everest. Take in all that is around you. It may not spike your adrenalin as much as other theme parks (with a couple notable exceptions), but Disney's Animal Kingdom is the most perfectly themed park of the four in central Florida. And the Oasis is where it all begins.

As you enter the park, cast members loiter about with cages containing exotic creatures. Don't pass up the opportunity for some early, up-close action.

Cracked and scarred pathways marked with animal tracks and floral imprints lead guests up into lush vegetation. Rock formations loom overhead, as animals begin to present themselves along the route. Assorted birds, wallabies and giant anteaters, roaming in natural-looking environments, line the route as it winds even further upward.

They key to this park is pacing. Go slowly. There are details around every corner. Wherever you find a patch of green, you're likely to find a new animal to observe and learn about. The best approach for Disney's Animal Kingdom is to put any traditional definitions of a theme park out of your

TEEN MOUSEJUNKIE RYAN Be sure to check out the various trails through each section of the park. Mousejunkie Jenna and I spent almost forty-five minutes watching a father vulture build a nest for the mother vulture, while a baby kangaroo hopped back and forth, back and forth, back and forth.

head. It's not about rushing from one thing to the next. It's about soaking everything in.

Crest the hill at the top of the Oasis and the massive, 145-foot tall Tree of Life rises up out of the surrounding verdant plant life that makes up the **Discovery Island** section of the park.

A massive, fourteen-story creation, the tree was engineered from an oil platform and has been the park's icon since opening in 1998. Disney set its Imaginers loose on it, and the result is a rather awe-inspiring piece of art that features more than 325 animals carved into its Kynar surface.

Mousejunkie U *Ten artists worked full-time for eighteen months to carve the 325 animals into the Tree of Life, which is topped by more than 103,000 artificial leaves.*

At the base of the tree, a number of animals are viewable in impressively themed enclosures. Once you're close enough to pick out beasts from the surface of the tree, it's time to start hitting attractions.

Here is a list of attractions that offer Fastpass at Disney's Animal Kingdom:

➤ Expedition Everest

➤ Kilimanjaro Safaris

➤ Dinosaur

➤ It's Tough to be a Bug!

➤ Kali River Rapids

➤ Primeval Whirl

Discovery Island is also where the attractions begin:

It's Tough to be a Bug! is located in a theater tucked inside the base of the Tree of Life. This 3-D, audio animatronic presentation is based on the Pixar film, *A Bug's Life*. The show's host, Flik (voiced by *Kids in the Hall's* Dave Foley), attempts to teach guests that bugs should be seen as beneficial, and not as pests.

It's a funny, inventive show that, like most of Disney's 3-D films, includes a few tangible smells, sights, sounds and unexpected tactile prods. However, every time I watch this film, there are always a couple youngsters who react by freaking out. The theater is plunged into virtual darkness at one point, and when the lights come back up there are a few new visitors that might send arachnophobes into fits. Fastpass is available for this attraction.

Duration: Nine minutes

Load: Medium. The theater empties and refills after each performance. However, if there is a bit of a line, do not back out. The queue winds around parts of the Tree of Life and offers a fantastic opportunity to view some of the stunning artwork carved into the surface.

Camp Minnie-Mickey is themed to evoke a rustic summer camp. It would essentially be an incredibly themed photo op (Mickey, Minnie, Goofy, Donald and others are available for safari-themed pics here), if it were not for one of the finest live performances on Disney property, the Festival of the Lion King.

The Festival of the Lion King—Puppetry, music, audience participation, dance, dramatic lighting, and acrobatics combine to create a sweeping, emotional celebration of African culture and mythology as told through the prism of Disney's film, *The Lion King.*

The performance is not a retelling of the film, but weaves its own tale based around the characters of Kiume, Kibibi, Zawadi and Nakawa. The four playfully poke at one another while involving the audience before launching into the show. Songs from the film make up the soundtrack to this Broadway-quality performance.

A visit to the park would not be complete without catching a performance of this masterful production.

Duration: Thirty minutes.

Loads: You know the drill by now—theater loading. When the show ends, the audience files out and the next group heads in. The enclosed, air conditioned theater can hold 1,450 guests, and lines tend to form throughout the day.

A few steps away is the completely immersive Africa, where the fictional village of Harambe hosts one of the park's signature attractions, the Kilimanjaro Safari.

Mousejunkie U *According to Imagineers, Harambe was at one time a Dutch colony, but broke away in 1963 to become self-governing.*

Kilimanjaro Safari: Board your safari truck and prepare for a two-week adventure across the Harambe Wildlife Preserve. (Or so the story goes.) Guests are driven across several African terrains: a forest, wetlands, and bush country. Giraffes, crocodiles, hippos, antelopes, lions, and elephants are among the animals you'll come across as they roam freely throughout the savanna. Disney's Imagineers have devised some ingenious ways to make sure the wildlife remains fairly visible throughout the day.

Duration: Twenty minutes.

Loads: Slowly. Fastpass is available, and can cut standby time down dramatically.

Awesome/Stupid Disney Idea *Make that brief musical interlude that comes into play near the elephant habitat—"Hapa Duniani" by African Dawn—a much longer part of the Kilimanjaro Safari. Its hypnotic, sets the mood, and is better than the evolving storyline that's become a bit convoluted through its recent iterations.*

Pangani Forest Exploration Trail—This walking tour, which begins outside the Kilimanjaro Safari exit, runs through a number of animal viewing areas, most notably the hippo pool, the meerkat grasslands, and the western lowland gorillas. The gorillas live in and around a rocky area that can be viewed from a glassed-in room, a bridge, and a few spots near some cliffs. Lucky guests can get up close and nearly personal to these absolutely massive animals if they happen to feel particularly social.

Rafiki's Planet Watch—The Wildlife Express steam train will take guests to Rafiki's Planet Watch, an interactive, backstage examination of the park's operations. There are hands-on displays, a chance to view animal care areas via the Animal Cam, and the Affection Section. (I'd call it a petting zoo, but I'm sure Disney' would say its "Nahtapettingzoo," to paraphrase its own marketing efforts.)

The first expansion to the park, opening in 1999, was the addition of the themed area, Asia. Centered around a fictional kingdom named Anandapur, guests tour between two villages: Anandapur itself and Serka Zong, which lies in the shadow of Mount Everest. (Just look up, you can't miss it.)

Here are the attractions you'll find in and around Asia:

Expedition Everest—Conquer the sacred mountain as a runaway train plunges guests into the world of the mythical Yeti.

This roller coaster, which climbs, twists, and turns through the mountain itself, reaches speeds of up to fifty m.p.h. forwards, and thirty m.p.h. backwards. Yes, backwards. When the Yeti is on the prowl and he shreds the tracks in front of you, there isn't much choice.

Disney Imagineers traveled to the real Himalayas to research this stunningly themed attraction. Actual props brought back from their journey are used as part of the ride queue, adding a sense of reality to the proceedings.

When it opened in 2006, Expedition Everest was awarded "World's Best New Theme Park Attraction" by Theme Park Insider.

This is a true gate buster. Like Soarin' or Splash Mountain, guests head straight for this towering structure the minute the park opens. Those who are fleet-of-foot can grab a Fastpass and then jump in the standby line.

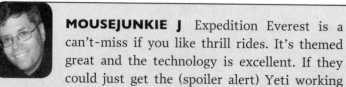

MOUSEJUNKIE J Expedition Everest is a can't-miss if you like thrill rides. It's themed great and the technology is excellent. If they could just get the (spoiler alert) Yeti working correctly. It's supposed to move, but it was breaking all the time. Most people don't notice this as they whiz by at forty m.p.h. in the dark, but he just stands there now and makes noise. This is the "B" mode. The "A" mode has him moving and swinging his paw at you. 'A' mode does not work so well.

Duration: Four minutes

Load: Moderately slowly. But again, the queue in this attraction is really half the experience.

Flights of Wonder—During my first visit to Disney's Animal Kingdom, I passed by the front of this attraction and said, "I'm not going to a stupid bird show."

I have been paying for that ill-informed remark ever since. Flights of Wonder is a hilarious, impressive production that showcases the surprising talents of some remarkable birds. And unlike the audio animatronic creatures of the Magic Kingdom's Tiki Room, these are real, live birds. Performed at an outdoor amphitheater, macaws and pelicans fly over head (and I mean *directly* overhead—just sit very still) and your guide, Guano Joe/Guano Jane learns to overcome his/her fear of feathered friends.

MOUSEJUNKIE J I never miss this interactive bird show. I choke-up every time they bring out the bald eagle. Also, be ready with a dollar bill when they ask. You can be part of the show when a small bird flies up to take it from you. (You get it back.)

Duration: Twenty-five minutes.

Loads: Typical theater load-in. If you get there and the previous show has just let out, you're in luck.

Kali River Rapids—Get whirled around, tossed up and down, and quite drenched in this rafting expedition along the fictional Chakranadi River.

Twelve-person rafts float guests past a number of staged scenes and ultimately drops them down a twenty-foot rapid. Themes of illegal logging are addressed, although I supposed they had to teach me something before whipping me down the whitewater.

There's a warning telling guests that they might get soaked on the ride. It should be amended to say "you will get soaked, so just deal with it."

If you're concerned about walking around sopping wet, consider wearing a bathing suit, water shoes (shoes are required in the loading area), and a spare t-shirt. You can rent a locker at the front of the park to store extra or dry clothing.

Duration: Five minutes

Loads: Fairly quickly. While it is among the more popular attractions, the theming in the queue helps alleviate any line fatigue.

Maharajah Jungle Trek: A wildlife trail similar to the Pangani Forest Exploration Trail, guests walk through a rain-forest setting to see tigers, gibbons, Komodo dragons, birds, and other creatures. Among the "other creatures" are the startlingly large Rodrigues fruit bats.

 MOUSEJUNKIE BARRY Someone should get those bats some chinos. How about a little modesty?

Nepal, India, Thailand, and Indonesia all are represented throughout the Maharajah Jungle Trek.

Guests who take the walk are treated to jaw-dropping views of Bengal tigers. The massive size of these cats becomes evident when you get to see them up close.

The final theme area in the park is **DinoLand U.S.A.** It's designed to evoke a carnival-like atmosphere, with midway games and a trashy, gaudy feel. Obviously, this is not the official description. Here's the lowdown on DinoLand U.S.A.: as much as I am completely enthralled with the rest of the park, this area leaves much to be desired. I get what they're going for. I'm just not a fan of it. I grew up in a somewhat broken-down seaside resort town that had seen better days, and it feels just like parts of DinoLand U.S.A. I don't harbor any bad feelings about where I grew up, I just don't want to be plunged back into it when I'm on vacation.

Needless to say, I don't spend a whole lot of time at Chester and Hester's Dino-Rama, an asphalt and particularly out-of-place section of Dinoland U.S.A. It's mainly a way to walk from "Finding Nemo: The Musical," to the Dinosaur attraction and then out.

 MOUSEJUNKIE J Chester and Hester's area is a shame in my opinion. Walt Disney World does such a nice job in theming, but this place is an abomination. Walt turned over in his grave when this place went up. It is a complete waste of space.

Here are the attractions you'll find in Dinoland U.S.A.:

Finding Nemo: The Musical—This live-action stage show based on the Pixar film, *Finding Nemo*, is a colorful, creative triumph. Original music was composed specifically for the show, and Michael Curry, who designed puppets for the stage version of *The Lion King* acted as leading puppet and production designer. The result? A show that looks like nothing else.

Duration: Forty minutes

Loads: Typical theater load-in. Only five shows are performed daily, so don't put it off if lines are beginning to form.

Dinosaur—A dark ride with teeth, Dinosaur shoots guests back to prehistoric times aboard a Time Rover to attempt to retrieve an Iguanodon.

The ride is fast, rough, and loud. Guests are whipped down unexpected drops, around corners, and away from hungry dinos. Most of the ride is in complete darkness, and the intensity may frighten younger children. However, it's a blast. It's funny and exciting and provides enough thrill to get my blood pumping.

Duration: Ten minutes

Loads: Quickly

Mousejunkie U *Do the actors in the pre-show look familiar? They should. That's Phylicia Rashad (The Cosby Show) and Wallace Langham (CSI: Crime Scene Investigation) debating your Cretaceous era safety.*

Primeval Whirl—Combine the teacups of The Mad Tea Party in the Magic Kingdom with an off-the-shelf, run-of-the-mill mini-coaster, and you've got Primeval Whirl. The ride car spins in circles while traveling along the tracks.

Duration: Ninety seconds

Loads: Quickly

 MOUSEJUNKIE J Primeval Whirl is an evil ride. This ride is a projectile vomiting machine for me. I got off it holding lunch back in my throat and had to sit for a good half hour to regain my dignity. If you like this type of spinning ride, take a shot. I avert my eyes from it when I enter the area.

Triceratops Spin—It's Dumbo the Flying Elephant, only it's dinosaurs.

Duration: Ninety seconds

Loads: Quickly

While the key to touring Animal Kingdom successfully is to take it at a leisurely pace, it is worth getting Expedition: Everest and Kilimanjaro Safari straight away. The best approach is to pick one, go directly to it and get a Fastpass. Then, walk across the park to the other attraction and get in the standby line. If it's taken care of quickly enough, the standby line could still be reasonable. Fastpasses are available for both of these attractions and Expedition Everest has a single rider line, which will cut your wait time down dramatically.

⭐ **The Straight Dope** *Head to the Kilimanjaro Safari early in the morning, or very late in the day. If you do it in the morning, they've just let animals out of enclosures into the display areas. The animals are wide awake, and they get them out there by using food so they're active. At the end of the day the animals are in transition, being prepared to be led back into the enclosures for the night, and you'll see a lot more activity.*

 MOUSEJUNKIE DEB   Animal Kingdom has pros and cons for me:

Pros:

➤ Expedition Everest—Awesome coaster
➤ Legend of the Lion King—Excellent show
➤ During Christmas, I love how all the characters have their own decorated trees in Camp Minnie-Mickey.
➤ The carvings in the Tree of Life are remarkable.
➤ Dinosaur is a cool ride, although not as cool as the Indiana Jones equivalent in Disneyland.
➤ Divine—a cast member on stilts costumed in remarkably camouflaged vines, leaves, and sticks—is very interesting to watch if you catch a glimpse of her.
➤ Theming is authentic.

Cons:

➤ I don't like seeing the creepy, crawly things in the glass boxes that cast members are holding in the morning when you walk in. Sure they're in glass, but if you dropped that thing...AAAHHHHH!!!!!

> ➤ I'm a night owl, not a morning person, so any park that's only open until 5 P.M. or 6 P.M. loses points in my book.
> ➤ No night hours, so no night show.
> ➤ It always seems to rain the day we go to Animal Kingdom. Probably not Disney's fault.
> ➤ Lack of dining options.
> ➤ Hester and Chester's Dino-Rama is too tacky for me.
> ➤ Theming is authentic.

Wild Africa Trek

A rickety rope bridge spans a chasm over the seemingly treacherous, crocodile-infested waters of the Safi River.

As adventurous souls step out onto its aged boards, the bridge creaks and twists just thirty feet above what would be certain death should one misstep send them hurtling into the middle of the nest of toothsome predators.

But that's not likely to happen.

This particular bridge, and the river it traverses, is located in Walt Disney World, where insurance liability considerations and guest thrills come in equal parts. The crocs and hippos along the path are quite real; it's just that the bridge may not be as rickety as it appears.

It's all part of the new Wild Africa Trek at Disney's Animal Kingdom theme park. A unique, three-hour tour designed to give guests a one-of-a-kind experience in deepest, darkest Walt Disney World, the Trek takes participants through sections of the park's Pangani Forest and through parts of the Harambe Wildlife Reserve not normally open to guests.

Disney's Animal Kingdom, the newest gate at the forty-seven square-mile central Florida Walt Disney World resort, is a five hundred-acre park themed around animals and conservation. It immerses guests in expertly-themed lands designed to recreate the natural habitat of its many animals. Guests can travel on a safari that runs through the theme park's Harambe Wildlife Reserve. Guides drive along washed-out and deeply rutted roads through forests, wetlands and open bush country to get as close to animals as safety allows. Just don't call it a zoo.

From the Kilimanjaro Safari, which takes visitors on an up-close tour through painstakingly recreated sections of an African savanna, to the village of Anandapur, which sits in the shadow of the imposing (and fairly credible reproduction of) Mount Everest, Disney's Imagineers have worked hard to steep the park in authentic experiences.

Which is where the Wild Africa Trek comes in. This VIP, expertly-guided expedition is no run-of-the-mill backstage tour. Forget well-worn sidewalks lined with gift shops. The pathways of the Wild Africa Trek wind through dense bamboo and fern forests, opening up into surprising and unexpected animal interactions. Every attraction at Animal Kingdom has a story to tell, and the Wild Africa Trek becomes part of that tale.

The Trek starts at the Outfitters' Post. Guests are geared-up with vests containing everything they might need, including a safety harness for some of the more "risky" moments. Tour groups are limited to twelve guests or fewer, allowing for a much-more personal experience where those taking part are woven into the storyline.

The section of the trail that winds through the Pangani Forest Exploration Trail offers amazing views of massive Western Lowland Gorillas as they move through and loll around a lush waterfall environment. The powerful animals move freely seemingly just beyond a fingertips' reach.

The trucks carting guests through the nearby Kilimanjaro Safari rumble in the distance as Trekkers strap their harnesses onto a safety rack and actually lean out over a cliff that overlooks a hippo enclosure.

And then there's that bridge. A thin, lengthy spit of rope and wood juts out over the Safi River, which is choked with floats of prehistoric-looking crocodiles. Wide, well-traveled bridges with obvious OSHA requirements are for amateurs. Disney's Imagineers have crafted a dilapidated-looking catwalk with missing boards and an aged feel that adds immeasurably to the ambience. A closer look reveals safety netting and a secure safety harness guaranteeing that adventurers make it safely to the other side.

Participants are afforded expansive views of the Harambe grasslands, populated by several species of antelopes, gazelle, wildebeests, okapis and elephants. The entire adventure culminates in an open-air meal at a private safari camp, featuring African-inspired cuisine.

Cameras and backpacks are not permitted, but Disney's photographers will capture the entire Trek and provide these images to participants at the end of the day. The cost of the digital images, available via Disney's Photopass system and viewable/downloadable online, is included with the entry fee. And because this is Disney, you can bet there is a fee attached to the new experience.

Walt Disney World offers any number of backstage-type tours, with wildly different prices ranging from tour-to-tour. The introductory price for the Animal Kingdom's Wild Africa Tour, however, is $129 per-person. For your money you get the expert-guided three-hour tour, all the photos and the 'tastes of Africa' finale.

As with most tours, a park-entry pass is necessary.

If you go: Reservations are necessary, and restricted to guests ages eight and older. There is a weight limit of 310 pounds for safety reasons, and guests should be healthy enough to walk the entire three-hour tour. Tours are held several times daily. Call 407-WDW-TOUR to book a Trek.

Disney's Hollywood Studios

THE SPECIAL BRAND OF Tinseltown glamour on display at Disney's Hollywood Studios never really existed.

Sure, the klieg lights lit up the stars, actresses stepped out in flowing gowns dripping with jewels, and square-jawed actors in tuxedos said things like, "Listen here, doll, we're going to put you in pictures, see?" But it was never really like this.

Instead, Old Hollywood—more an idealized frame of mind than an actual spot on a map—remains vital and very much alive in the streets and backlots of Disney's glitziest theme park.

Known as "a Hollywood that never was and always will be," the Studios represent all that is enchanting about starry-eyed dreams and movie magic.

Guests enter the park on **Hollywood Boulevard,** a glitzed-up version of Main Street U.S.A. Lined with shops, it leads to the park icon—the Sorcerer's Hat. Inspired by Mickey Mouse's lid in "the Sorcerer's Apprentice" segment of the 1940 film, *Fantasia*, the hat stands 122 feet tall and towers over a replica of the Chinese Theater behind it.

Mousejunkie U   *Mickey Mouse would have to stand 350 feet tall if he wanted to wear the massive Sorcerer's Hat.*

Inside the theater is **The Great Movie Ride**. A dark ride capable of seating 68 people in each ride vehicle, it takes guests on a tour through scenes of some of classic Hollywood's most famous movies. The host leads guests through musicals, gangster films, westerns, sci-fi, action/ adventure and fantasy films.

The pilot of the "moving theater" ride vehicle gets involved at one point, taking the audience along for an adventure within the attraction.

Duration: Twenty-five minutes.

Loads: Moderately slowly. The queue area can handle a massive crowd, but once inside guests are treated to trailers from classic Hollywood movies. This is great, although once I've been on the attraction I can't get "Gotta Dance" out of my head for a good hour.

Citizens of Hollywood: Cops, starlets, movie directors, and kitschy newspaper reporters wander up and down Hollywood Boulevard, putting on impromptu shows throughout the day.

Walk partway up the street to Sunset Boulevard on your right. This is the neighborhood where most of the park's heaviest hitters live.

Here's a list of attractions that offer Fastpass at Disney's Hollywood Studios:

➤ Toy Story Midway Mania
➤ The Twilight Zone Tower of Terror
➤ Rock 'n' Roller Coaster
➤ The Voyage of the Little Mermaid
➤ Star Tours

Here are the attractions you'll find on Sunset Boulevard:

The Twilight Zone Tower of Terror—Looming ominously over the entire park, the charred hulk of the Hollywood Tower Hotel dares guests to check-in for a brief stay.

This thrill ride starts in the intricately decorated lobby, leads down into the dank boiler-room basement, and then to the very top of the cursed hotel aboard a rather unreliable elevator. Unexpected shakes, special effects, and a random drop sequence will leave your stomach in your throat. Fastpass is available for this attraction.

Duration: Ten minutes

Loads: Slowly. Lines form early if there's any crowd at all.

 MOUSEJUNKIE RANDY A fantastically themed attraction, The Tower of Terror starts weaving its story immediately upon entering the queue. One of the little details I really like is that even when there is no wait, the standby wait time never goes below thirteen evil minutes.

Rock 'n' Roller Coaster starring Aerosmith—Zero to fifty-seven m.p.h. in 2.8 seconds, three inversions, and Steven Tyler screaming in your ear make this the most adrenaline-jacking attraction in the park.

Of course, this being Disney, there's more to it than that. The story goes like this: You're in the recording studio watching the Bad Boys from Boston lay down a few tracks. Their manager arrives and tells them they're late for a show. You, and everyone in your group, score some backstage passes at the Forum. This means you'll have to board a super stretch limo that'll get you to the venue.

Hold on, because your ride is certainly going to be interesting.

Duration: Four minutes (including preshow with the awesome acting by the boys from Aerosmith)

Loads: Slowly. This is one-half of the Tower of Terror/Rock 'n' Roller Coaster Fastpass shuffle.

MOUSEJUNKIE JOHN Meteor Moment: Earth is about to be destroyed by a giant meteor hurtling toward us at incredible speed. You have twenty-four hours left to live. What do you do? I buy a Corvette (do you accept personal checks?), drive to Disney World, and ride the Rock 'n' Roller Coaster one last time. (No, not Dinosaur. That would be way too ironic.) It's a masterful Disney combination of visuals, music, and accelerated heart rate. I've been on many coasters, but none satisfy more of the senses than this one: sight, sound, feel (it's not called GForce Records for nothing). If they could just pipe in the smell of bacon cooking, it would be perfect. They really need to update the intro of Aerosmith hanging out in the recording studio. Guys, you're still remixing "Walk This Way?" Really? Maybe they could recreate Steve Tyler's hip replacement surgery. A few more decades, and those cats will be ready for the Haunted Mansion.

Beauty and the Beast Live on Stage—Currently the longest-running stage-show at Walt Disney World, this Broadway-style show uses live performers, puppets, and special effects to present a musical stage version of the Disney film.

The songs performed during the show are:

➤ "Belle"
➤ "Be Our Guest"
➤ "Something There"
➤ "The Mob Song"
➤ "Beauty and the Beast"

Duration: Thirty minutes

Loads: Quickly. The Theater of the Stars can hold 1,500 people.

Fantasmic!—A nighttime spectacular telling the story of Mickey's dreams and a battle of good versus evil, this show uses live performers, fireworks, lasers, music, animation projected onto water, fire, boats, and a pile of Disney characters.

Stunts, choreography, running battles, and a giant snake all lead up to a fiery finale with a massive, fire-breathing dragon and the appearance of princes, princesses, and almost every Disney character you can think of. Fantasmic! is the only way to finish off a day at Disney's Hollywood Studios.

Duration: Twenty-five minutes

Loads: Quickly. The Hollywood Hills amphitheater seats 6,500 people.

To the left of Hollywood Boulevard is Echo Lake. It's identified by its, well, water.

Here are the attractions located around the Echo Lake area of Disney's Hollywood Studios:

The American Idol Experience—Inspired by the massively popular TV show, hopefuls are given the chance to sing in front of a live audience at several preliminary shows throughout the day. Guests then vote for their favorite, and a final show decides the winner, who is awarded a Dream Ticket—read: Fastpass for *American Idol*—when the TV show's judges roll through town.

The Superstar Television Theater has been rebuilt to represent the TV show's set, and it's all hosted with a very Ryan Seacrest-like cast member, who interacts with participants and three Idol-like judges who sit stage-left.

Duration: Thirty minutes

Loads: Quickly

Star Tours—A motion simulator that takes guests into the world of George Lucas's Star Wars films, Star Tours was due to open with a new storyline, new motion simulator and new technology in late 2011. The update is great news, because the old version had gotten more than a bit dog-eared.

Jedi Training Academy—A live action show located right next to Star Tours, the Jedi Training Academy allows young guests ("younglings"), to join a Jedi master to learn the ways of the force.

The younglings are brought up on stage and provided with Jedi robes and toy lightsabers. They're put through their paces before facing Darth Vader himself.

Even if you don't have a youngling of your own, this show is worth making time for. The lead cast member's interaction with the kids is often hilarious.

Duration: Twenty-five minutes.

Loads: N/A. It's an outdoor stage. You walk up and watch and laugh hysterically.

It's worth noting that the viewing area for this show is in the open with no shade. Make sure your sun block is doing its job and be sure to stay hydrated. The Florida sun can sear the unprepared in minutes.

Indiana Jones Epic Stunt Spectacular—Scenes inspired by the Indiana Jones film series are reenacted by stunt actors in this live-action theater show.

Indy outruns a giant boulder, dances between spears, goes toe-to-toe with a rather large opponent, and ultimately saves Marion.

The entire adventure is presented as if it's being shot as a film, with the director and camera operators taking part in the presentation.

Audience members can volunteer to play extras.

Duration: Twenty-five minutes

Loads: Quickly. The theater can hold two thousand people.

Wander just a bit further clockwise, and find yourself in the **Streets of America** section of the park. Forced perspective architecture and Imagineering ingenuity work to make this thoroughfare resemble urban streets in New York and San Francisco.

Here are the attractions you'll find around Streets of America:

Lights, Motors, Action! Extreme Stunt Show—Fast cars, running gun battles, motorcycle jumps, a guy falling off the top of a building, another one running around on fire, and explosions. That's a good afternoon at the Studios.

This show—presented as if it's being filmed, much like the Indiana Jones Stunt Spectacular—takes place on a six-acre set designed to look like a Mediterranean village square. Stunt drivers push cars to their limits as a storyline about an ongoing chase unfolds. Imported from Disneyland Paris, the show is exciting, funny, and holds a few surprises that I'll not spoil here.

Duration: Thirty-five minutes

Loads: Quickly. The stadium holds five thousand people.

Awesome/Stupid Disney Idea *The title of Countdown to Extinction at Disney's Animal Kingdom was shortened to Dinosaur. Why not shorten Lights, Motors, Action! Extreme Stunt Show to something you can say in one breath?*

I've never been in Disney's Hollywood Studios with any-one who referred to it by its full name, anyway. It's always, "Hey, let's go see Ready, Set, Car! or whatever it's called."

And now, a one-act play entitled, "Who has time for this?"

Sarah: Say, would you like to go see Lights, Motors, Action! Extreme Stunt Show?

Adam: No, I don't want to see Lights, Motors, Action! Extreme Stunt Show. I would like to do something else, and then maybe see Lights, Motors, Action! Extreme Stunt Show.

Sarah: Perhaps we could eat lunch and then see Lights, Motors, Action! Extreme Stunt Show.

Adam: Yes, that would be a better time to see Lights, Motors, Action! Extreme Stunt Show. I like Lights, Motors, Action! Extreme Stunt Show. Lights, Motors, Action! Extreme Stunt Show is an exciting show that features lights, motors and action. And it is extreme.

(End... Scene)

I've heard it referred to as "the car thing," "car show," "the stunt cars," and "that thing where the Golden Girls house used to be." Why not just paint some eyes on the wind-shields and call it Cars?

Studio Backlot Tour—This is a combination of a walking tour and a tram tour of the Studio's backlot area.

The first part of the tour, "Harbor Attack," shows how special effects are used to create an exciting action scene. Guest volunteers help act-out the attack.

The tram portion of the tour takes guests past the Boneyard, featuring a number of vehicles that have seen screen time. The big finish comes as the tram travels through Catastrophe Canyon, where there's a potentially catastrophic (thus the name) wall of water that narrowly misses your tram. And fire. There's fire and explosions. Again, you can't really go wrong if there are explosions involved.

Duration: Thirty-five minutes

Loads—Quickly

Muppet-Vision 3-D—This is a 3D film featuring classic humor from *The Muppets*. They're all here: Kermit, Miss Piggy, Gonzo, the Swedish Chef, Beaker—pretty much any other Muppet you can think of.

New, more advanced 3-D technology dates this attraction a bit. Mickey's Philharmagic and It's Tough to Be a Bug! look better, never mind big-budget advances like *Avatar*.

But none of those films have the Muppets—beloved creations that allow Jim Hensons heart and soul to shine through.

Duration: Twenty minutes

Loads: Quickly. But get there early for the preshow. It's loaded with Muppet humor and terrible, hilarious puns.

 MOUSEJUNKIE RANDY Muppet-Vision 3-D has a special place in my heart. This is the last thing that Jim Henson worked on before his untimely death. The premiere of the show was delayed until legal issues between Disney and the surviving family were resolved. This show just never gets old and really exhibits the genius of Jim Henson.

Cut back across the front of the Sorcerer's Hat and you'll find yourself facing the **Animation Courtyard**.

Here are the attractions that are located in and around the Animation Courtyard:

Voyage of the Little Mermaid—This stage show, using a combination of live action, film clips, lasers, lighting effects, and unique and innovative puppetry, re-tells the story of the Disney film, *The Little Mermaid*. Fastpass is available for this attraction.

Duration: Twenty minutes.

Loads: Quickly. Theater empties, next group files in.

Playhouse Disney Live!—This show brings your kids' favorite Playhouse Disney characters to life, using puppetry and special effects. A cast member host guides little ones through the story, and before long has them up dancing along with their favorite characters.

A refurb in 2008 brought new characters from these shows into the production: *My Friends Tigger and Pooh, Little Einsteins, Handy Manny,* and *Mickey Mouse Clubhouse.*

Duration: Twenty minutes

Loads: Quickly. Theater empties, next group files in. However, I recommend getting in as early as you can. There are benches located along the back and sides of the open room. I send Mousejunkie Amy and Katie up front, while I kick back on these incredibly convenient and comfortable benches. I can watch the show, see my wife and daughter, and park my butt for twenty blissful minutes.

Walt Disney: One Man's Dream—This walking, self-guided tour is essentially a museum dedicated to Walt Disney. It contains some great artifacts from his life and work, and features miniature models of some of Disney theme parks' instantly recognizable icons.

It ends with a short film detailing the life and legacy of Walt Disney.

Duration: The film at the end of the attraction runs fifteen minutes

Loads: Quickly. Well, as quickly as you can walk in.

The Straight Dope *There's a trivia quiz that goes along with this attraction. Are you Mousejunkie enough to take it? Just ask a cast member about it.*

The Magic of Disney Animation—Why didn't I go on this tour for the first seventeen trips I took to Walt Disney World? Because I'm an idiot.

This is a fascinating, interactive look at Disney animation. Cast members host a short film and exhibition about animation. Guests can then show off their art skills at an animator's workspace in the Animation Academy, or move into a room full of interactive exhibits and character meet-and-greet spaces.

Duration: The initial film is ten minutes long. The Animation Academy is fifteen minutes long.

Loads: Quickly

Mousejunkie U   *This tour is great, but there's a tinge of sadness about it. The studio was once a working animation studio where some magical and amazing art was created, including the film, Lilo and Stitch. The artists were laid off in 2003, however, and the studio shuttered when Disney Animation relocated to California. You can't see me right now, but I'm making faces of great consternation in the general direction of the former Walt Disney Feature Animation Florida.*

The final themed area in Disney's Hollywood Studio's is **Pixar Place**, home to the fantastic, addictive, superlative, nearly perfect dark ride/game, **Toy Story Midway Mania**.

Guests who have been "shrunk" down to toy size wind their way through a queue designed to look like Andy's room from the Disney/Pixar Toy Story films. An audio animatronic Mr. Potato Head (Don Rickles) entertains, guests pick up their 3-D glasses, twist up some stairs, over the attraction itself, and then down to the load area.

Guests then jump aboard the ride vehicle, where they are whipped through a series of carnival midway-type games. A firing controller hurls eggs, darts, and pies at various targets. The game keeps score, allowing for some good-natured trash talk when it's all over.

The attraction is colorful, exciting, and unique. The music is fantastic, the theming is perfect, and even the queue is fun. I've lost track of how many times I've heard people point to something and say, "I had that," while waiting in the always long line.

Duration: Six minutes.

Loads: Slowly. If you're not interested in experiencing Toy Story Midway Mania, you have problems, and Gatorland is fifteen miles down the I-4. Otherwise, head straight for Pixar Place as soon as the rope drops.

 MOUSEJUNKIE JENNA For the past couple of years, I have been telling my friends visiting Walt Disney World to follow my Toy Story Midway Mania strategy.

Bottom line—you're going to want to ride this and you're going to want to do it more than once. This is doubly true if you have kids, love the Toy Story movies, or enjoy playing video games. TSMM also has some of the most insane wait times of any ride at Disney World. So without further ado, here is my no-fail strategy:

First, you have to plan to get there early. Twenty minutes before park opening works for me. As soon as you've gotten through the turnstiles, give every park ticket in your party to the fastest and least encumbered (by children, spouse, or tendency toward distraction) person in the group. That person then needs to work their way toward the front of the crowd waiting for rope drop. It may be lonely, but don't stay with your group while waiting. Every person between you and rope drop becomes an obstacle to pass once the crowd starts moving. The fewer human slalom poles the better!

As soon as the rope drop ceremony is over—usually a funny "movie scene" with Otto Von Bonn Bahn, Flavio Fellini or Shelby Mayer—walk very, very quickly to Pixar Place and the TSMM Fastpass kiosks. Don't worry, you won't get lost. Eighty percent of the people in the rope drop crowd are going to the same place. Get your group's Fastpasses, then find your group.

Which leads me to part two of the strategy: just because the most fleet-of-foot person is heroically dashing off to get Fastpasses for everyone, it doesn't mean that the rest of the group gets to amble around leisurely. The key to getting everyone on the ride twice is to get every single person down to the ride as soon as possible. Go straight to TSMM. Do not stop in for coffee at Starring Rolls. Do not stop to watch hilarious police officers "just for a minute." It's go time, people!

If you time it just right, the entire party will arrive in Pixar Place just in time to see your forerunner finishing up with the Fastpass kiosks. I've never seen it, but

(Continued on next page)

the people to whom I am handing out Fastpasses tell me it's a wonderful sight. At that point, everyone gets in the stand-by line before it gets too long and enjoys the ride, knowing they can return later and walk right past all those people who didn't plan ahead and are stuck in a forty-five to one-hundred-twenty minute line.

And if you're traveling in a large group and it turns out that some people don't want to ride twice, well, Fastpasses are transferable. Teen Mousejunkie Ryan and I rode three times one day and ended up giving three extra Fastpasses to a family entering the line just as the wait time changed to ninety minutes.

At 3 P.M., Block Party Bash comes to life. A stage show and parade, it moves through the streets of Disney's Hollywood Studios before setting up performances in several areas throughout the park. Cast members perform dance numbers, interactive contests, and songs before packing the show up and moving along. Characters from Disney/Pixar films such as *The Incredibles*, the *Toy Story* movies, *Monsters, Inc.* and *A Bug's Life* are featured in this high-energy show.

The Straight Dope *It's worth trying to get a spot a little early for the Block Party Bash. Stake out an area near Sorcerer Mickey's hat (the giant, blue hat at the end of Hollywood Boulevard). Get a spot on the right-hand side. This will allow you to view the performance without looking straight into the sun. Additionally, the right-hand side offers* *a little more protection from the sun—which will fry you no matter what time of year it is.*

A day at Disney's Hollywood Studios should always end with a performance of Fantasmic! However, since the show's schedule has been reduced to just a couple of nights a week, be sure to check your park maps so you'll know when it's showing.

It's always crowded, and planning to sit in the center of the theater requires arriving at least one hour before show time. The Hollywood Hills Amphitheatre features metal benches that surround the performance area in a semi-circle. Your early arrival may get you a good, centrally located seat, but it's also going to guarantee you a numb rear end.

Avoid numb-butt by booking a Fantasmic! dinner package. This allows you to dine at specific times, and then arrive just before show time in a reserved seating area. (The reserved area is off to either the left or right side, but since the show is visible from any seat in the theater, that's not usually a problem.)

The Hollywood Hills Amphitheatre seats nearly ten thousand people. And when show is over, everyone leaves at once. The entire crowd is funneled into a single walkway, which is then split into to main exits. Being near the exit when the show ends can save a lot of time and aggravation.

★**The Straight Dope** *Many people will advise you to line up for Fantasmic extremely early. Here's why they're wrong: If its ten minutes until the show starts and they're* still letting people in, then by all means take a seat. The later you get there, the more likely it is that you will able to sit near the back and to the right. This is important for two reasons: You can see fine from anywhere, and—more importantly— you'll be near the exit.

Full disclosure: I put this practice to the test on a recent trip. We arrived late on purpose and ended up in the standing-room-only section behind the seating area. Other than my legs being a bit tired from a day at the park, it wasn't a bad experience. We could see fine, my daughter made a new little friend, and we were half-way home to our resort before the last person had left the theater.

If a seat up front or in the middle is important, this approach may not work for you. If you want to see the show and leave without going gray, it might be just the thing.

Mousejunkies Recreate

K<small>IDS ARE GREAT</small>, aren't they?

The magic in their eyes when they first catch a glimpse of Cinderella Castle or wrap their arms around Mickey Mouse is unforgettable.

Equally as unforgettable is when they throw up in line on a 100-degree day and it splashes all over your shoes. Or someone's doughy, moist, sticky-fingered cherub pushes by you in a queue, leaving behind great swaths of his DNA and God-knows-what disease on your leg. Or when they stand behind you in line and kick away at your calf until it feels like they may have fractured your tibia.

Yeah, kids are great. But occasionally the time comes to get very, very far away from them, lest the karate skills come into play and you end up in the most magical holding cell in Orange County.

(Editor's note: Mousejunkies does not condone karate chopping children. Usually.)

Walt Disney World has plenty of places where adults can put some distance between themselves and the theme parks. Water skiing, boating, golf, parasailing, fine dining, and my favorite, fishing, are all part of a Walt Disney World vacation.

Plus, you'll likely avoid being thrown up on unless you're recreating with a particularly odd adult.

Catching Nemo

It was cold. It was windy. Bay Lake was angry.

These were the conditions that met us as we prepared to launch the first annual Mousejunkies Invitational Fishing Derby at Walt Disney World. Participants flocked to the shores of Bay Lake behind Contemporary Resort. Walt Disney World has acres of waterways, from lakes and ponds to canals and rivers. And all of them are packed with aquatic life. Bass, bluegill, alligators, gar, and dozens of species of waterfowl thrive just outside the shadow of Cinderella Castle, and we were there to see what we could find.

At tournament time the roster of skilled and determined anglers was as follows: me and Some Guy Named Walt from Massachusetts. (Mousejunkie Walt, actually. But when it comes to competitive angling, he will be relegated to "Some Guy Named Walt.")

So to say that participants "flocked" to the location might be overstating it a bit. The unseasonably cool temperatures and windy conditions must have kept the hobbyists away, because there were very few other guests out fishing. Either that, or most people were a little smarter. It was rather raw.

Our guide was cast member and professional angler Carrie Bronson, who competes in the FLW tour. She was friendly, knowledgeable and determined to help us boat some of Disney's largemouth bass. Bronson fired up the engines on our pontoon boat, and brought us near the shores of the Wilderness Lodge resort.

Using live shiners, Some Guy Named Walt and I had our lines in the water and our game faces on. Within two minutes, Some Guy Named Walt's rod dipped, and he was reeling in the first catch of the day. He exuded confidence and sent some rather pointed trash talk my way. Bronson called the contest like a referee.

Having fished most of my life, I consider myself experienced, but out of practice in recent years. It would be a blow to my self image if I were to lose to a restaurateur from the North Shore. Just as I was beginning to doubt my skills, I felt a hit on the end of my line. I set the hook and cranked like my life depended on it. My catch was small, but Some Guy Names Walt and I were now tied up. Minutes later I boated a second largemouth, this one a bit larger. It was clear that the fish in Bay Lake were rather spirited. Our average so far weighed in between 1 to 2.5 pounds (a weight that did not reflect the fight in these fish.)

Disney offers a number of different fishing options daily, launching from several locations. Bronson said Bay Lake was her favorite spot, having seen a fourteen-plus pounder pulled from a point just next to the new Bay Lake Towers resort. The price ranges from $170 to $455, depending on time, location and number of anglers on board. Rods, reels, bait and drinks are provided, and guides will bait and cast the line for those who are queasy of touching the bait or have a little less experience. It's a strictly catch-and-release program, and guides outfit gear using circle hooks which provide an easy release. Guests are also given a free one-year subscription to Bass Magazine.

As I was asking Bronson questions about Disney's fishing program, Some Guy Named Walt managed to somehow hook into a larger fish, tying up the competition.

As the cold wind whipped across the lake, we tried other locations—alongside the former Discovery Island, and just next to the abandoned River Country. We didn't catch anymore of the many thousands of fish lurking just below the surface, so headed back to the dock with the results with a tie, the overall winner under review.

In the end, size mattered, as Some Guy Named Walt was named king of the day for landing the largest catch of the day. He accepted his coronation as champion of the first annual Mousejunkies Invitational Fishing Tournament with appropriate pride at the Rose and Crown Pub in the UK pavilion at Epcot.

To book a trip and have your friends crush your self-image, visit disneyworldfishing.com or call (407) 939-BASS (2277).

Bass fishing excursion prices: Two-hour excursions (boats can hold up to five guests)—$235 to $270. Four-hour excursions (boats can hold up to five guests)—$455

The Straight Dope *Annual Passholders enjoy a discount on guided fishing excursions, so make sure you mention it when booking.*

MOUSEJUNKIE WALT This was the second time I've gone on a fishing excursion at Walt Disney World. I enjoy fishing, but would I go every time I went to Walt Disney World? Not unless I was with people who have a passion for it. I like fishing, but I wouldn't go down there and say, "I've got to do that." If there was someone with me who wanted to, then sure. Of course it also makes it more fun when I win the contest.

The funny coincidence is that Carrie Bronson was our guide both times. And both times she was excellent. The fishing guides do a great job. They understand who they've got in the boat with them. When I was on a fishing excursion with my friend Michael, who is a serious angler, they had these in-depth conversations about lures. But yet she can still talk to a dummy like me.

As a postscript, Walt and I both got our butts kicked by Mousejunkie Amy a couple of years back during a guided Walt Disney World fishing excursion in the canals behind Port Orleans. It is a shame from which I have yet to recover.

Walt Disney World's most picturesque assets—its lakes, rivers, and canals—present a perfect opportunity to put some distance between you and the long lines.

Duffing at Disney:
A Golf Mancation at the World

MOUSEJUNKIE J Is Walt Disney World really the first location that jumps to mind when you want to get away with the guys for some male bonding?

It is for me, and I'll tell you why.

Say you want to get away on a golf trip. First, you need to convince the spouse that this trip will be good for both of you. Then there's just one major decision to make: Where to go? There are the classics—Vegas, Myrtle Beach—places like that. I say choose Walt Disney World, of course.

It may sound odd for four grown men to go to Walt Disney World, but it does make perfect sense. When Mousejunkie Deb announced she would be going on a spa weekend with the girls, the door swung open for my golf Mancation.

The guys I had slated for this trip are golfers, and that would be the focal point for the trip. Walt Disney World has five golf courses on property, two of which (Palm and Magnolia'o, host the PGA tour each year with the Children's Miracle Network Classic. Since all the members of the group have families and children heading to college, saving some money became an important factor. The cheapest hotel option for us would be using DVC points to stay at the Saratoga Springs Resort. Saratoga was the perfect choice since it is home to the Lake Buena Vista Course and would be a short walk to Downtown

Disney and all its restaurant choices each night after a full day of golfing. This would also provide us with free transfers to and from the airport with Magical Express. No need to rent a car.

In planning this trip, I would employ every money-saving trick I could muster. The major expense of any vacation is food. Annual Passholders are eligible to participate in the Tables in Wonderland program, which is a great money-saver. For $75, an Annual Passholder can buy a card that allows twenty percent off every table service meal and twenty percent off alcohol. The Tables in Wonderland card pays for itself after two meals. The discount can be applied for up to eight people in a dining party. It is good for a calendar year so even after the Mancation came to an end, I would be able to use the card for eleven more months.

For this vacation, the second big expense would be the golf. Normal rates at a Walt Disney World course can be as high as $159 for a round of golf. In order to save here, I bought a Disney Vacation Club golf membership for $50. This membership brought the cost of a round down to, on average, $90. The membership is also good for twelve months. Oddly enough, there would be no theme park time in this trip. The golf would consume our days and I was the only member of the party that had a park pass. As I have come to find over the years, great trips to Walt Disney World do not have to involve the theme parks.

It was just after lunch when we checked in at the Saratoga Springs Resort. I had requested the Congress

(Continued on next page)

Park section due to its proximity to Downtown Disney. We had no golf plans for the day so we headed over to Downtown Disney to grab lunch. After a short wait we were sitting in the T-Rex restaurant sipping on a draft. The golf trip was officially underway. Friday we had a tee time at Lake Buena Vista Course. Or so we thought.

Friday morning brought with it a deluge of rain. Luckily, the weather for Saturday looked perfect and we were going to be playing two full rounds of golf. It would be a long day ahead.

We awoke Saturday to gorgeous weather. After some waffles at Artist's Palette, we called for our free cab ride to the Palm course. When you stay on-property and golf, the greens fees include free cab rides to and from the courses.

We checked in at **Disney's Palm Golf Course** and went to the first tee. As we waited for our tee time we experienced our first magical moment of the trip. Two greens keepers came over and invited my friend Bob and I to choose the pin location on the eighteenth green. We selected the location, took some pictures and went back to tee off. Around the third hole, the men returned and presented us with personalized yardage book for the course with our names and dates. It was pretty neat to see that magical moments were not just for little kids in theme parks. We finished the round, then walked over to the Oak Trail course for the afternoon round.

Oak Trail is the nine hole walking course in between Palm and Magnolia. This course is inexpensive but it shows in the quality of the fairways and greens. It was like golfing back home in New England. Fortunately, it was only $20.

Sunday would be a full eighteen holes at **Disney's Magnolia Golf Course** and then a full eighteen holes at the **Lake Buena Vista Course**. We ate at Artist's palette and took a cab to Magnolia. With the Disney Vacation Club golf membership, our clubs were transferred from course to course for us at night for free. It is a great service if you are there to golf every day. We teed off and were on our way to a full day of golf. The weather was perfect and we had a great time. We left Magnolia a little after lunch and went back to our resort.

We had about an hour before tee off at Lake Buena Vista, so we grabbed lunch at Artist's Palette, which is a step above traditional Disney counter service. The food is great, isn't that expensive, and it qualifies for the Tables in Wonderland discount. At lunch they make their own potato chips that are to die for. We wiped our mouths with our sleeves since there were no wives around and went to the first tee.

Since it was the second round of the day, we thought team play using a best ball format would save us a bit of energy. The Lake Buena Vista course winds through the Saratoga Springs, Old Key West, and Port Orleans resorts. I love this aspect but a few members of the group who had errant tee shots that hit buildings and probably cars, did not like this. Our weary foursome finished the day eating out on the balcony at the Turf Club at our resort.

Monday was our last day. We were golfing at the Tom Fazio designed **Osprey Ridge Course**. It's the most well

(Continued on next page)

laid-out course and I love it. It's a challenging course where there are actually a few hills with elevated tee boxes—a rare sight in a flat state such as Florida. And yes, there are ospreys all over the place with manmade telephone pole perches that they can nest in. I witnessed one swoop in and grab an unsuspecting mouse for lunch. Mickey would disapprove.

This was also the second magical moment of the trip occurred. The greens keepers here asked our friends Hugh and Matt to select the pin placement on the eighteenth hole. They also received a personalized yardage book and a sign on the eighteenth tee box announcing who they were and where they were from.

The Straight Dope   *This is Florida, so alligators are among the residents who call this state home. But starters also caution golfers, especially out-of-state players, about the water moccasins. So rather than looking for your ball near a swampy area, it's best to pull another out of your bag.*

We finished up around 11A.M. and headed back to Saratoga Springs where our bags were in storage.

The golf trip had come to an end. It was compact and a bit tiring but we had a blast and didn't even see a theme park. If you want a great Mancation golf trip choose Walt Disney World. You won't be disappointed.

Winding Down

After a long day on the links, guests can head to one of two spas located on Disney property: the spa at the Grand Floridian or Disney's Saratoga Springs Resort & Spa.

The spa at the Saratoga Springs resort is tucked into the middle of the sprawling vacation club project, just across the lake from Downtown Disney. Surrounded by the Victorian architecture that evokes the horse-racing influence of the spa's upstate New York namesake, visitors will find an instantly relaxing atmosphere.

The opulence of the Grand Floridian carries over into its spa facility, a Victorian-themed ten-thousand square-foot expanse of relaxation and luxury just to the side of the main resort on the Seven Seas Lagoon.

The spa at the Grand Floridian offers an assortment of treatments, all of which soothe park-weary guests in a number of ways. The offerings include:

➤ **Massage therapies:** citrus zest massage, reflexology, sports massage, shiatsu, and personalized aromatherapy

➤ **Couples treatments:** In-room treatments are available, but the spa offers a candlelit room where couples can indulge themselves.

➤ **Hand and foot treatments:** Manicures, pedicures, and leg treatments.

➤ **Children's massage:** Mini massages, facials, manicures, and pedicures are offered for parents who want to bring the young ones along while they, well, get away from the kids. Other people's kids, I guess.

➤ **Water therapies:** Soothing soaks include Lavender Meadows baths, Secret Garden baths, and Gardenia bubble baths.

➤ **Facials:** Replenish your sun-baked skin with the spa's new Sodashi facial line. Stress recovery, antioxidant, and gentleman's facials are among the offerings.

⭐ **Awesome/Stupid Disney Idea** *Funnel cake aromatherapy.*

MOUSEJUNKIE WALT For years I wanted to try a massage but I just never did. Finally I got over my hesitance and tried it. Now I'm addicted. There's nothing better than relaxing and letting yourself be pampered. You get up feeling great.

I tried the spa at the Grand Floridian. It was just starting to rain the day of my appointment, so it was a perfect time to get inside and relax. I signed in and was brought into a room where everything was sparkling clean. Soft music was playing and I immediately started to unwind.

The facilities are beautiful and I enjoyed going over all the different options available. I chose a Swedish massage, which is what you think of when you hear 'massage.' My therapist asked what kind of pressure I was interested in, and I told her medium.

Another great thing is that once your massage is over, you have full access to the spa's facilities. I felt totally loose and fantastic, so I jumped in the Jacuzzi for a little while to complete the perfect hour-long appointment.

Would I do it again? Oh yeah. I'd like to give the spa at Saratoga Springs a try sometime.

Treatments at the Saratoga Springs's spa range from the standard manicure/pedicure to the more interesting Adirondack Stone Therapy, in which heated stones and oils are used to loosen stress points and knots. With nary a youngster in sight, the searing heat and daunting queues at the Disney World attractions couldn't seem farther away.

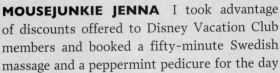 **MOUSEJUNKIE JENNA** I took advantage of discounts offered to Disney Vacation Club members and booked a fifty-minute Swedish massage and a peppermint pedicure for the day I arrived at Walt Disney World. It seemed like an excellent way to dive into vacation relaxation.

Saratoga Springs is a very calm and quiet resort in the first place, but the spa there is so far removed from Mickey Mouse, popcorn, and Fastpasses that it's almost spooky. It's a place of barely audible instrumental music, cotton waffle-weave robes, and pitchers of ice water served in a lounge where everyone whispers. It's a very relaxing atmosphere, but not somewhere to get excited about a Disney trip.

My first appointment was the Swedish massage. My massage therapist asked me some questions about allergies and trouble spots, and went to work on all those

(Continued on next page)

airplane coach seat knots. I think fifty minutes is just enough massage to relax without feeling ridiculous, though the spa offers shorter and longer massage times. I'm a bit chatty, so I just did not tune out, but if that's your thing, the atmosphere is perfect for it. Afterward, I had a ten-minute break in the lounge. The lounge has a special name—either Quiet Lounge or Meditation Room—which gives you a hint to its sole purpose. The room is quiet with dimmed lights, and ice water for drinking.

Soon the technician who would be doing my pedicure called me, and I fled the quiet room. I was fortunate enough to travel to Walt Disney World while the spa at Saratoga Springs was offering its Peppermint Pedicure. The Peppermint Pedicure is named after a special peppermint candy famous in Saratoga Springs (and sold in the Artist's Palette gift shop): the Peppermint Pig. The hand-and-foot treatment room has two pedicure chairs and two manicure tables. Additionally, they can set up a portable manicure station so guests getting a mani-pedi can get their fingers polished while their tootsies are soaking. The Peppermint Pedicure includes a soak in the foot spa, a massage with a tingly and fresh-smelling peppermint lotion, and the usual trim and polish. At fifty minutes, the pedicure lasted as long as the Swedish massage and I think I enjoyed it more. When I was done, my spa technician sent me off with all of the emory boards, buffing blocks, and toe separators she used on me, and tucked a nice-sized sample of the peppermint lotion for good measure.

It was a very relaxing visit to the spa, but I don't know that I can fully recommend it as a first-day treat. This was the second time that I have spent my first day at Walt Disney World at the spa. It was also the second time that I have left the spa worried that my luggage wouldn't be waiting in my new hotel room (it wasn't the first time) and that I'd show up late for dinner with massage oil in my hair and in the same tired clothes I flew down in.

If you want the relaxation of a spa visit to last, my advice is to schedule it in the middle of your vacation on a day when you have no concrete plans.

Date Night at Disney

There are literally scores of adult dining choices at Disney, but for the best views this side of Cinderella's Castle, head to the California Grill, located atop the Contemporary Hotel.

Guests also can enjoy an evening without the kids at Citricos at Disney's Grand Floridian Resort and Spa; Jiko— The Cooking Place at Disney's Animal Kingdom Lodge; Artist Point at Disney's Wilderness Lodge; Todd English's bluezoo at Walt Disney World Dolphin; and The Dining Room at Wolfgang Puck's in Downtown Disney.

Visitors wishing to truly upgrade their dining can opt to splurge at Victoria and Albert's at the Grand Floridian, a special-occasion restaurant designed to cater to the most discriminating culinary tastes. A customized seven-course gourmet meal is served each night in the intimate sixty-five-seat dining room. The wine cellar, with more than 700 selections on the menu and 4,200 in the cellar, has been recognized by *Wine Spectator* magazine with an Award of Excellence.

Of course, this being Disney, each waitress answers to Victoria, every waiter is known as Albert, and diners are presented with a personalized menu at the end of the meal. Dinner is $95 per person, $145 with a wine pairing. The coveted Chef's Table is $125 per person, $185 with a wine pairing.

Who Needs Theme Parks? Resort Recreation

MOUSEJUNKIE CAROL   Each Disney resort has its own hidden secrets. When checking in, take a look at the package of information you receive at the front desk. Each has activities planned throughout the day. Almost every pool on property has dance parties for the kids and games poolside around 3 P.M. The adults can lounge with a nice, refreshing pina co-lava the kids can be entertained by the Disney staff.

One day during an April vacation I was walking to my room at the Animal Kingdom Lodge when I noticed several televisions set up with life guards nearby ready for some gaming action. At Kidani Village, the lifeguards had set up some Wii stations ready to battle guests on the latest games. This time it happened to be a Wii game called "Just Dance." With some practice under my belt, I accepted the challenge and battled for the win. I forgot that the lifeguards are there daily and have many more hours of practice than I, but good times were had.

Most resorts have inflatable movie screens that play Disney movies after dark. My favorite resort to go to for this is the Beach and Yacht Club resorts. They set up the theater right on the beach and have a fire for roasting marshmallows and making s'mores.

Location is everything: after enjoying the movie I head over to the Boardwalk where the evening entertainment of jugglers and magicians take over for the perfect ending to an exhausting day.

Disney Recreation Checklist

- ❑ Golf reservations: (407) WDW-GOLF (4653)
- ❑ For group outings: (407) 938-3870
- ❑ To book a spa treatment at the Saratoga Springs Resort and Spa: (407) 827-4455
- ❑ To book a spa treatment at the Grand Floridian Resort: (407) 824-2332
- ❑ To book a parasailing excursion: (407) 939-0754
- ❑ Horseback riding at Fort Wilderness: (407) WDW-PLAY (939-7529)
- ❑ Richard Petty Driving Experience: (800) BE-PETTY (237-3889)
- ❑ SCUBA diving and SCUBA-assisted snorkeling: (407) WDW-TOUR (939-8687)
- ❑ Surfing lessons at Typhoon Lagoon: (407) WDW-PLAY (939-7529)
- ❑ Water skiing on Bay Lake: (407) 939-0754

Mousejunkies Procreate

At first I couldn't tell what had awakened me. All I knew was that one moment I was unconscious, and the next I was sitting up, staring into the darkness of our room at the Saratoga Springs resort.

In the span of about half a second, I did a rapid check of what was going on around me:

➤ No light coming in the window, so not time to get biscuits and gravy yet: check.
➤ I'm awake in a hotel room at Walt Disney World, yet Stacey isn't on the TV: odd, but check.
➤ Air conditioner is on. Room remains freezing cold: check.
➤ There's some little kid next to me and she's throwing up all over the bed: check. Wait, what?

I was starting to shake the cobwebs out of my head. Things were coming into focus.

Oh, right, I have a daughter, I remembered. That must be her.

Then the details came flooding back: We were on a Christmas season trip with family with whom we were sharing a two-bedroom suite at Saratoga Springs. Katie, Amy, and I were sharing a king-size bed. Which is what put me in the spray zone.

Amy bolted out of bed and hit the light switch, because evidently it's better to be able to see what's happening instead of lying back down and willing it to go away, which is usually my approach. She's always a lot quicker to react to these kinds of things than I am. I think it's a mother's skill. Dads are supposed to fumble around as they come out of a deep sleep, while moms spring into action. I was playing my role perfectly.

As the room became instantly illuminated and my eyeballs tried to dig a hole in the back of my head, an image was burned into my retinas just before I squeezed my eyes shut. It was of a little girl, my daughter Katie, reminding me that we had deep-fried Oreos for dessert at Boma earlier in the night.

How was she reminding me? She was showing them to me. And the sheets. And the bedspread. And the pillows.

Now I was fully awake.

Amy grabbed Katie and raced her into the bathroom. It was too late, however. There was a huge mess all over the bed. And since she was tending to the child, it was going to be my duty to begin the cleansing process.

But first, a thought crossed my mind that defined the entire incident: so this is what it's like when you come to Walt Disney World with kids.

I stripped the bed and did the best I could to scrub everything. After a quick bath and a few minutes to catch her breath, it appeared as if Katie was recovering nicely. She sat in a chair while Stacey babysat her from the television. Her mother and I started to put the room back together with clean bedding.

The thought kept coming: this is what it's like to go to Walt Disney World with kids.

It's certainly part of it. But of course it's not all 2 A.M. vomiting surprises. There are countless moments when an unforgettable memory is created and framed in the vacation slide deck of your mind.

I'm just saying that along with holding her hand as we walked up Main Street U.S.A. and seeing her meet her favorite princess for the first time, this would also be among those everlasting images. Its part of being a parent, and part of being a parent who goes to Walt Disney World frequently.

Our Disney habits had changed dramatically since Katie came into the world four years earlier. Where once we'd jump from park to park, doing whatever we felt like at the speed our legs would carry us, we now were forced to slow down considerably and factor-in the needs and best interests of a youngster.

Kidless, we would skip carelessly past exhausted looking parents who were trying to calm their red-faced, usually crying, and equally exhausted children. When we'd hear a young one throwing a fit somewhere nearby, we'd even be so cavalier as to jokingly say, "that kid hates Disney."

We thought it was funny then. Now I empathize with those parents. Having a child and bringing them along for the first time changes your Disney skill set entirely. There are dozens of things to think about that had never crossed our minds previously. Do we need a stroller? Did she get enough sleep? Will she be scared of certain characters or attractions? Is she hydrated enough? Why did she just throw up deep-fried Oreos at 2 A.M.? ("Because you fed her deep-fried Oreos, goofball," would be your answer. And you'd be right.)

But these were questions we never had to consider previously. We were now among those who we once stepped around to get to our next destination.

The Straight Dope *When it comes to character encounters, be patient. See how your child reacts the first time they see a character. If they act frightened, don't force it. Our little one was a little nervous as we were approaching Mickey in the Judge's Tent in Toontown, but the look of sheer joy on her face when she finally came around the corner and saw him was worth the gamble.*

Let's Nap-It-Out, Stitch

A little crankiness comes hand in hand with a Walt Disney World vacation. It's just a fact. It's usually hot, crowded, and often times you wake up early and stay out until very late. For a young kid, a schedule like that can be taxing. Heck, for a forty(mumble)-year-old it can be taxing.

It can be difficult to deal with, because a Walt Disney World vacation isn't the cheapest way to spend a week. But sometimes trying to talk sense to a slightly dehydrated, sleep-deprived toddler can be the wrong way to go. It gets especially tough when you see dollar signs floating away because your kid insists on going back to the pool instead of using your rather expensive park passes to stay in the theme park. On every trip I see far too many parents trying to berate their kids into having fun, which almost always results in a general meltdown.

Consider the nap: A mid-day respite, spent huddled under the covers in complete darkness. (It might be 112 degrees outside, but I keep our room's air conditioning frigid at all times.) I know it can seem like a waste of time. While you're lying in a darkened room back at the resort, the rest of the World is going on just minutes away. Parades, character meet and greets, shows—everything you want to get done on your vacation is still happening. But you're prone and motionless as the daylight hours tick away.

A much-needed nap, however, can save an entire day. It's impossible to scream a kid into a good mood, so rather than battle back and forth in the heat and the crowds, pack it in and grab some down time. A recharge of the batteries and a splash of water on the face can do wonders for a little one's mood. And her Mom's.

I am often the butt of some pointed Mousejunkie barbs because of my nap routine. But I swear by it.

An ode to the nap, as expressed through ancient art of haiku:
Bus back to the room
Ice-cold air conditioning
No one is crying

A Lack of Character Is Not Such a Bad Thing

The next thing we learned is not to base our vacation around Disney's colorful and conveniently available characters. They certainly are part of the Walt Disney World experience, but standing in long lines to get a picture with a character is not an efficient use of time.

We haven't put a number on how many character interactions of photos are enough, it's just a matter of getting a feel for how the day is going.

When I look back at my old trip photos, or someone else's the least-interesting ones are the posed character pictures. It looks like everyone is lined up for execution at dawn, and there's usually very little emotion outside of a wave and a smile.

I took a picture of Cinderella Castle in 1981. I took another one in 1998, and yet another in 2010. Guess what? It hasn't really changed. The people standing in front if it, however, have changed. And that's what it's all about, in the end. I put more value in photos of my daughter's reactions to unexpected events or resting in her mother's arms after a long day. If you still feel like you need your character interaction, and don't misunderstand me—it's still a great part of a Walt Disney World vacation—let them come to you.

★ **The Straight Dope** *Book a couple of character meals. The characters come to you. It's much easier and it all takes place inside—so it's air conditioned. Plus, food.*

Strollers Are Your Friend

If you think your child might need a stroller, bring it. You can pack your own or rent one at the parks. Stroller rentals are available at all four theme parks: $15 per day, or $31 for a double-stroller per day. We always brought our own, and I'm very happy we did. While it can be a pain to get it on and off the Disney buses, it looks different from the vast fleet of hard plastic rental strollers that converge in alarming numbers in Fantasyland, and is therefore easier to find after exiting an attraction.

It's also more common for the Disney rental strollers to be stolen. You can't tell them apart, so it'd be hard to identify it as yours.

The Straight Dope *Having your stroller stolen is a hazard every parent must face, but here's a unique strategy that may lessen the chances of this happening. It's simple: Take a diaper, put it in a see-through freezer bag, pour some root beer into the bag and hang it from your stroller's handle. Voila—the "soiled diaper gambit" keeps your property safer from stroller poachers.*

I get totally wiped out walking around all day, so the last thing I want to do is carry my daughter around all night. Putting her in the stroller conserved her energy, it helped us keep track of where she was all the time, and it gave us a place to put stuff—cameras, souvenirs, and so forth. Not to mention it preserved her dad's back for a few more years.

The Straight Dope *Mark your stroller with something that's easy to spot. We use a neon-orange Mickey-shaped luggage tag. It makes your stroller much easier to locate after riding an attraction, especially if it was moved from where you parked it on the way in.*

Stroller parking areas are located throughout the parks. Just because you left your stroller in a certain place when you went into an attraction, doesn't mean it'll be in that same spot when you come out. It doesn't necessarily mean someone took it, however. Cast members often have to relocate strollers to make room for others or to clear a pedestrian area.

On a related note, don't leave anything of value in the stroller when you park it and walk away. Take any digital cameras, park passes, or pocketbooks with you.

Stroller Rental Locations

The Magic Kingdom: The first level of the Main Street Railroad station.

Epcot: At the main entrance, just to the right. International Gateway—on the left before the turnstiles.

Animal Kingdom: Go through the turnstiles and go right.

Disney's Hollywood Studios: At Oscar's Super Service—just look for the gas station on the right after you walk through the turnstiles.

A length-of-stay stroller rental is also available. Guests make a one-time payment for as many days as will be needed

at a rate of $13 a day (saving $2 a day), and double strollers
for $27 a day (saving $4 a day.) Just show your receipt at the
stroller rental location and you'll be on your way.

Tackling the Magic Kingdom

The Magic Kingdom is the Holy Grail for the younger set. It
is the iconic park and it has the most attractions appropriate for children.

The Straight Dope *If your child shows fear or starts
to cry while in line at an attraction, consider skipping it. It's
not worth the frustration involved as you attempt to calm an
upset child while adding up the cost of the trip in your head.*

When we first took our daughter to Walt Disney World,
she was three years old. She was afraid of the dark rides, primarily because we'd get into a ride vehicle and be taken into
a dark tunnel. Yet she loved any of the attractions that were
located outside.

When I asked her to review Magic Kingdom attractions
after that first trip, most of her comments contained the
words, "no," "scary," and "never again."

But that was years ago. She's braver now, and generally
wants to ride anything she's tall enough to get on, which
brings with it its own set of restrictions.

A list of Magic Kingdom attractions with height restrictions:

Land	Attraction	Height restriction
Tomorrowland	Space Mountain	44 inches
Tomorrowland	Stitch's Great Escape	40 inches
Tomorrowland	Tomorrowland Speedway	32 inches to ride, 54 inches to drive
Frontierland	Big Thunder Mountain Railroad	40 inches
Frontierland	Splash Mountain	40 inches

The Straight Dope *Use the "baby swap" to experience any attractions you might want to, but your child does not (or is too short for). It works like this: Parents and child queue up together. Parent A rides first, while parent B stands to one side with the child. Once the ride is over, the parents trade places and parent B gets to ride the attraction without waiting through the entire line again.*

Approaching the Magic Kingdom with Kids

Get to the park early. You'll get to see the opening show, and you'll get a jump on all those other people who are still abed while you're storming the Castle.

Attack **Fantasyland** first. It's tailor-made for kids, but the beauty of it is that parents can ride-along on every attraction without feeling awkward or outsized. If you've got youngsters along, get Fantasyland out of the way as soon as possible. I'm not saying to run from attraction to attraction, but focusing on the slower-loading kid magnets early will save you from unnecessary stress later in the day. Specifically target Dumbo, Peter Pan's Flight, the Many Adventures of Winnie the Pooh, the Mad Tea Party, and—working toward Tomorrowland—the Tomorrowland Speedway. Lines can form quickly at these attractions in particular, and it's best to get to them as early as you can.

If the kids are older, follow the crowds to **Splash Mountain and Big Thunder Mountain Railroad**. Fastpass one, standby the other. **Space Mountain** also packs them in early, so prioritize and execute.

If the **3 P.M. parade** is kicking off and you're stuck in the back of the crowd near Main Street, consider relocating to Frontierland near the bridge at Splash Mountain. The crowds are usually much thinner there and little ones will have a better chance to see what's happening.

Need some room to breathe by mid-day? Raft over to Tom Sawyer's Island, hop on the Walt Disney World railroad for a few loops, grab a seat in the Hall of Presidents or catch the Country Bear Jamboree to power down with the kids.

If your kids will sit still long enough and you'd like a front-row seat to the evening parade and **Wishes**, pull up a curb on Main Street or the Hub in front of Cinderella Castle about at least an hour before show time.

One of our favorite viewing spots for **Spectromagic/ Main Street Electric Parade and Wishes** is from the second floor of the Main Street train station facing the Castle.

If you want to catch everything from there, plan on arriving a couple hours early.

Epcot with Kids

At first glance, Epcot has less to offer the little ones than the Magic Kingdom—what with the learning and lectures and such. Beyond the initial impression, however, there lies a full day of things to do for parents and children.

Here's what we've found works best when touring Epcot with youngsters:

You've heard it before, but it works: arrive at the park before it opens. When the ropes drop and everyone makes a mad-dash to get their Fastpass for Soarin', head straight for the **Character Connection** (located near the Fountainview Café) for some (normally) easy access to characters.

Activity areas spread throughout Future World and the World Showcase—**Kidcot Fun Stops**—are a great way for kids to feel involved in the park, and to accidentally learn something. The Kidcot Fun Stops are designated on park maps with a big "K" in a red square. There are sixteen of them located throughout Futureworld and the World Showcase. Children receive a cutout mask that they can color and decorate as they stop at each Fun Stop. The Kidcot Fun Stop activity areas are staffed by cast members native to the specific country, who will stamp the child's mask and often will write something in their native language. Kids can also purchase an Epcot passport, which cast members stamp at each country they visit.

The Kidcot Fun Stops are free, and if you don't point it out, the kids may not notice that they also are educational. It forces you to seek out the activity tables, drawing you deeper into the World Showcase pavilions. It provides a better opportunity to uncover details and interact with cast members. In Future World, the Kidcot Fun Stops are located in The Land, Test Track, Innoventions East and West, and The Seas with Nemo and Friends. They're also located in each country of the World Showcase.

The Living Seas with Nemo and Friends, based on the Disney/Pixar film, *Finding Nemo*, is a natural when traveling with children, and getting there is half the fun. After winding through an imaginatively designed queue area, guests board appropriately themed "clamobiles" where they'll travel along with Marlin and Dory in search of Nemo, who has gone missing again. A little further along, guests encounter Mr. Ray instructing his students, and then come upon a school of jellyfish. An anglerfish pierces the darkness—one of the only moments that may spook skittish children—leading to Bruce the Great White and Chum the Mako.

The clamobiles then get swept into the undersea current with Nemo (found), Crushn and Squirt. "In the Big Blue World," a song written for the Animal Kingdom's Finding Nemo: the Musical, rounds it all out.

During the adventure, visitors glide by displays that use new animation techniques that project characters from the film into tanks of actual aquatic creatures.

Headlining the pavilion is the interactive **Turtle Talk with Crush**. Crush, the stoner/surfer character from *Finding Nemo* treats guests to ten-minute shows where he interacts with, talks to, and messes with the audience. No two shows are alike, and it's a clever, customized attraction perfect for kids.

The entire Living Seas complex is tucked into a series of tanks that make up a 5.7-million-gallon marine environment—one of the largest of its kind anywhere. Kids can take their time watching scores of different types of aquatic life from a myriad of viewing areas.

The Straight Dope *Children get a kick out of the IBM Internet Postcards, located in Innoventions West. It allows families to take a picture of themselves and then send it via e-mail to friends back home. The postcards are available in several languages.*

The **World Showcase** has several experiences that target youngsters in particular. A **hedge maze** in the United Kingdom is just the right size for younger children. Kids can join the **fife and drum corps** outside the American Experience as they recite the Pledge of Allegiance. A miniature **train display** next to the Germany pavilion can keep kids entertained for a few minutes. A stand of **hand drums** at the African village is very likely to keep youngsters attention for a bit longer. They can bang away for as long as they like. Dancing and making a God-awful cacophony is not only OK here, it's encouraged.

A list of attractions at Epcot with height restrictions:

Land	Attraction	Height restriction
Future World	Mission: Space	44 inches
Future World	Soarin'	40 inches
Future World	Test Track	40 inches

Strollers in the Studios

Disney's Hollywood Studios is the home of **Playhouse Disney Live!** That, alone, is enough of a reason to point the stroller at this theme park and begin marching.

Characters from a number of The Disney Channel's shows take the stage live, in a singing, dancing, and storytelling performance that urges the tykes to get up and take part. The show is geared toward preschool-aged audiences, and is located in the Animation Courtyard.

A refurb brought new characters from Playhouse Disney shows into the production, including familiar faces from *My Friends Tigger and Pooh*, *Little Einsteins*, *Handy Manny*, and *Mickey Mouse Clubhouse*.

Stage shows, including **Beauty and the Beast**, located on Sunset Boulevard just before the Twilight Zone Tower of Terror, and **Voyage of the Little Mermaid**, located in the Animation Courtyard, are both musical, entertaining shows not to be missed.

Beauty and the Beast is a Broadway-style spectacle, while Voyage of the Little Mermaid combines live actors, animation, laser displays and some incredibly innovative puppeteers to tell Ariel's story. This seventeen-minute production often draws crowds, but the theater can hold a substantial number of people so the wait time (the queue is covered, protecting little ones from direct sun and rain) tends to be reasonable.

If there's a wait at **Muppet Vision 3-D**, consider yourself lucky. The preshow contains dozens of puns and jokes—particular to the Muppets' sense of humor—that will entertain parents, and keep youngsters occupied.

The show is very similar in execution to Mickey's Philharmagic in the Magic Kingdom, and It's Tough to be a Bug in Disney's Animal Kingdom. Where Bug might frighten children, Muppet Vision 3-D is mild and funny enough to keep everyone in the family happy.

Disney's Imagineers are constantly pushing the envelope, coming up with inventive ways to entertain guests, and using the latest technologies to wow visitors. So what do younger kids find the most fun? Water fountains and playgrounds. Just like the ones they could've played at down the street for a lot less money and effort. Regardless, there are several scattered throughout the Studios, and in every theme park, and they can be a fantastic way to cool off and get off our feet for a few.

For slightly older kids, the **Great Movie Ride** can be fun. It's in the reproduction of Mann's Chinese Theater at the end of Hollywood Boulevard. (Walk toward the Sorcerer Mickey hat and keep going.) Just because there aren't any people waiting outside the theater doesn't mean a queue hasn't formed. This attraction can hold a great many people inside.

The twenty-minute guided tour through movie history is entertaining, but easily spooked youngsters may find the *Alien* portion of the attraction a bit unsettling.

A list of attractions at Disney's Hollywood Studios with height restrictions:

Area	Attraction	Heigh restriction
Sunset Blvd.	Rock'n'Roller Coaster	48 inches
Echo Lake	Star Tours	40 inches
Sunset Blvd.	Tower of Terror	40 inches

Animal Kingdom with Kids

Thrill rides, learning experiences, and stage shows now make this park a must-do for anyone spending time at Walt Disney World. Activities for children abound:

The **Festival of the Lion King** is, hands down, the single best stage show on Disney property, and appropriate for all ages. A Broadway-caliber show based on the film, this production features live singing performances, acrobatic displays, wire acts, dancing, and audience participation.

The Straight Dope *Try to sit as close to the front as possible if you bring a child to Festival of the Lion King. Near the end of the performance, cast members pull children up from the audience to take part in the finale.*

MOUSEJUNKIE BARRY One of my fondest memories from our first trip to Disney with the kids is when my daughters Maddie and Emma were picked from the crowd to participate in "Festival of the Lion King" show at Disney's Animal Kingdom. The smiles on their faces could not have been any broader as they marched around with their maracas and danced. They both have acted in local theater since that visit, and I wouldn't be surprised if that first little taste of the spotlight lit the fire for them.

Head to the opposite end of the park for **Finding Nemo: The Musical**. Brightly costumed cast members manipulate puppets across a massive stage. The music is catchy and the cast of characters is extensive. This performance is fine for all ages, but may do best with younger children.

Kilimanjaro Safaris remains a must-do attraction for all ages, providing an amazing experience for adults as well as children. Aboard a large safari truck, guests go on a guided tour of a 100-acre East African savanna that is home to dozens of species of animals. You have a chance to catch an extreme close-up of elephants, giraffes, antelope, lions, hippos, cheetahs, and rhinos, among other beasts. This nearly twenty-minute ride through a small re-creation of Africa is an enthralling experience for all ages.

Youngsters can spend hours playing in the **Boneyard**, and meeting Disney characters at the various **character greeting trails**.

Flights of Wonder, a stage show featuring trained birds, would be easy to pass off as a simple parrot showcase. But deeper conservation themes, surprisingly funny cast members, and breathtaking stunts by trained hawks, cranes, owls, and other fowl make this show one of the strongest in the entire park. Youngsters love the up-close encounters and their parents will enjoy the quick-witted host, Guano Joe. There are audience-participation opportunities for brave kids.

While there are plenty of activities and attractions that parents and children can take part in together, there are a few the skittish should avoid. Obviously, the more thrilling attractions like Expedition Everest would not be a wise choice for little ones. But there is one attraction that draws kids like flies (you'll get that clever turn of phrase in a moment) and one parents should think twice about.

The Straight Dope *Avoid taking easily-scared tykes to see It's Tough to be a Bug—a 3-D experience located inside the lower portion of the Tree of Life. While the 3-D bug glasses may seem silly, the show always seems to frighten youngsters in the audience.*

Every performance of **It's Tough to be a Bug** I've attended has resulted in at least one absolute freak-out by a startled child. Large spiders descend from the ceiling, and several tactile surprises jar little ones unexpectedly. However, older children may love the show.

A list of attractions at Disney's Animal Kingdom with height restrictions:

Land	Attraction	Height restriction
Dinoland U.S.A.	Dinosaur	40 inches
Anandapur	Expedition Everest	44 inches
Asia	Kali River Rapids	38 inches
Dinoland U.S.A.	Primeval Whirl	48 inches

14 Mousejunkies Expectorate

IT WAS ABOUT 11 P.M. when I hit rock bottom.

My lungs were full of fluid, I had a mind-shattering head-ache, and I fixated on the bedspread. But then, taking three times as much cold medicine as you're supposed to will do that to a person. I am the Keith Richards of Nyquil.

The lights in the room were turned off. The TV flickered, casting oddly shaped shadows onto the bed. There was a man with a pork-pie hat. Another wailing on a trombone. Yet another was cutting a rug in front of a 1950s juke box and I think a woman who looked like Billie Holiday was talking to me. Thank you, Nyquil.

It's been years, but I can still see the figures that deco-rated the wallpaper and bedspread in my room at the All-Star Music resort as clear as day. That's because I spent about forty-eight hours memorizing it under the influence of some awesome cough medicine and cursing my bad luck.

I had anticipated, scrimped, and saved to be at my favor-ite vacation destination for nearly a year. Yet here I was, immobile, wracked with coughing, and not going anywhere. It felt as if pneumonia had settled in. I was stuck in my room wheezing and watching *The White Shadow* reruns, while my companions were out exploring theme parks and soaking up Disney magic.

I got up at one point, determined to get myself together and meet my fellow travelers out in the parks. I got about three minutes into my effort when I said—and I want to quote this accurately: "Bleeauurrrgggghmagical."

I heaved, but it was a Disney heave. In short, I wasn't going anywhere.

For a Mousejunkie, there could be no worse torture. So I decided to soak up what I could—mainly antihistamines. If a little would help, maybe a lot would get me on my feet so I could join my friends the next day. I had opted to write off one day, but there was no way I was going to miss our final day at the Magic Kingdom.

Anyone in their right mind knows that's not exactly a winning approach, but I wasn't in my right mind, and I didn't really know what to do.

First—don't pity my pathetic condition. I've had dozens of trips since then, so I think I've more than made up for those miserable few days.

Second—I've learned something over many trips to central Florida: Sometimes people get sick. And sometimes people get sick at Walt Disney World. And nearly overdosing on cold medicine isn't going to help.

The epilogue of that particular episode was that I forced myself to get out of bed the next day and walked in forty-foot jaunts before I had to stop for a rest. It took forever to get where I was going, but I did get to bask in the Magic Kingdom before heading home. I wasn't going to allow a collapsed lung to get between me and another ride on Big Thunder Mountain. Basically, if you can die from stubbornness, I probably will.

Unfortunately, I've had a few occasions to hone my "getting sick at Disney" skills. And it wasn't until one of my most recent trips that I discovered a few helpful things.

We had booked a trip to the Wilderness Lodge Villas in January. January is also known as "Bill Gets Bronchitisuary" around our house. I got bronchitis a couple weeks before the trip, got a little better, and then flew to Walt Disney World. My prescriptions had run out on the day we left, but it felt as if I may have gotten through the worst of things.

Our second day there I learned I was wrong. It came back full force, and I was stranded far away from my doctor and my pharmacy. I panicked a little as the memories of that bedspread hallucination trip were still with me. I visited the concierge, who suggested I call my doctor back home and have him call in a prescription to Turner Drug, a pharmacy nearby that delivers to Walt Disney World resorts.

The darkness lifted. I felt as though I might be able to ward off the worst of the bronchitis if I could get some medication in me. I made a few calls, spoke with Turner Drug, and heard these magic words: "We'll be there within an hour."

They were, and I began the process of expelling the bronchitis from my lungs. It took longer than I would have liked, but I firmly believe I was saved from dropping further into sickness by the kindness of that concierge, and the existence of Turner Drug.

We don't usually have a car at Walt Disney World, so when a pharmaceutical need became necessary I never really considered what to do. I just figured I'd get through the rest of the trip and visit the doctor when I got back home. However, Turner Drug delivering to Disney resorts can be an invaluable resource should you be stricken by an ill-timed malady.

To contact Turner Drug: 407-828-8125

Avoiding Epcrotch

It's no secret that there's a lot of walking involved during a Walt Disney World vacation. And everyone knows the central Florida climate approximates a blast furnace for nine months out of the year. Combine those two and you've got something that could potentially turn an enjoyable vacation at Walt Disney World into a remarkably painful death march.

Of course, I speak of the worst possible sentence that can be passed on an unprepared park visitor: Epcrotch.

Epcrotch is the chafing that occurs only in the confines of Walt Disney World. Heat plus extensive walking plus ill-fitting underclothes equals a pain only Disney guests know.

This isn't the normal chafing associated with long-distance runners or triathletes. Those guys have it easy. They don't have to get from the Main Street train station to the Crystal Palace during Spectromagic with their inner thighs aflame with the heat of a thousand suns.

Epcrotch is an aggressive, flesh-searing strain of chafing that strikes at the least convenient time. Because no matter when it starts to peel away layers of skin and rub raw, you've got days of walking ahead of you. Once it sets in, there's not a lot you can do. It's already too late. On a vacation built around walking, it can interrupt even the best-laid plans.

No one is immune to Epcrotch. This objectionable condition isn't relegated to the overweight or those who wear their shorts too tight (though, don't do that.) It can strike anyone in the Florida heat.

There is only one way to protect oneself from this debilitating and mentally scarring pain—and its closely-related cousin, blisters—and that is proper preparation.

There may be other options, but I have come across an extremely successful manner of banishing Epcrotch from my vacations: Bodyglide Anti-chafe balm.

Bodyglide comes in a stick resembling deodorant. It is applied in a similar manner to any area that may experience chafing or blisters. Through repeated research, I've found that it completely prevents chafing and blisters. It works. It's your friend.

Slather it on first thing in the morning before leaving your resort. One application is enough to keep the thigh fires at bay. It can, literally, save a vacation.

Canada Attacks!

Over the course of the Mousejunkies' combined vacations, there have even been a few more urgent medical situations.

MOUSEJUNKIE WALT Let me tell you about the dangers of park touring: I bought a pair of sandals that I insisted on calling "the best investment I ever made" through one entire Disney World trip. The people I was with got sick of hearing me say that, and it would come back to haunt me. I hadn't owned a pair since I was a kid, so just before the trip I went out and bought a pair and brought them with me.

When I got to Disney World I put them on and walked around. I loved them. And I had to keep saying it: "These are the best investment I ever made."

We were in Epcot, walking through the Canada pavilion when we got to the stone steps that lead up to the upper level. There was a baby sitting on the step, and as I went to step up, the baby darted in front of me. I tried to get out of way and my foot came down with a lot of force. The sandal went one way and my foot, which was driven into the jagged edge of stairs, went the other.

Still, I didn't step on the baby, so I didn't think anything of it. We continued to walk, and as that foot came forward I noticed a stream of blood sprayed out in front of me. I took another step and another spurt of blood shot out in front of me. It was then I realized how badly I was bleeding. I sat down and got a look at how deeply I was cut. I thought Mousejunkie Deb was going to pass out.

It was funny in a way, because I became an attraction for a bit. People were stopping and looking at all the blood. And it's also funny because you don't know who the managers and emergency responders are, but they

(Continued on next page)

are always there. In my case, they arrived on the scene within seconds. A woman came over—she was manager of the Canada pavilion—and a few seconds later EMTs were there. They put hydrogen peroxide on it, wrapped it up and suggested I go to the nearby hospital.

That was when I quite literally put my non bleeding foot down. It was our last full day at Walt Disney World, and I wasn't about to spend it sitting in an emergency room. I signed a release saying I wouldn't sue Disney, they got me a wheelchair, and before too long we were back on track.

That's not to say I wasn't in pain, because I was. J had to push me around in the wheelchair. I thought I was going to be able to push the wheelchair by my own power, and I did for about fifty feet, but then my arms got tired and I let J push me around the park.

It's impressive how quickly the cast members responded and took care of me. They do a great job.

But that wasn't the end of Mousejunkie Walt's adventures. A year later he was standing in line at Starring Rolls Café in Disney's Hollywood Studios. A woman standing in line in front of him turned quickly and spilled an entire cup of steaming coffee down his leg.

I watched it happen as if in slow motion, but from where I was sitting I couldn't see the seriousness of it until he limped painfully over to the table. His entire leg was glowing an angry red color. And again, Disney's cast members leapt into action. Within seconds workers arrived with cold compresses and a bag of ice. Meanwhile the coffee flinger paid for Walt's breakfast and begged forgiveness. Since we were in a Disney frame of mind—incredibly painful burns or not—Walt magnanimously let the woman off the hook.

"It was the very next trip after I cut my foot open," he said. "I swear I thought I was going to get hurt on every Disney trip from then on."

Thankfully, most of Walt's limbs remain intact, and he hasn't needed major reconstructive surgery. Yet.

Health and Well-Being Checklist

❑ Aspirin packed
❑ Antacid packed
❑ CPAP machine packed (for sleep apnea patients)
❑ Bodyglide packed
❑ Prescription drugs packed
❑ Stitches packed (If you're Mousejunkie Walt)
❑ Turner Drug (will deliver to Walt Disney World resorts): 407-828-8125
❑ Celebration Health hospital in Celebration, Florida (407) 303-4000

15 Mousejunkies Marry

IT'S A MIRACLE THAT I belong to Disney Vacation Club.

Right now you're saying to yourself, "You're a sick man with an unhealthy attachment to Disney. Why wouldn't you belong to Disney Vacation Club?"

Because I am married to Mousejunkie Amy, the reluctant Mousejunkie. She is a delightful person who loves the magic as much as anyone I know. It's just that she cares about our family's financial health as well.

She's the smart one. I'm the fun one.

So when we took the Disney Vacation Club tour in 2005 (only to score the $100 promised by the marketing department), I was a little more than shocked when she said the whole deal made sense. Hey, if she says so, I'm on board.

We've since spent many nights in one of the several DVC resorts scattered around the property. We've used points, borrowed points, banked points, rented points and yearned for more points. The point? We're happy with our decision. In the long run, it'll save us money. In the short run (or, the way I see things), it'll allow us to return to Walt Disney World twice a year for pretty much the rest of my life. (Assuming I live to be a healthy eighty-something-year-old Mousejunkie.)

Here's a basic rundown of how it works:

Disney Vacation Club is a timeshare-like operation, allowing members to buy a real estate interest through a one-time purchase of "vacation points." Members use points to pay for accommodations at one of the DVC resorts. Members can use the points, bank them for future use, borrow from future use years, or transfer them in or out of their account. The points renew every year. When making a reservation, members are charged points. The number of points depends on what kind of room, what resort, and what time of year the reservations are for. Members can book a reservation at their "home resort" up to twelve months in advance, or at any other resort up to seven months in advance.

MOUSEJUNKIE DEB Although I've enjoyed every trip, our first time staying on WDW property was when I really started to love the whole theming immersion and realized we'd be coming back often. We stayed at Port Orleans Riverside (Dixie Landings at the time) and have never stayed off property since, buying into Disney Vacation Club and into a lifetime of memories. We vacation at many other places and always will, but DVC's "home away from home" mantra is a reality for us. People have beach houses on the Jersey Shore, time shares in Cabo, points and comps in Vegas, and we have our DVC.

MOUSEJUNKIE CAROL It's probably the easiest way to spend around $20,000 that I have ever experienced. Randy (my husband) had gone on the DVC tour a few times. He was having a tough time convincing me that it was the way to go, so eventually he got me to go on a tour. (I will admit the free $100 in Disney dollars for taking the tour was my real enticement).

At the end of the tour, our salesman, Marshal (how many people fondly remember the name of the guy who convinced them to buy a timeshare) worked with us and talked about the different number of points we might want to buy. A quick 220 points later and we were out of there. Now I do think it was the best thing and the worst thing we have ever done. It's the best in that we do save money in hotels every time we visit. It's the worst, because, well, let's say that we tend to go more than our allotted 220 points will allow. So what do we do? We are now in a network where we will buy someone else's unused points for the year, transfer into our accounts and we're good to go one more time. DVC has really just been an instrument to bring us to Disney at least three times a year and if we can do so, four to five times a year.

Members can use their points at one of several Disney Vacation Club resorts around the property, and a few off property. The resorts range from quite nice to extravagant.

But the latest DVC news involves a new Hawaiian resort.

Mahalo, Mickey

Aulani, a Disney Resort and Spa, is a twenty-one-acre ocean-front getaway on the island of Oahu in Ko Olina, Hawaii. That's a long way from Orlando. Let's face it, it's a long way from any Disney park. But the long arm of Disney reached across the Pacific, dropped off some Imagineers, and suddenly there's a DVC resort in the middle of the Pacific.

Renderings show an open-ended spacious lobby—in no small part cousin to the Animal Kingdom Lodge. Hawaiian art is spread throughout the "Maka'ala," the grand lobby. The grounds feature the lush greenery native to the area, with trees, bushes, and grassy areas filling in between the two resort towers.

Aulani will have 359 rooms and 481 two-bedroom villas in two towers. Each tower features angled rooms with views of the ocean, mountains, and the surrounding grounds.

The resort will include an eighteen thousand square-foot spa, two restaurants, a wedding lawn, a themed pool area, a kids' club, a snorkel lagoon and hot tubs built to face the sunset.

A groundbreaking and blessing ceremony took place in November of 2008. The resort will throw open its doors to its first guests on Aug. 29, 2011.

This being Disney, there's a little more to the place than just a Hawaiian beachfront resort. Imagineers have intertwined Hawaiian culture and stories throughout the place.

Disney is also offering several unique tours and experiences, including:

➤ A tour of the island guided by storytellers
➤ Catching your own fish, harvesting fresh ingredients, and cooking it under the tutelage of a Hawiian chef
➤ Kayaking through protected coves
➤ Taking a catamaran out onto the ocean (According to Disney, the trip will be "among playful pods of dolphins." I don't see how you can guarantee that. It's the ocean. "Playful pods of dolphins" can just as easily become "lifeless bobbing flotsam" or "ravenous packs of orca." Then again, we're talking about the company that stuck a giraffe outside my balcony every morning at the Animal Kingdom Lodge.)
➤ Surfing Hawaii's famous waves

Rooms will start $399 a night with ocean views more expensive. For DVC members, an ocean-view studio will run from 175 to 217 points weekly; a one-bedroom ocean-view room will run 322 to 434 points weekly; a two-bedroom ocean view will run 441 to 595 weekly.

It can be affordable, however. If you're not overly concerned with the view out your window, a standard view studio will run 126 to 168 points weekly.

The resort is seventeen miles from Honolulu International Airport.

Here's a look at Disney's Vacation Club's Walt Disney World resorts:

Old Key West: A sprawling resort inspired by the architecture and spirit of the Florida Keys, Old Key West was the first Disney Vacation Club resort to be constructed. It costs the fewest amount of points of all the DVC resorts, yet offers the largest rooms.

Old Key West has one table-service restaurant, Olivia's, and the Gurgling Suitcase bar. Guests can rent boats or catch a water ferry down the Sassagoula River to Downtown Disney.

Old Key West still represents a fantastic value if measured by points used to the quality of the resort.

Beach Club Villas: Designed to look and feel like a New England seaside resort, the driveway into the Beach Club is a toll road, each guest gets a copy of the Herald and a scratch ticket. Concierge cast members are required to end every sentence with "Sox rule."

OK, not really. But that'd make it pretty authentic.

The Beach Club Villas are a top-notch DVC option. The Beach Club shares the best hotel pool on property, Stormalong Bay, with its sister resort, the Yacht Club. (Where the Bahnies[1] stay, according to my friend from Somerville.)

The most important amenity at the Beach Club is its location: just a short walk to Epcot's International Gateway, and a quick boat ride to Disney's Hollywood Studios.

The Villas at Wilderness Lodge: Tall trees and thick woodlands surround this majestic resort, which is themed to look

---

1 Bahnies, or "Barnies" are considered upwardly mobile residents contributing to the gentrification of the formerly blue-collar city of Somerville.

like a National Park Service lodge. The DVC villas are integrated into the resort, attached to the main lobby by a short walkway. A massive lobby welcomes guests, with rough-hewn exposed logs and an eighty-foot-tall fireplace dominating the space.

The Iron Spike Room boasts an impressive collection of Walt Disney's train memorabilia and deep, luxurious leather chairs in which to contemplate said collection. If you go at Christmas time, the lobby is worth a visit whether or not you are a guest at the resort. A massive Christmas tree shoots up into the cavernous entryway, in an impressive and festive display.

Boardwalk Villas: A favorite to almost anyone who stays there, the Boardwalk is a true showpiece among Disney's resorts. Designed in the image of a turn-of-the-century Atlantic seashore hotel, the stately yet whimsical Boardwalk is among the most picturesque of all Disney's resorts.

If location is important, the Boardwalk is for you. If perfect theming is something you look for, the Boardwalk is for you. Want to feel pampered and be right in the middle of everything? You want to stay at the Boardwalk Villas. The Boardwalk boasts its own entertainment district, with musicians, magicians, and showmen roaming the boardwalk throughout the night, passing by one of the several restaurants and snack bars that dot the lakefront space.

While much of the nightly hubbub that goes on out in front of the guest rooms is filtered out, visitors will not be able to ignore the nightly fireworks at the adjoining Epcot theme park. Any thoughts of turning in early to get some rest will be sharply interrupted by the sound of IllumiNations going off nightly at 9 P.M.

Saratoga Springs Resort and Spa: The upstate New York horseracing destination has been faithfully recreated at the site of the former Disney Institute. A massive complex, Saratoga Springs Resort and Spa features themed pools, Victorian architecture, various springs, and fantastic views of Downtown Disney—which is located just across the lake. A short walk or ferry ride and you're right in the middle of the shopping, dining, or people-watching action.

Not surprisingly, Saratoga Springs is a beautiful resort. The grounds are immaculate, the lobby is bright and clean, the main themed pool feels like a natural lake amidst large rock formations, and horse-racing themes abound. It is a pleasure to stay at this resort.

Saratoga Springs is a large resort. Plan to leave plenty of travel time when heading out for any scheduled plans. We usually end up breaking one of our cardinal rules if we stay at Saratoga Springs: We rent a car. I normally would never consider it, but being able to come and go when we want makes for a more convenient experience when the alternative is standing at a bus stop for forty minutes as the advanced dining reservation you made 180 days ago goes by.

Saratoga Springs is broken up into five areas:

➤ **The Grandstand**—Across a parking lot from the main lobby, this area features a barbecue grill area and the Backstretch pool bar.

➤ **The Paddock**—The Paddock runs along Union Avenue and has two bus stops.

➤ **The Carousel**—These rooms are the furthest from the Carriage House.

➤ **The Springs**—The Springs are closest to the Carriage House lobby, the High Rock Spring theme pool, arcade, spa, and many of the resort's amenities.

➤ **Congress Park**—Congress Park is the area of Saratoga Springs that sits closest Downtown Disney. The buildings closest to Buena Vista Drive offer easy walking access to Downtown Disney, and its bus stops.

➤ **The Treehouses at Saratoga Springs:** Every one of these elevated vacation homes was constructed off-site, and then trucked-in to replace the old octagonal treehouses that stood on the same spot.

Disney calls them "cabin casual." These three-bedroom, two-bath treehouses stand ten-feet off the ground and feature flat-screen TVs and granite countertops.

MOUSEJUNKIE J The treehouses have their benefits and drawbacks.

The good: Two-bedroom points for a three bedroom unit: brand new—nicely decorated, vaulted ceilings; detached units—no neighbors banging on the ceilings, walls, floors, etc.

The not-so-good: Location, Location, Location. It's not a bad spot if you like Downtown Disney and spend time there. We lucked out and got the primo location so it was manageable. We never took the internal bus because it was a short walk to the Grandstand bus station at Saratoga Springs from our villa. But people at the other end of the Treehouses would have a long walk. The internal bus was running on time but it is still another bus that you have to transfer to. We avoided it.

The boat was OK if you wanted to go to Downtown Disney. It was always on time and dropped you off at Pleasure Island near the old Rockin' Roll Beach Club. It's really not a nice place to just hang out. The deck is nice but the bugs are out in the wooded areas. It's not like sitting on the balcony at Boardwalk. You can't people watch at all.

I would not stay in them again. I would choose a two bedroom at Old Key West first.

Animal Kingdom Villas: The Animal Kingdom Lodge villas are located both in the existing Animal Kingdom Lodge and in the new Kidani Village. The new units more than double the current size of the resort and include a children's water play area, a new restaurant—Sanaa—and its own savanna.

Staying at the Animal Kingdom Lodge is everything it's purported to be. A savanna-view room allows guests to start the day with a stunning view of animals in their natural habitat. Sunrises and sunsets explode through the Jambo House lobby, bathing the authentic African art in a golden glow. One end of the massive, six-story lobby is glass-enclosed, providing a bright, naturally lit atmosphere.

Kidani Village, located just next door to the Animal Kingdom Lodge, has a similar, yet much smaller lobby. It lends the resort a more intimate feel. Disney calls the Vacation Club resorts "home away from home." Kidani Village lives up to this description more than any other. It feels like home.

> **MOUSEJUNKIE RANDY** Carol and I recently stayed at Kidani Village. We had just added an additional 125 DVC vacation points at Kidani and were excited to try out this new resort. Since it was the first time using our points at Kidani Village, we splurged and got a savanna view. The view was well worth the additional points.
>
> We did learn some additional things about the resort on this trip. It's huge—much more spread out than Jambo House. The best rooms are on any floor between the lobby and the pool. This location gives you easy access to the bus stop, which is right off the lobby, and quick access to the pool, which is where all the activity happens at the resort.

I have one question for the Imagineers at Disney: How am I ever supposed to get any sleep with a perfect Eden outside my balcony?

We were on the fifth floor of Kidani Village, so I thought I'd get up with the sun to see the savanna come to life. Little did I know that it would affect my sleeping habits for the rest of our ten-day trip.

I've been to WDW many times, and sometimes you just start to expect amazing moments. But this was better than I could have imagined.

We snagged a nice Savanna-view room, so the idea was to take advantage of our elevated position by watching the sun rise. I awoke in the early morning darkness, whipped up some coffee and took my seat on our balcony. Everyone else was still asleep, and it was very quiet and incredibly peaceful. Very slowly the stars grew dimmer as the sky started to get almost imperceptibly brighter. I could see the smoke from the Jambo House kitchens to my right wafting dreamily up over the thatched dome of the resort.

As it grew lighter, a trio of massive Ankole Cattle revealed itself right outside our room. They lay huddled in a small circle unaware of—or more likely undisturbed by— my presence just a few feet away. Every once in a while one of them would move its head around, reminding me of just how huge these animals, and their distinctive horns, can be.

A slight fog made everything in the distance look a little soft. Bit by bit, the sun peeked up over the thatched roof directly across from our section of the resort. The placement of our room, totally random, could not have been more perfect.

And then it happened: One of those moments that can occur at Walt Disney World that illustrates how it can be more than just a collection of attractions and gift shops. The warming sunlight, the totally convincing Savanna, the animals opening their eyes to a new day and the feeling that I was totally alone in this experience, deepened my connection to the place.

It also could've been the caffeine now coursing through me. I didn't care. I was sharing the birth of a new day with exotic beasts I thought I'd never see in person, and I knew there was no way I was going to miss another sunrise as long as we were housed in this amazing resort.

Bay Lake Tower: Ultramodern (read: a little cold, according to some), Bay Lake Tower sits just outside the Magic Kingdom and on top of what used to be the Contemporary Resort's north garden wing. A coveted Magic Kingdom view is part of the new tower, making it a much sought-after booking.

The interior features abstract Disney art, and bright, clean lines and colors. A sixteenth floor Top of the World Lounge provides amazing views of the property, and of the Magic Kingdom, in particular. Only guests staying on points are provided access to the Top of the World Lounge.

The resort is secure, accessible only to members staying at the tower.

In addition to the Aulani resort, Disney Vacation Club also operates two additional off-site resorts: Disney's **Hilton Head Island Resort** in South Carolina, and Disney's **Vero Beach Resort**, on Florida's Atlantic coast.

In each of the DVC resorts, guests can choose from one of four room types:

A studio room, essentially a standard hotel room that can sleep four people

A one-bedroom vacation home with a master suite, living room, kitchen and a patio sleeps up to five people

A two-bedroom vacation home (also referred to as a two-bedroom lock-off), which is the same as a one bedroom unit and has a second bedroom attached. A two-bedroom unit can sleep up to eight people.

The grand villa: the granddaddy of all DVC units. The villa is luxury, convenience, and comfort all in one. The grand villa has three bedrooms, three baths, is a two-story unit and can sleep upwards of twelve people comfortably. While the Boardwalk grand villa is a one-story unit, and the Wilderness Lodge and the Beach Club do not offer grand villas, the top of the line unit at Old Key West is bigger than many private homes.

Renting The Secret

Disney Vacation Club counts more than 300,000 people among its members. Quite often, members end up with points they won't be able to use during a designated use year. This glut is a bonus for visitors to Walt Disney World, who can rent points from members and stay at a deluxe resort for a fraction of the cost. The transaction, normally conducted completely online, requires a bit of trust, but it results in a much less expensive room rate.

MOUSEJUNKIE BARRY I am of the shameful branch of the Mousejunkies family tree that doesn't belong to Disney Vacation Club. This, however, hasn't prevented me from enjoying the spoils of a greatly discounted resort room.

My last visit to Disney found me back at the Wilderness Lodge Resort, where my family stayed during our first

(Continued on next page)

trip. Since we were traveling with another family, we figured that it made sense to book one of the Wilderness Lodge Villas. Problem was, a mere mortal such as I can't book one of those prized rooms, only those aligned with DVC have that honor. After a bit of research, I discovered that there are some DVCers out there with such an abundance of points that they have been known to rent those points to others. They benefit because they don't waste the points and I benefit because I wind up a) staying at a DVC resort and b) saving quite a bit of cash that I can later spend on bottomless milkshakes and ribs. Actually, I could probably afford to buy a fancy monocle and top hat to wear while I gorge myself on those ribs.

All told, I ended up paying considerably less for the Villa than I did in staying in a regular room in the Lodge some fourteen months prior. Renting points *is* on the honor system, but the overwhelming majority of folks reporting online on their experiences with these transactions have only positive things to say. Why pay full price when you can pocket the extra hundreds—maybe thousands—of dollars. It just makes sense."

The transaction works like this: The owner of the points—the DVC member—agrees to reserve a room in the renter's name in exchange for a cash payment. The trust element comes into play because the renter, assuming he or she is not a DVC member, has no control over the points. An unscrupulous DVC member could potentially play havoc with a trusting vacationer's plans and funds. While it has happened, it appears to be an uncommon occurrence. The average price-per-point rate ranges from $8 to $12, and sometimes slightly more.

The Straight Dope *At an average rate of $10 per point, it would cost $80 per night (during the week) for the month of January to stay in a studio-sized room at the Old Key West resort. Visitors paying cash would pay $285 a night for the same room. Renting points would allow a guest to stay at the Villas at Wilderness Lodge during the same time period for an average of $120 a night. Guests paying cash would pay $225 to $385 a night for the same room. Arrange to rent points at sites such as dvcrequest.com, disboards.com, mouseowners.com, or dvctrader.com.*

In addition to reduced rates at the deluxe level, there are members-only perks. DVC members enjoy discounts while shopping, dining, and booking entertainment and recreation options. The most valuable perk, however, is the reduced rate on an Annual Pass. Annual Passholders enjoy entrance to all four theme parks for one calendar year, access to special "Passholder-only" events, and occasional discounts on rooms, merchandise, and dining.

The Straight Dope *Will you be visiting a Walt Disney World theme park more than 11 days in a one-year period? If so, pick up an Annual Pass. DVC members enjoy a $100 discount.*

16 Mousejunkie Dreams

THERE ARE THOSE WHO dream about dropping everything and moving to within close proximity of Walt Disney World, and there are those who actually do it.

I fall into the former group. Each time we visit, we choose our "retirement job." We fantasize about retiring, moving to Florida, and working for Walt Disney World. My retirement job usually changes from trip to trip. Most of the time I want to work on the steam trains at the Magic Kingdom. Other times, though, it's monorail pilot. I'm probably too much of an introvert to try out for Mayor of Main Street, and as I've mentioned earlier my dance skills would get me banished from Disney property if I ever conned my way into entertainment.

But it remains all speculation and daydreaming at this point.

The Mouse in Retirement

MOUSEJUNKIE CAROL When I first started going to Disney I wanted to be Goofy. The older I get the more appealing any job in air conditioning looks. But currently, I would love to work at Goofy's Candy Store and make candy apples.

MOUSEJUNKIE JENNA At one point, my dream retirement job was "maid" at the Haunted Mansion because I could really see myself in a hat-with-a-bat. However, I have since decided that the job I would most want is Fairy Godmother. I already know all of the words to "Bibbidi-bobbidi-boo" and I happen to look fantastic in that shade of blue.

MOUSEJUNKIE J Practically speaking it would have to be a bag-drop person at one of the Walt Disney World golf courses. It'd be pretty easy, and you get tips and free golf.

A job with a bit more responsibility, thus more stress, would be piloting one of the Friendship launches. I think it would be cool *if*, and it's a big *if*, you were paired with someone you liked. I see the dynamic between some of the pairs on these boats and they range from non-speaking to laughing and whooping it up. Although driving the monorail would be neat for a day or two, there is now no riding up front so you really wouldn't get to interact with guests."

TEEN MOUSEJUNKIE RYAN I want to be one of the ghost hosts at the Haunted Mansion, or a Tower of Terror bellhop. What does it say about me? Am I morbid? Nah. I just like Halloween a lot.

MOUSEJUNKIE AMY   I would like to work on one of the gardening and landscaping crews. I'd like to tend to the flowers all through the parks and resorts. Being able to create hidden Mickeys with different colored flowers would be creative and fun. It would be relaxing because they'd have to do most of it at night and the crowds would be gone.

MOUSEJUNKIE DEB   You're going to laugh, but I'd prefer to work somewhere that I didn't have to wear a uniform, because let's face it, most of them are goofy looking and made of uncomfortable polyester material.

➤ First choice: Tinkerbell zip-lining from Cinderella Castle nightly. Else:

➤ I'd like to be a lifeguard so I could hang out at the pool, but if it was truly a retirement job, I'd be old and wrinkly. If I ran away now, though, I may do that.

➤ I'm a planner, so I'd actually enjoy being a Disney wedding planner.

➤ I think it would be fun to be a bartender in the Bellevue Room at Boardwalk .

➤ Golf cart girl selling drinks and snacks—the courses are beautiful.

➤ If my husband Mousejunkie J were there too, I would work at the funnel cake cart on the Boardwalk so I could see him a lot.

MOUSEJUNKIE WALT I would like to start a new tour. I would be the ultimate tour guide for Drink around the World on a Segway. Might be a little dangerous, but it would be lots of fun."

MOUSEJUNKIE RANDY My dream job would be to be a Disney World host. Being able to interact with the guest and share the magic of the parks.

Walking through the parks and conjuring up scenarios where we help guests or get to learn the deep secrets behind the scenes is always fun. But for the Demeritt family, formerly of Nashua, N.H., it became very real.

The World Is Ours

A sagging job market in the northeast combined with a real case of Disney addiction prompted Stephen and Judy Demeritt to actually consider chasing that dream.

"Being close to Walt Disney World was definitely our dream," Judy said. "It's something we've talked about since our first trip together in 2002. We had always talked about 'some day' moving to be closer to the magic."

That day arrived in early July 2010. The couple, married nine years, packed as many of their belongings into their car as they could, pointed south, and kept going until they saw those Purple signs.

"The drive down here felt like an adventure," Judy said. "The morning we got in the car in Nashua and got on the highway it started. Once we crossed the border into Florida we immediately felt like, 'Oh my God, we did it.'"

Disney had always been a part of the Demeritt's lives. Long before the two even met, it was as though their futures were in sync and everything was headed toward this big move.

"Growing up Disney was a staple on Sunday nights," Stephen said. "We would have dinner at our grandparents' house and watch *Wonderful World of Disney* after supper."

And Judy?

"Sunday nights were all about *Wonderful World of Disney*. *Growing* up I always wanted to go to the places we saw on Sunday nights."

So when the two married, there was only one obvious choice for the honeymoon destination.

"I fell in love with the magic of Disney on our first trip," Stephen said of their honeymoon visit. "There are so many stories to tell. So many great memories to remember. It brought back memories of childhood where everything was new and wonderful. For me, that is the magic of Disney."

When the couple divulged to family members that they were planning to "run away to Disney," the news was met with mostly positive reactions.

"They know how we feel about Disney and know that this is where we are meant to be," Judy said.

Then the research began in earnest. The two would scour the Internet every day for tips and information on living in the Orlando area. They scouted possible jobs and decided on a place to live. As with all adventures, however, there were setbacks.

"The day we arrived we learned you can't always trust the Internet all the time," Judy said. "The first place we had booked to stay temporarily was an absolute nightmare in a horrible area. It was not the same place that was pictured on line."

Some quick shuffling got the two into more acceptable living conditions. First they unpacked. Then they got their Florida driver's licenses. Next? The Florida state resident's Premium Annual Pass to Walt Disney World.

The next step came straight out of the couples' dream: A celebration dinner at 'Ohana followed by the Wishes fireworks on the beach. All the planning, hoping, believing, and trusting each other had worked. They had made it, and their new life was about to begin.

"We know we're crazy, but that's what made the decision to do this so easy," Judy said. "It was an 'all-in' situation. Of course there were doubts, especially since we arrived unemployed and we both have to find jobs. Sometimes we think, 'Did we make a mistake coming down here?' It's been a total leap of faith for us, but we feel like we are where we belong and are determined to make it work.

"It feels like the World is really ours now. After a day of job hunting it's great to be able to go to the Magic Kingdom to see the fireworks or to head over to Downtown Disney for dinner at Raglan Road. It's a completely different feeling being here as a resident instead of a tourist. To be able to walk around the parks stress free and not have that feeling of rushing around before you have to leave is the best feeling in the world."

What about adding children to the mix?

Craig and Amy Petermann of Appleton, Wisconsin, also dreamed of making the move. Craig, 35, and Amy, 36, are the parents of two young daughters. The dream, then, became a family affair.

"Craig brought it up years ago, but more seriously after our last trip in June of 2009," Amy said. "At first, the plan was to wait until both kids graduated high school, but 2011 seemed to be a better fit. Craig was more gung-ho than I in the beginning, but I liked the idea more and more as time passed."

The couple, married for nearly seventeen years, each caught the bug young. As they began to take family vacations there, they began to experience the dreaded Disney Withdrawal.

"It was the way the place made us feel," Amy said. "I never felt like that on any other vacation in my life. Every time we would leave Walt Disney World we would be severely depressed."

The Plan, of course, would solve that.

"Craig hopes to go down for a month, establish employment and residency and then come back for us."

The two spend much of their time researching the next step online. ("Do you know how many apartments there are in the Orlando area? Google it sometime. It's ridiculous.") But each day that goes by brings them closer to "selling it all, packing up both vehicles, and saying goodbye to Wisconsin," Amy said. "Most people are supportive, but you do have the naysayers who point out every possible bad thing that could happen."

Craig envisions a career in Information Technology at Walt Disney World, while Amy sees herself earning her wings at Soarin'.

Surely there are some doubts. Could there be a tiny inkling in the back of their minds, reminding them that maybe the Wisconsin winters might not be all that bad? That the twice-a-year Love Bug invasion in central Florida could be rather uncomfortable? That the humidity could sap their thick Midwestern blood?

"No doubts whatsoever," Amy said. "It's where we want to be."

17 **Mousejunkies Confess**

I INITIALLY FELL IN LOVE with Walt Disney World in a nondescript hallway during the preshow of a now-defunct attraction. But the moment when I was absolutely convinced I was helpless in the face of Walt Disney World came on our second trip.

We were walking through the World Showcase at Epcot, when an announcement was made that a parade would be starting soon. Knowing this would likely slow our walk to a crawl, we found a bench just to the side of the Germany pavilion, cuddled up with a pint of Beck's and waited for the undoubtedly garish display to get out of our way so we could continue on to the next country.

But a funny thing happened on the way to parking my butt. I sat down an enthusiast, but when I stood twenty minutes later my transformation into absolute Disney freak had taken place. I surrendered.

The Tapestry of Nations parade took its colorful, theatrical beauty and smashed me in the mind. It left me woozy (though it could've been the Beck's) and shockingly, touched.

The first time I experienced this parade I had no idea what to expect or what was going on. A majestic, towering

figure in a flowing robe trimmed with gold alchemy sym-
bols came walking out of a gate directly in front of me. That
got my attention rather quickly. He gave a monologue about
world peace (delivered via one of 416 speakers cleverly hidden around the World Showcase) then disappeared. He was
trailed by a line of inventive, completely unique flowing
puppets that would interact with guests and dance in time
to a rhythmic, hypnotic soundtrack. The music had no dis-
cernable lyrics, but it spoke to me. It swelled and grew quiet.
It exploded again majestically as drummers on giant wheels
rolled by, beating out the pulse of this otherworldly performance. I was speechless as the dramatic procession played
out in front of me. I had fallen in love with Walt Disney
World about a year earlier, but this was the moment that
would cement the obsession.

For each Mousejunkie, without exception, there is a similar experience.

The Lightning Bolt Moment

Matt Saunders, Stratham, N.H.: I was a Disney skeptic,
almost aggressive in my disdain for anything other than the
classic movies. When my wife suggested we take our five-
year-old to Disney World, I wasn't terribly keen on the idea.
Disney was too cheesy, too hyper-happy, too plastic—the
very opposite of what I look for in entertainment. I expected
a glorified version of Storyland or something like that. Now
I'm a complete convert. My friends can't get me to shut up
about the place.

The lightning bolt for me was Peter Pan's Flight. I get chills when I think about the moment Peter says "Here we go!" and we burst into the night over London. It's one of the most amazing things I've ever experienced. That one ride made it crystal clear to me that Disney operates on an entirely different level from the rest of the world.

Jean Jarvis, Willowbrook, Ill.: We were having breakfast at Cinderella's Royal Table and mentioned to one of the princesses that the one character we wanted to meet most was Maleficent. She told us that sometimes if you go to city hall, they can arrange for a special meeting. We never thought in a million years that it would happen, but a superb cast member called my cell phone about an hour later and told us to be at city hall after the 3 P.M. parade. We walked into city hall, were escorted behind the desk and into a small room, and there she was in all of her wicked glory! We had a good ten minutes alone with her where she took pictures with us and informed us that we should be very grateful that she allowed us in her presence. She was amazing, and it was such a special moment that was created just for us. Imagine all of the planning that was involved in getting the whole thing set up. We were so grateful to that wonderful cast member.

Katie Hall, Evans, Ga.: It wasn't until I became an adult and planned a trip to Disney World with my husband and parents that Disney really hit me. That trip to Disney is one that I will never forget. I cried so many times—tears of happiness of course. I cried as soon as we walked under the train station and stepped onto Main Street U.S.A. I cried during the Wishes fireworks. Of course, I also cried a few tears of self pity when we had to leave. I know this may make me sound like I have emotional problems, but honestly I am not that much of a crier. There was just so much happiness in one place. Disney does everything with such attention to detail, and the quality of everything they do never ceases to amaze me. They truly know how to bring out the child in every one of us. I watched my mom talk to Alice in Wonderland at the character breakfast and I saw her as a little girl. I watched my husband have the time of his life playing at Innoventions. I basically felt like I had electricity pulsing through my body the entire time I was there. If I had to pick one singular moment, it was going to "Walt Disney: One Man's Dream" at Disney's Hollywood Studios. I am sure for many people this exhibit is one to pass up in favor of Tower of Terror or another ride with a Fastpass. For me, this attraction was life changing. I never fully appreciated that the entire Disney Corporation owes its very existence to one man and a mouse.

Judy Minton, Memphis, Tenn.: Our magical moment was in September 2009 when we were treated like royalty right from the start. We got a hotel upgrade, and then met "Wally," the manager of Main Street U.S.A. (Let the super magic begin.) He chatted us up for a while when we were standing for the Boo To You parade during Mickey's Not So Scary Halloween Party. Before we knew it he was asked if we wanted VIP seating for the parade. It was just one more of those moments that leave you feeling like Cinderella. We go to Walt Disney World every year for our wedding anniversary. We honeymooned there, and no matter where else in the world we go we always look at each other and say, "I wish we had gone to Disney instead."

Marilyn Robles, Hawthorne, NJ.: I've been going to Walt Disney World since I was a young girl. But my moment came in May of 2007 when I went with my husband and daughter. I was excited that we were going, but I wasn't truly in love with Walt Disney World until the moment that we stepped onto the pavement in the Magic Kingdom. I remember from previous trips when we would get there my father would always do the triumphant pose of having both his arms raised in the air right in front of the castle. My father has passed and for a split second I saw another man do the same thing with his family looking on. It just sent butterflies to my stomach. It made me realize that another family is now starting their own love affair with Disney. That moment bought a tear to my eye and has since every time I see the castle. It's just the atmosphere and feeling that you get when you are in Disney that makes you fall in love every time you are there.

Molly DeVuono, Naperville, Ill.: My moment was on the first evening of my honeymoon in 2008, standing together, hand in hand, while watching the evening Wishes fireworks. The emotion of the show and the magic of the castle all right there was overwhelming. I couldn't imagine a more perfect time. Looking at my husband, I saw that he, too, had a few tears reflecting in the color bursts of the fireworks. It was so powerful, and I knew that we were both hooked for life.

Nicole Caswell, Danville, NH: My first experience at Walt Disney World was when I was about six, but it was far from the wonderful childhood memory most have. I got food poisoning and had to be pushed around the parks in a wheelchair. Despite the sickness there was one moment that made me really feel the magic. While watching It's Tough to be a Bug, I felt like something bit me in my chair. While this is a part of the show, I felt like it was magic and that Disney had somehow been able to bring me into the attraction. It was such a little thing but because I was unable to experience the bigger things at the time I was in awe of it. I have been to Disney several times since but that moment—a time when Disney put a smile on my face in the simplest of ways—still stands out.

Tricia-Ann Maher, Buffalo, NY: When I first took my two daughters, then four and two, I had an amazing experience. My oldest, Gabby, and I were sitting on the Disney bus to the Magic Kingdom. We came up the hill and she exclaimed, "Look Mama, it's Cinderella's Castle!" and she turned to me with tears streaming down her face. It was almost as if she didn't believe it was happening until that very moment. Needless to say, I started to tear up myself, as did all the people around us. It's a moment I will never forget.

Julie Kimball, Methuen, Mass.: My lightning bolt moment occurred on my honeymoon. My husband and I were in line for my favorite ride, the Twilight Zone Tower of Terror at Disney's Hollywood Studios. We were not in any way obvious about it being our honeymoon; no bride-and-groom mouse ears, no T-shirts, no buttons declaring our newly minted marital bliss. But when we got to the front of the line, the bellhop working our elevator looked at us and said in traditional Tower of Terror creepy fashion: "Newlyweds? Congratulations." Oliver and I looked at each other dumbfounded. I started thinking maybe Disney puts out some kind of list of people on their honeymoons with pictures of us. But then the bellhop looked at Oliver and said "Play with your wedding ring much, sir?" Oliver had been twirling his ring on his finger and didn't even realize he was doing it. The bellhop, in true Disney attention to detail, noticed this and correctly surmised that he was recently married and not used to wearing a wedding band. It was such a great moment that made a huge difference to us. We will never forget it.

Kim Griffith, Atlanta, Ga.: I fell in love with Disney on my honeymoon. We had flown in from Atlanta and taken the Mears shuttle to the Caribbean Beach Resort. We had reservations our first night at the San Angel Inn in the Mexico Pavilion. We arrived at Epcot and made our way through Future World just after dark. As we got closer to the World Showcase we could hear some wonderful music. When we walked into the World Showcase it was like being in another world completely. We were in the midst of the Tapestry of Nations parade and it was just unbelievable. The sights and sounds of that parade just enveloped you and we couldn't help but smile. To this day when I hear the music from that parade, tears come to my eyes and I relive that moment. It is something I will never forget.

Mary Barry, Round Lake, Il.: A trip to Disneyland in the 1960s when I was about ten years old became a lifelong love of Disney. My dad bought me one of the huge Mickey Mouse stuffed dolls inside the park. We had driven from Chicago to California, so on packing day, I wanted my "Big Mickey" to sit with me. When I got to the car, my "Big Mickey" was no where to be seen. My dad put him in the truck with the luggage! Upset that "Big Mickey" couldn't breathe in the truck, I made a big enough stink to get the stuffed doll to ride all the way from California to Chicago with my two brothers, me, and my parents! I still have the now-tattered Big Mickey and knew from that moment on, my dad had turned me into a lifelong Mousejunkie.

Christopher Owens, Lowell, Mass.: The moment that I fell in love with the park was in July of 2005. My wife, my father-in-law and I took my two children, then four and seven, for their first visits. For me it had been some thirteen years since my last visit. I felt myself falling for this magical world as we passed under the Main Street train station and got that glimpse of Main Street U.S.A. with Cinderella Castle standing elegantly between the buildings at the end. I felt as if all the stresses of life were lifted and one could now relax and be wrapped up in the magic that was present all around us.

Don Quashne, Newark, Del.: My moment was when my wife Cathy and I had our wedding at the Walt Disney World wedding pavilion. The wedding went as planned, but when the moment came to shoot a photo session, Cathy's flowers had wilted just a bit. The staff of the Grand Floridian took the bouquet and freshened it up without even being asked. After that I walked over to the registration desk and asked about staying an extra night. (Our original plan was to stay somewhere near the airport.) The reply: "No problem Mr. Quashne, we have arranged for you to stay in the same room." At that moment I fell in love with Disney.

Angela Marriner, New Whiteland, Ind.: I think my lightning bolt moment came when we traveled to Walt Disney World for Christmas in 2008 after my husband returned from a fifteen month tour in Iraq with the Army. We were celebrating Christmas, his safe return, and our honeymoon all in one vacation.

We started a conversation with a cast member at the entrance of the Magic Kingdom while we waited for the gates to open. We mentioned that my husband had just returned from Iraq and we were celebrating everything that we had missed. She thanked my husband for his service and then asked us if we had our tickets handy. We gave them to her and she scanned them and let us in the park one hour early. She told us that it was a wedding present from her.

My husband was lucky enough to be the veteran chosen to take part in the flag retreat ceremony on Main Street U.S.A. that day. Once the ceremony started it was so emotional. They announced his name and where he was stationed and that he had just returned from Iraq. Everyone started applauding and I was speechless. I recorded the event since we may never get the chance to experience it again. They folded the flag and presented it to my husband along with a certificate. The entire family was the main focus of the retreat parade down Main Street.

Karen Gabriel, Aurora, Ill.: Our first trip was three years ago, and we had just gotten through a rough year with sick family members. People had told me how magical Disney was, but I thought they were full of bologna. I told my husband and son that we were going to go all out for this trip because it was the one and only time we were doing Disney. Well, we were sitting on the curb front and center of the castle when the Wishes fireworks were going off around us. There's me on the curb crying saying, "We're coming back next year. This is just too magical!" We've been back every year since. Disney is really an addiction.

Shari Matz, Adamstown, Penn.: The first time I went to Disney World I was twenty-six. I took my five-year-old daughter, because that's what you are supposed to do, right? I was excited, as this was all new to me. I studied the books, web sites, magazines. I got all sorts of tips from friends. I prepared myself for the magic. Or so I thought. We took the ferry across to Magic Kingdom, and I was taking pictures like every other tourist. We saw the opening show, which I enjoyed. But then it happened...I walked underneath the railroad bridge, and saw it. Here was one man's dream come true. And as I walked down Main Street, I got teary-eyed (and still do to this day), and I knew that this would be the place that I call home. The place to which I would go when I take my vacations. The place at which I will one day work. I have fallen in love with Disney World. I have fallen in love with everything Disney. How could I not?

Lori Fernald, Hudson, N.H.: My sister Denise and I were in Disney one December. I was there on business and we only had a few hours to see the Magic Kingdom and Epcot. We didn't want to leave the Magic Kingdom until the Christmas lights came on, but it was getting late. As we were leaving Main Street, we noticed a crowd had gathered under and around the train platform. There was a hush over the crowd, and then Mickey and Minnie appeared on the platform above. They counted down from five and whoosh! All of Main Street lit up for Christmas. We were so overcome by the beauty and joy of what we were witnessing that my sister and I, both in our thirties, held hands and cried.

Why We Go

Something happens when the blazing Florida sun dips below the horizon and darkness begins to settle in.

Twinkling lights blink to life, illuminating the too-perfect surroundings in a way that makes everything even more magical. Main Street U.S.A. takes on a new, golden glow. Tiny lights resembling fireflies flicker in the trees.

Cinderella Castle is bathed in ever-changing colors, dressed in her evening best.

It makes even the most jaded adult stop for a moment to take in the wonder. That perfect hour between dusk and when the stars seem to paint a backdrop specifically for your own personal moment is something that can't be explained to the uninitiated.

Try to explain that when the lights blink on and the park puts on an entirely new face, the dream-like environment combines with hypnotic music to create a euphoric feeling.

Try to explain that when you walk under the train station on your way out of the Magic Kingdom for the last time, it's usually in silence. What can you say when you turn your back on a world built from the blueprints of your childhood dreams and walk away?

Try to explain to someone who's never experienced Walt Disney World that you actually feel sadness when the end arrives. I tend to try to fight it off as long as I can by clinging to everything around me. But when the Magical Express bus passes under the Walt Disney World sign and we turn onto the interstate on our way to the airport, it all seems to disappear.

It's never fun when a vacation comes to an end. But a Walt Disney World vacation finale is different. Packing up and heading home also means leaving behind unforgettable experiences and unexpected feelings. Because somehow, the cast members and Imagineers have created a world where guests— even repeat guests—can be surprised by sometimes subtle, sometimes profound moments that leave them breathless.

MOUSEJUNKIE JENNA I have a wonderful picture of my parents from our most recent trip together. We were at Cinderella's Royal Table for dinner on the first night of our trip, and in the picture they're looking at each other like a couple of lovesick newlyweds. My parents were married forty-six years and nine days before that picture was taken.

On the way into the park, I stopped off at the town hall to pick up a pair of Happy Anniversary buttons. Besides wearing the buttons, I also noted to the hostess that my parents were celebrating their anniversary. Rather than the usual meet-and-greet kind of character dinner, dinner at Cinderella's Royal Table is a show featuring the Fairy Godmother, and Suzy and Perla the mice. It's all about wishes coming true and true love and happy ever after. At the end of the show, the Fairy Godmother asks if anyone is celebrating their marriage, and all the guests applaud the newlyweds. Then they ask for anniversaries and everyone shares how many years they're celebrating. At this particular dinner, my parents just happened to be the longest married, so the Fairy Godmother really oohed and aahed over them. It was obviously something that made them feel really special. It made me feel special, too, because I was a part of their celebration, not just as their child, but as a witness to their happiness and their love.

My parents are the ones who introduced me to Disney as a child. I'm the one who keeps the love of Disney going. That dinner was a great example of why I'll never lose that love for Disney. Any place that can make my parents look at each other with that kind of love and happiness, after all these years and after all the changes in their lives, that's some place I want to keep in all of our lives as much as possible.

MOUSEJUNKIE JOHN   Fine. I'll admit it: Finding Nemo: The Musical at Animal Kingdom. My eyes started tearing up at the end. Is that emotional enough? The dad gets his son back. I was moved. Those Disney Pixar people sure know how to turn a grown man into a real Sally. We went to a nearby drive-in to see *Toy Story 3* with my teenage daughters and both of their boyfriends, and oh man! The whole time in my head, "I'm not gonna cry at the end, I'm not gonna cry at the end." Came close, but I held it back.

TEEN MOUSEJUNKIE RYAN   When I was a wee one, my favorite Disney movie was *The Lion King*. My dad and I watched it every single weekend for many years. Thus, during my very first trip to Disney, I sprinted straight to the Festival of the Lion King show at Disney's Animal Kingdom. I have never felt more wonder or amazement than seeing my favorite Disney characters brought to life in such a beautiful way. The music, the dancing, and the costumes blew me away. I make sure to return every trip to see the show that turned me into the Mousejunkie I am today."

MOUSEJUNKIE J While Walt Disney World is referred to as a "Magical Place" it really does go beyond just a marketing campaign.

During a recent trip I witnessed a moment that showed how moving it can be. I was standing in front of Mission: Space with friends waiting for the braver souls in our group to experience this newest Disney thrill ride. Mickey and Pluto came out dressed in space suits to sign autographs and take pictures. I told the couple I was with, Jen and Jason, to get in line so I could get a picture.

I wasn't paying that much attention at first but started to notice that the kids with Mickey and Pluto were taking a long time. Just as I started to get annoyed, I realized the young boy was blind. Since he could not see, he needed to feel. The characters had already figured this out and they were going the extra mile to ensure this boy enjoyed the full experience.

This six-year-old blind boy was more excited with simply touching Pluto's ear than a life-long Red Sox fan was after winning the 2004 Championship. He was so excited to feel the characters, he could barely contain himself. Watching him find Mickey's ears and grab onto his nose was incredible to watch. I was floored. While telling the story to my wife back in our hotel room, Jen started to tear up again. Jason and I were not far behind her. The simple act of Mickey and Pluto getting down on their knees and taking the time so this boy could feel every part of their faces was truly magical. It is something I will have a hard time forgetting.

MOUSEJUNKIE AMY The first time we were going to bring our daughter down to Disney, I wanted her to be old enough to remember it and cherish it the way we do.

When an opportunity came to bring her sooner than I'd hoped, I wasn't sure she'd understand what was going on. She was three years old, and younger than I would have liked.

It was made all worthwhile when after a dance party in Epcot, we were ushered out to see the IllumiNations show during a dessert buffet at a Magical Gathering. The look of wonder as she watched the fireworks will stay with me forever. You could see the wonderment of a child seeing fireworks for the first time. I was able to hold her in my arms and let her see it all.

MOUSEJUNKIE DEB I can't think of one specific thing that touches me. It's all the little things that get you: seeing an excited child meet a character; seeing a photo being taken of many generations of a family on vacation together; or just the way the setting makes me feel while I'm sitting and relaxing, looking out over Bay Lake or the World Showcase Lagoon or walking down Main Street at night all lit up.

Although Beverly brings me to tears each time I try it.

MOUSEJUNKIE WALT For me it's the American Adventure in the World Showcase at Epcot. When it comes to America and when it comes to patriotism, I get really corny. When I go to a sporting event, I like to make sure I'm in my seat and standing for the National Anthem. I get emotional about that stuff, and I think that's why the American Adventure has such a strong effect on me.

When I see the struggles that the settlers in this country went through, it reminds me of where we all came from. So when the end comes and *Golden Dreams* is playing and all the scenes throughout American history, I find it very touching.

That's why I keep returning. Walt Disney World isn't about standing in line and getting a picture with Mickey Mouse—though that's fine, too. It's about how it always finds a way to touch me.

There's always a twinge of sadness as I'm leaving. It's weird, because I know I'm coming back, it's just that the whole escape is over. When I'm there totally immersed in that world. When I come out of it, it's like, "Oh yeah. This is what the world is.

When I leave, I always stop and take one last look at Cinderella Castle to say goodbye.

When I'm preparing for a Walt Disney World vacation, I get the same questions: "You're going again? Doesn't it get boring? Are you going to wear pants this time?"

Anyone who wears the title of Mousejunkie faces similar questions. Unless someone has touched, or has been touched by a small piece of Walt Disney's imagination, it's difficult to explain. Perhaps that's why I love going on vacation with someone who has never been to Walt Disney World before. It's an incredible experience to introduce someone the Castle for the first time; to watch them stand in awe of the Tree of Life; to walk the streets of old Hollywood; or to actually feel the concussions of Illuminations: Reflections of Earth as it displays a future of hope and light.

I go back for the chance to feel like a kid again. And to see the look on my daughter's face as she sees her dreams literally come to life. To eat too much, drink too much, and to laugh too much.

The park's heart pulses through those twinkling lights that bathe the central Florida night in an ethereal wash. Stirring music flits up and around, alternately playful and profoundly moving, as I wonder what Walt Disney would have thought had he lived long enough to see his creation come to life.

Could he have seen the Florida Project blossom into a massive resort offering dreams come true to anyone who crossed into the playground of his imagination? Is Epcot what he imagined it might be one day? Would he recognize the glitz of Hollywood Boulevard or could he have foreseen the virtual veld that is now home to the scores of animals who played such an important role in Disney's world?

He may not have survived to see the resort named in his honor completed, but his fingerprints are all over that wonderful world.

There's a quote attributed to Walt Disney that goes like this: "It is my wish to delight all members of the family, young and old, parent and child."

Dozens of trips. Thousands of memories made with my wife, my daughter, family members, and some of my closest friends. I've seen grandfathers sitting alongside grandsons and great-grandsons on the same attraction. On more than one occasion I've stood by as a young man drops to one knee and proposes to his fiancée in the shadow of the Partners statue in the Magic Kingdom. But maybe most profoundly I've seen families with young children fighting terrible diseases treated like royalty by Disney cast members. And for that brief time it's as if they don't have a care in the world.

Memo to Walt: Mission accomplished.

Resources

Finding Others of Our Kind

Four theme parks, twenty-two resorts, scores of restaurants, five championship golf courses, dozens of recreation opportunities and endless shopping spread across forty-seven square miles.

This is what you're attempting to get your arms around when you book a trip to Walt Disney World. It can leave even the hardiest vacationer beaten. I've seen them. They pay full price for everything, they spend too much time standing in line and their chafed and blistered bodies are strewn from one end of Fantasyland to the other. You can identify them by the tell-tale stroller tire marks across their backs. They leave tired, frustrated and broke.

I know because all of these things have happened to me at some point in my Disney addiction. I'm not free of its grip, but I have gotten a little better at navigating Walt Disney World.

It can be daunting, but there are some great resources to help ensure you don't become a casualty.

➤ **Mousejunkies.com:** Let's just get this out of the way—I write a supplemental blog attached to the "Mousejunkies" books. It has words like "mayhem," "splurge" and "droppings," which, in context can be quite amusing. (Mousejunkies.com)

There is a community of on Disney journalists, and they are special people who are friendly, helpful and are an endless font of valuable information. The following are the kings of online Disney information:

➤ **WDWToday:** Mike Scopa, Matt Hochberg, Mike Newell and Len Testa lead an interactive Webcast/Podcast that airs new episodes three times a week. They are funny, smart, and a can't-miss. Their collective experience is invaluable when planning a Disney vacation. Listen in a few times and you'll be considering them friends. Every time I fly to Walt Disney World, I load up my MP3 player with episodes of the WDWToday Podcast to pass the time. It's a great way to get into the proper mindset for the upcoming trip. (WDWToday.com)

➤ **WDWRadio:** Lou Mongello is the iron man of online Disney information. The hardest working man in WebDizBiz, Lou has won the 2006, 2007, 2008 and 2009 awards for Best Travel Podcast. He's branched out to video reports, live broadcasts and in-park meet-and-greets. Do yourself a favor and dive into WDWRadio.com.

➤ **JimHillMedia.com:** Who has better sources than Jim Hill? No one. Jim gives his view on all doings at Walt Disney World, and the Disney company as a whole. His dogged reporting has got to have Disney execs scratching their heads and wondering how he keeps breaking news. (JimHillMedia.com)

➤ **Mickeyxtreme.com:** Great info, another great online personality, and the most up to date collection of Walt Disney World News. Julian's news section is like a Drudge Report of Disney news. I visit this site daily. (Mickeyxtreme.com)

There are a million online Disney forums, but the grand-daddy of them all is the DISBoards. It is the largest, most expansive online Disney community on earth. Need to find out about theme park strategies? Dining information? Renting Disney Vacation Club points? You can find it all here. If you have a question about planning a vacation, search the forums here. (Disboards.com)

And of course there's the official Walt Disney World site, which is really good at getting you to throw caution to the wind and your money down the rabbit hole. And I wouldn't have it any other way. (WaltDisneyWorld.com)

Important and Useful Phone Numbers

General Information

Walt Disney World: (407) W-DISNEY
Annual Passholder information: (407) 560-PASS
Disney College Program, U.S. students: (407) 828-3091
Disney College Program, students outside the U.S.:
(407) 828-2850

Cirque du Soleil—La Nouba: (407) 939-7600
Walt Disney World golf: (407) WDW-GOLF
Disney guest relations: (407) 824-4321
Fireworks cruises: (407) WDW-PLAY
Lost and found: (407) 824-4245
Walt Disney World tours: (407) WDW-TOUR

Walt Disney World Resorts

All Star Movies: (407) 939-7000
All Star Music: (407) 939-6000
All Star Sports: (407) 939-5000
Animal Kingdom Lodge: (407) 938-3000
Beach Club: (407) 934-8000
Boardwalk Inn: (407) 939-5100
Boardwalk Villas: (407) 939-5100
Caribbean Beach: (407) 934-3400
Contemporary: (407) 824-1000
Coronado Springs: (407) 939-1000
Fort Wilderness: (407) 824-2900
Grand Floridian: (407) 824-3000
Old Key West: (407) 827-7700
Polynesian: (407) 824-2000
Pop Century: (407) 938-4000
Port Orleans French Quarter: (407) 934-5000
Port Orleans Riverside: (407) 934-6000
Saratoga Springs Resort and Spa (407) 827-1100
Shades of Green: (407) 824-3600
Walt Disney World Swan: (407) 934-3000
Walt Disney World Dolphin: (407) 934-4000

Wilderness Lodge: (407) 824-3200
Wilderness Lodge Villas: (407) 938-4300
Yacht Club: (407) 934-7000

Walt Disney World Dining

Dining Reservations: (407) WDW-DINE
Disney Dinning Experience: (407) 566-5858
Same-Day Advanced Dining Reservations, on-site
   guests: 55 from hotel
Same-Day Advanced Dining Reservations, off-site
   guests: (407) 824-2858

Glossary

Mousejunkies—people who are obsessed with all things Walt Disney World—can sometimes seem to have their own language. Acronyms, nicknames, and shortened versions of longer titles pepper their conversations. Venture onto any Disney-related online community and you'll be overwhelmed by Mousejunkie-speak.

To help readers navigate the pixie dust-clouded waters of Disney lingo, here is a glossary of some of the more common terms and acronyms found in this book and often used in online Walt Disney World correspondence:

AA: The American Adventure. An attraction at Epcot.

AA: Audio Animatronics. Lifelike figures of animals or humans used throughout the parks.

ADR: Advanced Dining Reservations. Guests who call to reserve a dinner reservation are actually making an Advanced Dining Reservation. To make an ADR, call (407) WDW-DINE.

AK: Disney's Animal Kingdom theme park. See also, DAK

All Star Resorts: The term "All Stars" refers to three of Disney's value level resorts—All Star Music, All Star Sports, and All Star Movies. The three resorts are located next to one another near Disney's Animal Kingdom theme park.

Animal Kingdom Lodge: A deluxe level resort that opened in 2001, the Animal Kingdom Lodge (AKL) is situated around a savannah where giraffes, zebras, and other wild animals graze.

AP: Annual Pass

Bay Lake: A lake located east of the Magic Kingdom and just behind the Contemporary Resort. It connects to the nearby Seven Seas Lagoon. Fishing excursions, parasailing, and boating activities are offered on Bay Lake.

Beach Club: The Beach Club Resort (**BC**) is a deluxe level resort located near the Epcot theme park. It is themed to look like turn-of-the-century seaside Atlantic cottages.

Boardwalk Resort: The Boardwalk Resort (often shortened to **BW, BWI** for Boardwalk Inn, or **BWV** for Boardwalk Villa), is a deluxe level resort designed to look like a 1920s Atlantic boardwalk.

Candlelight Processional: A massed-choir and orchestral performance of the Christmas story performed at Epcot during the holiday season.

Caribbean Beach Resort: A moderate level resort opened in 1988, the Caribbean Beach Resort (**CBR**) is located near Epcot, and features a Caribbean theme throughout. The buildings encircle a small lake Barefoot Bay.

Cast member: An employee of Walt Disney World. Often shortened to **CM**.

Character meal: A dining option where Disney characters make their way around the room for photo and interaction opportunities with diners.

Contemporary Resort: One of the original resorts at the Walt Disney World resort, the Contemporary (**CR**) was built using modular construction. Prebuilt rooms were placed into the building's frame by a crane. A bit of trivia: President Richard Nixon gave his "I'm not a crook" speech at the Contemporary Resort in 1973.

Coronado Springs Resort: Opened in 1997, this moderate level resort has a southwestern theme and features a pool in the shadow of a Mayan pyramid. Coronado Springs Resort (**CSR**) has a large convention center and often hosts trade shows.

Disney's Animal Kingdom: The fourth theme park built at the Walt Disney World resort, Animal Kingdom (**AK** or **DAK**) opened in 1997.

Disney's Hollywood Studios: The third theme park built at the Walt Disney World resort, it was opened as Disney-MGM Studios in 1989. The name was changed to Disney's Hollywood Studios (**DHS**) in January of 2007.

Disney's Magical Express: Guests staying at a Walt Disney World resort can use Disney's Magical Express buses (**DME**) to travel from Orlando International Airport to their resort for free.

Disney Vacation Club: Often referred to simply as **DVC**, Disney Vacation Club is essentially a vacation timeshare, allowing people to purchase a real estate interest in one of the DVC resorts. Members purchase points that are used to make reservations at a DVC resort. The points are renewed annually.

Dolphin: The Walt Disney World Dolphin hotel is located in the Boardwalk resort area. It is operated by Starwood Hotels and Resorts Worldwide under the Sheraton Hotels brand. It is decorated in 'Floribbean' style, using nautical themes in varying shades of pink and coral. It is adjacent to the similarly themed Walt Disney World Swan hotel.

Downtown Disney: An outdoor shopping, dining, and entertainment complex at the Walt Disney World resort. It features several themed and chain restaurants like the Rainforest Café, House of Blues, and Planet Hollywood, as well as the Cirque du Soleil theater where *La Nouba* is performed. Downtown Disney (**DTD**) is divided into three sections: the Marketplace, Pleasure Island, and the West Side.

ECV: Electric convenience vehicle. The scooters those with mobility issues can take advantage of.

Epcot: The second theme park built at the Walt Disney World resort, Epcot opened in 1982. Originally named Epcot Center, its name was shortened to Epcot in 1994.

Epcrotch: The chafing that occurs while vacationing at Walt Disney World.

Extra Magic Hours: One of the Walt Disney World theme parks opens early or stays open after regular park closing hours every day. Guests staying at a Walt Disney World resort can take advantage of Extra Magic Hours (**EMH**), enjoying, in theory, shorter wait times and lighter crowds.

Expedition Everest: An expertly themed roller coaster at Disney's Animal Kingdom. Expedition Everest (**EE**) was built to resemble Mount Everest, complete with snowy peaks and jagged rock formations.

Fastpass: Disney's Fastpass (**FP**) is a virtual queuing system wherein guests insert their park tickets into a kiosk that then distributes a small ticket with a return time stamped on it. Guests return to that specific attraction at the prescribed time, thus bypassing the sometimes lengthy standby line. Guests are allowed to have only one Fastpass per park ticket at one time.

Festival of the Lion King: A can't-miss musical performance at Disney's Animal Kingdom.

Fort Wilderness: A resort with campsites that allow guests to tent, use their own camper or recreation vehicle, or stay in a cabin. Fort Wilderness (FW) opened just weeks after the Magic Kingdom in 1971.

Friendship Launch: Boats that shuttle guests around the Epcot theme park and resort area. The Friendships travel from one side of the World Showcase Lagoon to the other, and from the Boardwalk area resorts—including the Boardwalk, Yacht Club, Beach Club, and the Swan and

Dolphin hotels—to Epcot and Disney's Hollywood Studios theme park.

Future World: An area of Epcot located adjacent to the World Showcase. Spaceship Earth, Soarin', Test Track, and Mission: Space are among the more prominent attractions located in Future World (**FW**).

Grand Floridian: Disney's Grand Floridian Resort and Spa (**GF**) is a deluxe level resort across the Seven Seas Lagoon from the Magic Kingdom. Its look was inspired by the beach resorts of Florida's East Coast.

Great Movie Ride: This attraction (**GMR**) takes guests on a tour through memorable films throughout Hollywood history.

Hidden Mickey: A cleverly disguised shape in the form of Mickey Mouse's head. Disney's Imagineers sometimes work them into attractions or theming as a way of "signing" their work.

Hoop-Dee-Doo Musical Review: A dinner show held at Pioneer Hall on the grounds of Fort Wilderness, the Hoop-Dee-Doo Musical Review (HDDMR) is a Wild West vaudeville review. The shows run approximately two hours.

International Gateway: A back-door entrance to the Epcot theme park, the International Gateway is accessible through the Boardwalk area resorts. Entering through the International Gateway puts visitors into the United Kingdom pavilion in the World Showcase.

It's a Small World: Classic attraction at the Magic Kingdom, sometimes shortened to **IaSW**.

Kidcot Fun Stops: There are sixteen Kidcot Fun Stops located in the Epcot theme park throughout Future World and the World Showcase. Children are given a cutout mask which they can color and decorate as they stop at each of the locations throughout the park. Cast members will also stamp the mask at each country or Kidcot Fun Stop.

Magic Kingdom: The Magic Kingdom (MK), which opened in 1971, was the first theme park at the Walt Disney World resort.

Magic Your Way: What Disney calls its theme park tickets. Guests can buy the base Magic Your Way ticket, or add several options, such as Park Hopping or No Expiration.

MCO: Orlando International Airport.

MNSSHP: Mickey's Not So Scary Halloween Party. A hard-ticket, after-hours event at the Magic Kingdom, celebrating the Halloween season.

Mousejunkie: Anyone interested in or obsessed with Walt Disney World. Someone of high standards, great knowledge, a sense of humor, a yearning for fun, who is normally extremely attractive and intelligent.

MVMCP: Mickey's Very Merry Christmas Party. An after hours, hard-ticket event at the Magic Kingdom celebrating the holiday season.

Old Key West: The original Disney Vacation Club resort, Old Key West (OKW) opened in 1991 and evokes a Key West theme.

Park Hopping: The act of leaving one Walt Disney World theme park and going to another in a single day. Guests must purchase the Magic Your Way Park Hopper option in order to move between two or more theme parks in one day.

Pop Century: A value resort, Pop Century has 2,880 rooms in ten separate, themed buildings.

Polynesian: Disney's Polynesian Resort (often referred to in the shorthand, "the Poly"), opened in 1971 on the shores of the Seven Seas Lagoon. It reflects a Hawaiian theme, and is one of the original Magic Kingdom area resorts.

Port Orleans French Quarter/Riverside: A moderate level resort, the French Quarter (POFQ) and Riverside (POR) were once two separate resorts. They were combined in 2001.

Reedy Creek Improvement District: Sometimes shortened to **RCID**, it is the governmental structure overseeing the property of Walt Disney World.

Saratoga Springs: The Saratoga Springs Resort and Spa (**SSR**) is located across the Lake Buena Vista Lagoon from Downtown Disney, and was built to look like the upstate New York spa and horseracing town. It is the largest of the Disney Vacation Club resorts.

Seven Seas Lagoon: The man-made body of water located in front of the Magic Kingdom.

Spaceship Earth: The geodesic sphere (the giant golfball) that functions as the Epcot theme park's icon, Spaceship Earth (**SE**) stands eighteen-stories tall and houses a thirteen-minute dark ride that takes guests through the history of human communication.

Swan: The Walt Disney World Swan hotel is located in the Boardwalk resort area. It is operated by Starwood Hotels and Resorts Worldwide under the Sheraton Hotels brand. It is decorated in "Floribbean" style, using nautical themes in varying shades of pink and coral. It is adjacent to the similarly-themed Walt Disney World Dolphin hotel.

Tree of Life: A fourteen-story artificial tree that acts as Disney's Animal Kingdom's park icon. Images of more than 325 animals are carved into its trunk, and the structure houses a 3-D movie, *It's Tough To Be a Bug*.

TTC: The Ticket and Transportation Center is located between the Magic Kingdom parking area and the Seven Seas Lagoon. At the TTC you can board a monorail to Epcot or the Magic Kingdom, or a ferry boat to the Magic Kingdom. The Magic Kingdom Kennels are also located there.

Wilderness Lodge: Disney's Wilderness Lodge Resort (WL) is a deluxe level resort on the shores of Bay Lake. It look was inspired by the great lodges of the Pacific Northwest.

World Showcase Lagoon: The body of water around which Epcot's World Showcase is situated. Epcot's IllumiNations: Reflections of Earth show is displayed over the World

Showcase Lagoon nightly. The World Showcase Lagoon has a perimeter of 1.2 miles.

Yacht Club: Designed to look like a New England seaside retreat, the Yacht Club (YC) is located in the Boardwalk area near the Epcot theme park.

The Mousejunkie Lexicon

There's an even deeper level of communication. We Disney people have our own language. We know what HDDMR is. We throw around terms like ADR or ASMu as if they were normal parts of everyday speech.

But there's another layer of language that the deepest Disney enthusiasts know. It's a way of speaking that communicates nuance and subtext in a way that others of our kind completely understand. Reader submitted, this is the **Mousejunkie Lexicon**. Add to the Lexicon. Submit your entries to bill@mousejunkies.com.

Disney-pendent: One who's happiness generally hinges on a human-sized Mouse with red pants and white gloves, and his many theme parks, films, TV shows and Web sites.

Magicate: The uncontrollable urge to relay vast amounts of knowledge and trivia about Walt Disney World to those who may or may not be interested in visiting the resort. Or to correct any errors you may overhear in others' conversations while waiting in line for an attraction. ie: Its Brer Rabbit not Briar Rabbit! (Shawn Byrley)

Mouse-a-thon(ers): A person or family that tries to do it all, see it all, ride it all and fit it all in on their vacation. No time for food, bathroom, naps, or shopping breaks, just go... go...go! You will see this family rushing around like they are on a stuffed french toast sugar high. (Dawn)

Mousejunkie: One who is devoted to, and expresses a physical and emotional need for, Walt Disney World. The Mousejunkie is usually extremely clever and incredibly good-looking. (See also: Disney-pendent)

Scerred: When the clueless drivers of the electric carts get WAAAAYYY TOOOO CLOSE!!! (See also: Kamikaze Granny, video above) (Marilyn Kane)

Sherpavigate: A mix of Sherpa and navigate. Most often associated with an adults-only group of Disneyphiles attempting to find the shortest, most direct route to Expedition Everest after arriving at the Animal Kingdom. (See also: Kiss My Sherpa) (Christopher Ashby)

Kiss My Sherpa: The reaction of the wise guy/gal from the group when he or she realizes there is no such short, direct route. (Christopher Ashby)

Stop the Clock: The first words out of our mouths after checking in to our Resort, and the refusal to leave even when the Magical Disney Express pulls up on the last day. (Judy Minton)

Stroller Kamikaze: Stroller operators moving through crowds at a high velocity without regard for pedestrian wellbeing, often resulting in bruised ankles and shins of aforementioned pedestrians. (The only known method of avoiding stroller kamikazes is to dive rapidly out of their flight plan or to wear shinguards.) Most commonly encountered in the Magic Kingdom at the conclusion of Wishes. (See also Kamikaze Granny—the noticeable difference being this kamikaze is behind the wheel of a motorized chair and not behind a stroller.) (Amanda Koeppen)

The Cote Pace: The otherworldly speed at which one navigates the "World" by foot alone. (Mike Downer)

Touristerol: A small group of tourists who decide to stop smack dab in the middle of a main traffic route, causing a major pedestrian blockage (and, frequently, chest pains in those being blocked). Usually followed by the unfolding of a park map and an argument. (John Cortes)

Wishdrawals: The process of of often painful physical and psychological symptoms that follows discontinuance of a Walt Disney World vacation, particularly related to the Magic Kingdom and its nightly fireworks display. (Corey Townsend)

Zip-a-dee-doo-da-brew-haha: Epcot World travelers that happily sample brews from country to country until they become quite "Mad hatterish. " (Even venturing to eat the scorpion at the bottom of their glass-yes you know who you are...next time right?) (Scott and Dawn Mazur)

Acknowledgements

The following people have been extremely important in helping bring this all together: Amy and Katie Burke, Randy and Carol Houle, J and Deb Cote, Jenna Petroskey, Ryan Elizabeth Foley, Walter Pomerleau, John Cortes, Barry Kane, Judy and Stephen Demeritt, Charles Stovall, Rose Monahan, Patrick LaKemper, Julian Pupo, John and Melanie Swoap, Blue Sky Journeys, Kevin Linn, Adam and Sarah Powers, and God.